KIDNAPPED

Conflict Resolution in Hostage Situations

LUIS FERNANDO TEJADA YEPES

Index

1. Introduction to Hostage Negotiation 3

2. History of Hostage Negotiation ....……..18

3. Basic Principles in Hostage Negotiation ....……..32

4. Hostage Negotiator Profile ....……..46

5. Types of Hostages and Hostage Situations ....……..61

6. Preparation for Hostage Negotiation ....……..73

7. Effective Communication in Hostage Situations 89

8. Communication Strategies ....…..103

9. Hostage Situation Assessment ....…..120

10. Establishing a Hostage Negotiation Team ....…..132

11. Hostage Negotiators' Training ....……..147

12. Decision-Making in Hostage Situations ....……157

13. Psychology of Kidnappers and Hostages ....…..173

14. Persuasion and Reverse Persuasion Techniques 185

15. Crisis Management in Hostage Situations ....…..192

16. Conflict Resolution in Hostage Situations ....….205

17. The Importance of Empathy in Hostage Negotiation 220

18. Media in Hostage Negotiations ....…….229

19. Negotiating with Terrorist Groups ....……..237

20. Famous Hostage Negotiation Cases ....…….251

21. Hostage Release and Post-Negotiation ....……260

22. Explosive Device Deactivation Techniques 266

23. Negotiation in Virtual Kidnapping Situations 276

24. Hostage Negotiation in the Business Environment 286

25. Legal and Ethical Aspects of Hostage Negotiation 300

26. The Importance of Intelligence in Hostage Negotiation 315

27. Hostage Negotiation in the International Context ....……..324

28. Long-Term Psychological Impact on Hostages and families……..336

1.Introduction to Hostage Negotiation

The history of hostage negotiation dates back to the dawn of civilization, marking a pivotal chapter in the evolution of diplomacy and crisis management. From ancient civilizations to the present day, this subtle and risky art has been a constant in the human narrative, facing changing challenges and stretching the imagination in extreme situations.

The earliest evidence of hostage-taking can be traced back to antiquity, where empires and kingdoms employed the practice as a means to ensure that agreements and treaties were upheld. Hostages, often members of the nobility, found themselves in a delicate balance, representing a link between two conflicting parties. The fate of these hostages depended largely on the outcome of negotiations and the behavior of both parties.

As history progressed, hostage-taking tactics evolved and became a common resource in political and military conflicts. From ancient Rome to medieval Europe, hostage-taking became a deeply-rooted practice in diplomacy, often used to secure peace treaties or ransom payments.

The true transformation in hostage negotiation occurred with the rise of modern diplomacy and the formation of international bodies. The 20th century witnessed the birth of the League of Nations and subsequently the United Nations, which played a crucial role in resolving international crises and negotiating the release of hostages. As the world became more complex and globalized, hostage situations also became more intricate and challenging.

Kidnappings in the context of political terrorism and insurgency became a distinctive feature of the 20th and 21st centuries, with extremist groups resorting to these tactics to advance their political goals. Hostage negotiation became a matter of national security and a highly specialized field.

Famous cases throughout history, such as the 1979 American embassy hostage crisis in Iran or the 1996 hostage-taking at the residence of the Japanese ambassador in Lima, have left a profound mark on the global consciousness and shed light on the complexity of hostage negotiation.

This book delves into this rich history, exploring how hostage negotiation has evolved over the centuries and the lessons we can learn from these past events. As we progress through the pages, we will examine the unique challenges faced by diplomacy in critical situations and how this discipline continues to play a vital role in crisis management in our modern world. The history of hostage negotiation is a testament to human adaptability and perseverance in the face of adversity, and this work adds to the ever-evolving narrative of this essential field.

Diplomacy, as a tool for conflict management and international relations, has undergone a remarkable evolution throughout history. From the early negotiations between tribes and civilizations to the complex political and commercial agreements of today, diplomacy has been the means by which nations have resolved differences, promoted cooperation, and, in critical situations, safeguarded peace.

The history of diplomacy dates back to antiquity when Mesopotamian, Egyptian, and Greek civilizations sent envoys and ambassadors to establish relations, exchange information, and negotiate treaties. These early diplomats acted as intermediaries and ambassadors of peace, resolving conflicts through dialogue and negotiation.

In Mesopotamia, one of the oldest civilizations, envoys were employed to manage trade and political agreements, as well as to settle territorial disputes. Egyptians, on the other hand, used diplomats to maintain relations with neighboring nations and manage issues like trade and peace. In ancient Greece, where the term "diplomacy" was coined from the Greek word "diplōma," ambassadors were sent to other city-states to negotiate treaties and alliances.

These early diplomats played a crucial role in conflict prevention and the promotion of cooperation between nations, setting a precedent for diplomacy as a means of peacefully resolving disputes instead of resorting to war. Over the centuries, diplomatic practices evolved and formalized, laying the foundation for the development of modern diplomacy and its role in managing critical situations and international relations.

As civilizations grew and connected through trade and conquest, diplomacy became a fundamental pillar of international relations. In ancient Rome, for example, the concept of "ius gentium" (law of nations) was developed to regulate diplomatic relations between states. As civilizations expanded, diplomacy became even more essential for managing increasingly complex international relations and resolving conflicts peacefully. In ancient Rome, one of the most notable examples of this evolution, the concept of "ius gentium," which translates to "law of nations" or "law of peoples," played a crucial role in regulating diplomatic relations between states and creating a legal system that transcended borders.

The "ius gentium" in Rome established a legal framework for interactions between Rome and other nations, including treaties and trade agreements. It set rules and procedures for the treatment of foreigners and ambassadors and also outlined the rights and duties of the parties involved in international relations. This emphasis on legality and mutual respect laid the foundation for the later development of diplomacy as a specialized field.

The notion of international law governing relations between nations became a fundamental concept throughout the history of diplomacy and has influenced the development of international treaties and agreements in the modern era. Diplomacy has transformed from an informal practice in antiquity into a system regulated by international laws and agreements that address a wide range of issues, from conflict resolution to trade and human rights.

This emphasis on international law and diplomacy as a means of dispute resolution and the promotion of cooperation has endured through the centuries, becoming an essential component of modern international politics and a key tool for managing critical global situations.

The Renaissance marked a period of flourishing diplomacy in Europe, with the establishment of permanent embassies and the emergence of figures like the renowned Italian diplomat Niccolò Machiavelli. During this era, ambassadors played a crucial role in conflict resolution and alliance-building.

The Renaissance, a period of significant cultural and political transformation in Europe that occurred approximately between the 14th and 17th centuries, played a crucial role in the evolution of diplomacy. During this time, significant advances were made in how international relations were conducted, and the foundations of modern diplomacy were laid.

One of the most notable changes during the Renaissance was the establishment of permanent embassies, marking a departure from the temporary diplomatic missions used previously. Permanent embassies allowed for continuous communication between states, resulting in greater stability and better mutual understanding.

Italian diplomat Niccolò Machiavelli is a prominent figure of this era and an important precursor in the theory of diplomacy. His work "The Prince" and his writings on diplomacy offered a pragmatic and realistic perspective on international relations. Machiavelli emphasized the importance of cunning and adaptability in diplomacy, as well as the need to strike a balance between power and morality.

During the Renaissance, ambassadors played a crucial role in conflict resolution and alliance-building. They acted as intermediaries between states, negotiating treaties and agreements, and served as sources of information and analysis for their home governments. Diplomatic skills such as oratory and negotiation became valuable assets during this time.

The Renaissance was a period of diplomatic flourishing in Europe, characterized by the establishment of permanent embassies and the rise of influential figures like Niccolò Machiavelli. These developments laid the groundwork for modern diplomacy and the way international relations are managed today.

The 19th century saw the emergence of a more formalized diplomatic system with the Congress of Vienna in 1815. This event laid the foundations for modern diplomacy and the balance of power in Europe. As industrialized nations competed for resources and territories, diplomacy became even more crucial for preventing conflicts and promoting peace.

The 19th century witnessed a significant milestone in the evolution of diplomacy with the Congress of Vienna in 1815. This event marked a turning point in European diplomacy and laid the groundwork for modern diplomacy and the maintenance of peace on the continent.

The Congress of Vienna was an international conference that brought together major European powers after the Napoleonic Wars with the goal of reorganizing the political map of Europe. During this conference, the principles of the balance of power were established, involving the equitable distribution of power among European nations to prevent any one nation from becoming too dominant and triggering conflicts.

Additionally, the notion of legitimacy was introduced, implying that legitimate leaders and monarchs should be restored to power in nations affected by the Napoleonic wars. This focus on legitimacy and the balance of power aimed to maintain stability and prevent future conflicts in Europe.

The Congress of Vienna also promoted the idea of ongoing diplomatic cooperation and the use of international conferences to address disputes and matters of common interest. This formalized approach to diplomacy and multilateralism laid the groundwork for the modern diplomatic system, which has evolved into a vital component of international relations.

The 19th century was a time of intense competition among industrialized nations for resources and territories, making diplomacy even more crucial for preventing conflicts and promoting peace. The system of alliances and bilateral and multilateral treaties became a distinctive feature of diplomacy at the time and played a fundamental role in maintaining European stability for much of the century.

The Congress of Vienna and the focus on the balance of power, legitimacy, and formalized diplomacy marked a significant milestone in the history of diplomacy and laid the foundations for modern diplomacy in a rapidly changing world.

The 20th century brought drastic changes in diplomacy due to the two World Wars and the emergence of international organizations such as the League of Nations and the United Nations. These institutions played a crucial role in international conflict resolution and the promotion of global cooperation.

In more recent times, diplomacy has evolved to address a variety of complex global challenges, from nuclear proliferation to climate change and cyberspace. Instant communication and globalization have altered the way diplomatic negotiations are conducted, making transparency and collaboration more important than ever.

In recent times, diplomacy has undergone a notable evolution to address an increasingly complex array of global challenges. These challenges include nuclear proliferation, climate change, cybersecurity, and various transnational issues that require effective international cooperation.

Nuclear proliferation is a critical issue for international security, and diplomacy plays a pivotal role in preventing the spread of nuclear weapons.

Agreements like the Nuclear Non-Proliferation Treaty (NPT) and nuclear agreements with North Korea and Iran underscore the importance of diplomacy in managing these global risks.

Climate change is another urgent challenge that demands coordinated diplomatic action. International agreements, such as the Paris Agreement, exemplify how diplomacy is used to address global environmental issues and promote the reduction of greenhouse gas emissions.

Cybersecurity has become a hot topic in modern diplomacy, as cyberattacks can have significant repercussions on a country's security and economy. Cyber diplomacy involves negotiating international norms and agreements to address these challenges and establish clear rules for behavior in cyberspace.

Globalization and instant communication have transformed the way diplomatic negotiations take place. The speed at which information spreads and the ability of non-state actors to influence diplomacy have created a more complex environment. Transparency and collaboration are now more crucial than ever, and social media and public diplomacy play a significant role in promoting policies and generating public support.

Diplomacy has also become more diverse and multilateral in response to these global challenges. Agreements and treaties often involve multiple stakeholders and require closer cooperation between countries and international organizations.

Diplomacy has evolved to address a variety of global challenges in more recent times and remains essential for conflict prevention, the promotion of international cooperation, and finding solutions to problems affecting the global community. Adaptability and collaboration are now key components of modern diplomacy.

Today, diplomacy is an essential tool in conflict resolution, the promotion of human rights, and the fostering of international cooperation. In critical situations, diplomats play a crucial role in preventing armed conflicts and seeking peaceful solutions. Currently, diplomacy is an essential tool in promoting peace, conflict resolution, and the promotion of human rights on a global scale. Diplomats and diplomatic missions play a crucial role in preventing armed conflicts and seeking peaceful solutions in critical situations.

Conflict Resolution: Diplomats work in conflict prevention and resolution, whether through mediating peace negotiations, promoting diplomatic agreements, or facilitating conversations between conflicting parties. Diplomacy contributes to reducing tensions and preventing armed conflicts.

Conflict resolution is one of the central roles of diplomacy in the modern world. Diplomats play an essential role in preventing and resolving conflicts, contributing to the reduction of tensions and the maintenance of peace.

Mediation in Peace Negotiations: Diplomats often act as mediators in peace negotiations between conflicting parties. This role involves facilitating dialogue between the conflicting parties, helping identify areas of compromise, and working toward the development of sustainable peace agreements. Diplomatic mediation can be crucial in preventing armed conflicts and promoting peaceful resolution.

Promotion of Diplomatic Agreements: Diplomats work on negotiating and promoting diplomatic agreements and treaties that can help resolve conflicts. These agreements can address a wide range of issues, from border delineation and trade to security cooperation. Diplomatic treaties and agreements often lay the foundations for long-term peace and cooperation.

Facilitation of Conversations: In conflict situations, diplomats often serve as facilitators of conversations between conflicting parties. This role involves creating a conducive environment for dialogue and ensuring that the parties feel heard and respected. Diplomacy facilitates communication and bridge-building between conflicting parties.

Prevention of Escalation of Tensions: Diplomacy also plays a significant role in preventing the escalation of tensions. Diplomats can intervene early in conflict situations to calm the waters and prevent the situation from worsening. Preventive diplomacy focuses on identifying and addressing the underlying causes of conflicts before they escalate into major crises.

Peace Diplomacy: In some cases, diplomatic peace missions are established, where diplomats are sent to conflict zones to promote reconciliation, disarmament, and stabilization. These missions aim to build bridges between conflicting parties and pave the way for a peaceful resolution.

Diplomacy significantly contributes to conflict prevention and resolution, helping to avert armed conflicts and promote peace. Diplomats, through their crisis management expertise and their ability to facilitate dialogue, are key actors in building a more peaceful and stable world.

Promotion of Human Rights: Diplomacy plays a significant role in the international promotion of human rights. Diplomats advocate for justice, equality, and the respect of fundamental rights in their bilateral relationships and in international forums.

The promotion of human rights is an essential component of contemporary diplomacy, and diplomats play a crucial role in advocating for justice, equality, and the respect of fundamental rights worldwide.

Human Rights Diplomacy: States send diplomats to international missions and intergovernmental organizations dedicated to the promotion and protection of human rights, such as the United Nations and the International Court of Justice. These diplomats work to influence the development of policies, resolutions, and treaties that uphold human rights at the global level.

Bilateral Diplomacy: In their bilateral relationships with other countries, diplomats advocate for human rights, discuss areas of concern, and promote policies and practices that respect fundamental rights. This can include discussions of specific cases of human rights abuses or cooperation in projects and programs aimed at improving the human rights situation.

Women's Rights Diplomacy: Diplomacy has been instrumental in promoting women's rights, gender equality, and the fight against gender-based violence. Diplomats advocate for policies and international agreements that promote gender equality and work to influence laws and practices in this area.

Peace and Human Rights Diplomacy: In conflict situations, peace diplomacy is often combined with the promotion of human rights. Diplomats work to ensure that the rights of people in conflict zones are respected and protected, seeking justice and accountability for human rights abuses.

Public Diplomacy and Human Rights: Public diplomacy involves interacting with civil society, the media, and public opinion to promote policies that respect human rights. Diplomats often engage in the promotion of human rights through speeches, press releases, and public education programs.

Promotion of Rights in Agreements and Treaties: In the negotiation of agreements and treaties, diplomats can ensure that human rights are an integral part of these agreements. This may include provisions on labor rights, minority rights, refugee protection, and more.

Promoting human rights through diplomacy is essential to ensure that states fulfill their obligations under international human rights treaties and uphold universal principles of human rights. Diplomats play a fundamental role in building a world where all individuals enjoy their fundamental rights and live with dignity.

International Cooperation: Diplomacy fosters cooperation between nations on a wide range of issues, from poverty reduction and climate change to managing health crises and security collaboration.

International cooperation is a central component of modern diplomacy, and diplomats work tirelessly to promote collaboration between nations on a wide range of issues that affect the global community.

Poverty Alleviation and Development: Diplomacy plays an essential role in promoting cooperation to address poverty and promote sustainable development worldwide. Diplomats negotiate assistance agreements and collaborate on development programs that seek to improve the living conditions of vulnerable populations.

Climate Change and Environment: International cooperation is essential in the fight against climate change and the protection of the environment. Diplomats participate in international agreements and treaties, such as the Paris Agreement, to address global environmental issues and promote sustainable practices.

Health Crises: In situations of global health crises, such as pandemics, diplomats work to coordinate international responses. This includes collaboration in the distribution of medical resources, promotion of scientific research, and implementation of measures to contain the spread of diseases.

Security Collaboration: Diplomacy plays a fundamental role in promoting international security. Diplomats work on negotiating arms control treaties, conflict prevention, and stability promotion in crisis areas.

International Trade: Diplomacy is essential in international trade negotiations. Diplomats negotiate bilateral and multilateral trade agreements that promote market openness, economic growth, and job creation.

Human Rights and Justice: International cooperation on human rights and justice matters is fundamental. Diplomats work to establish standards and treaties that promote justice, equality, and accountability for human rights violations.

Education and Culture: Diplomacy also fosters collaboration in educational and cultural areas. This includes student exchange programs, the promotion of cultural diversity, and the protection of cultural heritage.

Humanitarian Assistance: Diplomats play a significant role in coordinating humanitarian assistance efforts in crisis situations, such as natural disasters and conflicts. This includes mobilizing resources and delivering aid to affected populations.

International cooperation through diplomacy is essential for addressing global challenges and promoting a safer, more sustainable, and just world. Diplomats play a key role in building bridges between nations and seeking solutions to problems that affect humanity as a whole.

Negotiation of Agreements and Treaties: Diplomats are responsible for negotiating and agreeing on bilateral and multilateral treaties and agreements that address global issues such as trade, the environment, security, and cooperation in science and technology.

The negotiation of agreements and treaties is one of the central roles of diplomats and a fundamental part of international diplomacy. Diplomats work to negotiate, agree upon, and promote a wide variety of treaties and agreements that address globally significant issues.

International Trade: International trade agreements are a significant example of diplomats' work. They negotiate free trade agreements, investment agreements, and other trade-related agreements that aim to promote market openness and facilitate the exchange of goods and services between countries.

Environment: Diplomats work on negotiating treaties and agreements related to the environment, such as the Paris Agreement on climate change. These agreements seek to address global environmental issues and promote sustainable practices.

Security and Disarmament: Diplomats participate in arms control treaties and disarmament agreements that aim to promote international security and reduce the proliferation of nuclear and conventional weapons.

Science and Technology: Cooperation in science and technology is another area where diplomats work to foster international collaboration. This can include agreements for joint research, knowledge and technology exchange, and cooperation in areas such as space exploration.

Human Rights: Diplomats can participate in the negotiation of treaties and agreements that promote human rights and seek to establish standards and principles to ensure justice, equality, and the protection of fundamental rights.

International Security: Security agreements, such as mutual defense treaties, are negotiated by diplomats to promote international stability and cooperation in the field of international security.

Arms Trade and Nuclear Non-Proliferation: Diplomats also work on negotiating agreements related to arms trade and nuclear non-proliferation, seeking to control the transfer of weapons and prevent the spread of nuclear weapons.

Bilateral Assistance and Cooperation: In addition to multilateral treaties, diplomats also negotiate bilateral agreements between countries on various topics, from economic assistance to education cooperation and security collaboration.

The negotiation of agreements and treaties is essential for international cooperation and for establishing legal frameworks and standards that govern relations between nations. Diplomats play a fundamental role in building these agreements, which often have a significant impact on peace, security, trade, the environment, and other aspects of international policy.

Public Diplomacy: Public diplomacy involves direct interaction with civil society, the media, and public opinion to explain and promote a country's policies and objectives. Diplomats play an important role in building bridges and creating understanding between nations and their citizens.

Public diplomacy is an essential tool of modern diplomacy that focuses on direct interaction with civil society, the media, and public opinion both in the home country and abroad. Diplomats play a crucial role in building bridges and promoting understanding between nations and their citizens through various strategies and activities. The following are key aspects of public diplomacy:

Communication and Promotion: Diplomats act as spokespersons for their country abroad, explaining their government's policies and objectives to foreign audiences. This may include speeches, press releases, interviews, and the promotion of initiatives and programs.

Culture and Education: The promotion of culture and education is an important part of public diplomacy. Diplomats can organize cultural events, exhibitions, concerts, and educational activities to promote intercultural understanding and knowledge exchange.

Academic and Student Exchange: Academic and student exchange programs, such as Fulbright scholarships, are a significant aspect of public diplomacy. They facilitate the exchange of students, scholars, and professionals between countries, promoting mutual understanding and learning.

International Visitor Programs: Diplomats can coordinate programs that bring foreign leaders and professionals to their home country to exchange ideas and knowledge. This fosters collaboration and dialogue between countries.

Digital Diplomacy: Public diplomacy often leverages digital platforms, and diplomats use social media such as Twitter, Facebook, and Instagram to reach broader audiences and promote messages and policies.

Promotion of Investment and Trade: Public diplomacy can include efforts to promote investment and trade opportunities in the home country. This may involve organizing business events and promoting economic advantages.

Citizen Diplomacy: Diplomats may also interact with their country's citizens abroad and expatriate communities to maintain cultural ties, provide consular assistance, and promote cooperation among nationals living abroad.

Crisis Management and Emergency Communication: In times of crises, such as natural disasters or medical emergencies, diplomats play a crucial role in emergency communication and assisting citizens abroad.

Public diplomacy is essential for building a country's image and influence abroad, promoting mutual understanding, and strengthening bilateral relationships. Through a variety of strategies, diplomats work to build bridges and establish strong relations between nations and their citizens, contributing to international peace and cooperation.

Crisis Prevention: Diplomacy also focuses on crisis prevention and early identification of potential conflicts. Diplomats can intervene before a critical situation escalates into a full-blown conflict.

Crisis prevention is a critical component of modern diplomacy, and diplomats play a vital role in early detection of potential conflicts and taking steps to prevent a critical situation from escalating into a full-blown conflict.

Early Detection: Diplomats work closely with intelligence agencies and information networks to identify early signs of potential conflicts. This may include monitoring political, social, or ethnic tensions, assessing risks, and identifying possible triggers.

Preventive Diplomacy: Preventive diplomacy involves proactive diplomatic intervention to prevent a critical situation from deteriorating. Diplomats may engage in dialogue, mediation, and facilitation of discussions between conflicting parties before the situation turns violent.

Multilateral Cooperation: Multilateral diplomacy plays a significant role in crisis prevention. Diplomats work in international forums and regional organizations to address issues that could lead to conflicts and promote peaceful solutions.

Promotion of Preventive Diplomacy: Diplomats can advocate for the importance of preventive diplomacy at the political level and within the international community. This involves raising awareness among leaders and the public about the need to address conflicts before they become more severe.

Mediation and Facilitation: Diplomats often act as mediators or facilitators in crisis situations. They work to reduce tensions, promote dialogue, and assist conflicting parties in finding peaceful solutions.

Diplomacy in Crisis Zones: In some situations, special diplomatic missions can be established in crisis zones to monitor the situation and provide guidance to the parties in conflict.

Crisis Management: In situations where a crisis has already erupted, diplomats work to manage the crisis and prevent escalation. This may include the evacuation of citizens, mediating in the conflict, and seeking short-term solutions.

Crisis prevention is essential for maintaining peace and stability in an ever-changing world. Diplomats play a significant role in identifying and addressing tensions and conflicts early and working towards peaceful solutions to international challenges. Crisis prevention is an example of how diplomacy can contribute to the security and well-being of the global community.

In an increasingly interconnected and ever-changing world, diplomacy remains an essential tool for addressing global challenges and promoting peace and cooperation. Diplomats play a fundamental role in building bridges between nations and seeking peaceful solutions to the world's most pressing issues.

This journey through the evolution of diplomacy in critical situations shows how this discipline has transitioned from an informal dialogue process to a vital part of modern international politics. Diplomacy, in all its forms, continues to be a fundamental pillar for peace and stability in a world that often faces complex and evolving challenges.

2.History of Hostage Negotiation

The history of hostage negotiation dates back to the dawn of civilization, marking a fundamental chapter in the evolution of diplomacy and crisis management. From ancient civilizations to the present day, this subtle and perilous art has been a constant in the human narrative, facing changing challenges and pushing the boundaries of imagination in extreme situations.

The earliest evidence of hostage-taking dates back to antiquity, where empires and kingdoms used the practice as a means to ensure that agreements and treaties were upheld. Hostages, often members of the nobility, found themselves in a delicate balance, representing a link between two conflicting parties. The fate of these hostages depended largely on the outcome of negotiations and the behavior of both parties.

As history progressed, hostage-taking tactics evolved and became a common resource in political and military conflicts. From ancient Rome to medieval Europe, hostage-taking became deeply rooted in diplomacy, often used to guarantee peace treaties or the payment of ransoms.

The true transformation in hostage negotiation came with the emergence of modern diplomacy and the formation of international organizations. The 20th century witnessed the birth of the League of Nations and later the United Nations, both of which played a crucial role in resolving international crises and negotiating the release of hostages. As the world became more complex and globalized, hostage situations also became more intricate and challenging.

Kidnappings in the context of political terrorism and insurgency became a distinctive feature of the 20th and 21st centuries, with extremist groups resorting to these tactics to advance their political goals. Hostage negotiation became a matter of national security and a highly specialized field.

Famous cases throughout history, such as the 1979 American embassy hostage crisis in Iran or the hostage-taking at the residence of the Japanese ambassador in Lima in 1996, have left a profound mark on the global consciousness and shed light on the complexity of hostage negotiation.

This book delves into this rich history, exploring how hostage negotiation has evolved over the centuries and the lessons we can learn from these past events. As we progress through the pages, we will analyze the unique challenges faced by diplomacy in critical situations and how this discipline continues to play a vital role in crisis management in our modern world. The history of hostage negotiation is a testament to human adaptability and perseverance in the face of adversity, and this work contributes to the ever-evolving narrative of this essential field.

Diplomacy, as a tool for conflict management and international relations, has undergone a remarkable evolution throughout history. From the earliest negotiations between tribes and civilizations to today's complex political and commercial agreements, diplomacy has been the means through which nations have resolved differences, promoted cooperation, and, in critical situations, safeguarded peace.

The history of diplomacy can be traced back to antiquity when Mesopotamian, Egyptian, and Greek civilizations sent envoys and ambassadors to establish relationships, exchange information, and negotiate treaties. These early diplomats acted as intermediaries and ambassadors of peace, resolving conflicts through dialogue and negotiation.

The history of diplomacy dates back to ancient civilizations in Mesopotamia, Egypt, and Greece, where the earliest diplomatic practices developed. These civilizations used envoys and ambassadors to establish relations with other nations and address matters of common interest. The early diplomats in history acted as intermediaries and ambassadors of peace, playing a crucial role in conflict resolution through dialogue and negotiation.

In Mesopotamia, one of the oldest civilizations, envoys were employed to manage trade and political agreements, as well as to resolve territorial disputes. The Egyptians, on the other hand, used diplomats to maintain relations with their neighbors and manage issues such as trade and peace. In ancient Greece, where the term "diplomacy" originated from the Greek word "diplōma," ambassadors were sent to other city-states to negotiate treaties and alliances.

These early diplomats played a vital role in preventing conflicts and promoting cooperation among nations, setting a precedent for diplomacy as a means of peacefully resolving disputes rather than resorting to war. Over the centuries, diplomatic practices evolved and formalized, laying the foundations for the development of modern diplomacy and its role in managing critical situations and international relations.

As civilizations grew and connected through trade and conquest, diplomacy became an essential pillar of international relations. In ancient Rome, for example, the concept of "ius gentium" (law of nations) was developed to regulate diplomatic relations between states. As civilizations continued to grow and expand, diplomacy became even more crucial for managing the increasing international relations and resolving conflicts peacefully. In ancient Rome, one of the most notable examples of this evolution, the concept of "ius gentium," translated as "law of nations" or "law of peoples," was developed. This concept played a fundamental role in regulating diplomatic relations between states and creating a legal system that transcended borders.

The "ius gentium" in Rome established a legal framework for interactions between Rome and other nations, including treaties and trade agreements. It set rules and procedures for the treatment of foreigners and ambassadors and also established the rights and duties of the parties involved in international relations. This emphasis on legality and mutual respect laid the groundwork for the subsequent development of diplomacy as a specialized field.

The idea of international law governing relations between nations became a fundamental concept throughout the history of diplomacy and influenced the development of international treaties and agreements in the modern era. Diplomacy transformed from an informal practice in antiquity into a system regulated by international laws and agreements addressing a wide range of issues, from conflict resolution to trade and human rights.

This emphasis on international law and diplomacy as a means of resolving disputes and promoting cooperation has endured through the centuries, becoming an essential component of modern international politics and a key tool for managing critical situations on a global scale.

The Renaissance marked a period of flourishing diplomacy in Europe, with the establishment of permanent embassies and the rise of figures such as the renowned Italian diplomat Niccolò Machiavelli. During this era, ambassadors played a crucial role in conflict resolution and the creation of alliances.

The Renaissance, a period of significant cultural and political transformation in Europe that unfolded roughly between the 14th and 17th centuries, played a pivotal role in the evolution of diplomacy. During this era, significant advances were made in the way international relations were conducted, laying the foundations for modern diplomacy.

One of the most notable changes during the Renaissance was the establishment of permanent embassies, marking a departure from the temporary diplomatic missions that had been used previously. Permanent embassies allowed for continuous communication between states, resulting in greater stability and improved mutual understanding.

Italian diplomat Niccolò Machiavelli is a prominent figure of this era and an important precursor in the theory of diplomacy. His work "The Prince" and his writings on diplomacy offered a pragmatic and realistic perspective on international relations. Machiavelli emphasized the importance of cunning and adaptability in diplomacy, as well as the need to maintain a balance between power and morality.

During the Renaissance, ambassadors played a pivotal role in conflict resolution and the formation of alliances. They acted as intermediaries between states, negotiating treaties and agreements, and served as sources of information and analysis for their home governments. Diplomatic skills, such as oratory and negotiation, became valuable assets during this period.

The Renaissance was a period of diplomatic flourishing in Europe, marked by the establishment of permanent embassies and the emergence of influential figures like Niccolò Machiavelli. These developments laid the foundations for modern diplomacy and the way international relations are managed today.

The 19th century witnessed a significant milestone in the evolution of diplomacy with the Congress of Vienna in 1815. This event marked a turning point in European diplomacy and laid the groundwork for modern diplomacy and peace maintenance on the continent.

The Congress of Vienna was an international conference that brought together the major European powers after the Napoleonic Wars with the goal of reorganizing the political map of Europe. During this conference, the principles of the balance of power were established, involving the equitable distribution of power among European nations to prevent any single nation from becoming too dominant and triggering conflicts.

Furthermore, the notion of legitimacy was introduced, implying that legitimate leaders and monarchs should be restored to power in nations affected by the Napoleonic Wars. This focus on legitimacy and the balance of power aimed to maintain stability and prevent future conflicts in Europe.

The Congress of Vienna also promoted the idea of ongoing diplomatic cooperation and the use of international conferences to address disputes and matters of common interest. This formalized focus on diplomacy and multilateralism laid the foundations for the modern diplomatic system, which has evolved into a vital component of international relations.

The 19th century was a time of intense competition among industrialized nations for resources and territories, making diplomacy even more crucial in preventing conflicts and promoting peace. The system of alliances and bilateral and multilateral treaties became a distinctive feature of diplomacy during this era and played a fundamental role in maintaining European stability for much of the century.

The Congress of Vienna and the emphasis on the balance of power, legitimacy, and formalized diplomacy marked a significant milestone in the history of diplomacy and laid the foundations for modern diplomacy in a rapidly changing world.

The 20th century brought drastic changes in diplomacy due to the two world wars and the emergence of international organizations like the League of Nations and the United Nations. These institutions played a crucial role in resolving international conflicts and promoting global cooperation.

In more recent times, diplomacy has evolved to address a variety of complex global challenges, including nuclear proliferation, climate change, and the cyberspace. Instant communication and globalization have altered the way diplomatic negotiations are conducted, making transparency and collaboration more important than ever.

In more recent times, diplomacy has undergone a remarkable evolution to address an array of increasingly complex global challenges. These challenges include nuclear proliferation, climate change, cybersecurity, and a range of transnational issues that require effective international cooperation.

Nuclear proliferation is a critical issue for international security, and diplomacy plays a fundamental role in preventing the spread of nuclear weapons. Agreements such as the Treaty on the Non-Proliferation of Nuclear Weapons (NPT) and nuclear agreements with North Korea and Iran highlight the importance of diplomacy in managing these global risks.

Climate change is another urgent challenge that requires coordinated diplomatic action. International agreements such as the Paris Agreement are examples of how diplomacy is used to address environmental issues on a global scale and promote the reduction of greenhouse gas emissions.

Cybersecurity has become a hot topic in modern diplomacy, as cyberattacks can have significant implications for a country's security and economy. Cyber diplomacy involves negotiating international norms and agreements to address these challenges and establish clear rules for behavior in cyberspace.

Globalization and instant communication have transformed the way diplomatic negotiations are conducted. The speed at which information spreads and the ability of non-state actors to influence diplomacy have created a more complex environment. Transparency and collaboration are now more important than ever, and social media and public diplomacy play a significant role in advocating policies and generating public support.

Diplomacy has also become more diverse and multilateral in response to these global challenges. Agreements and treaties often involve multiple stakeholders and require closer cooperation between countries and international organizations.

Diplomacy has evolved to address a variety of global challenges in more recent times and remains essential for conflict prevention, the promotion of international cooperation, and the search for solutions to issues affecting the global community. Adaptability and collaboration are now key components of modern diplomacy.

Today, diplomacy is an essential tool in conflict resolution, the promotion of human rights, and the fostering of international cooperation. In critical situations, diplomats play a crucial role in preventing armed conflicts and seeking peaceful solutions. Diplomacy is a vital instrument for promoting peace, resolving conflicts, and advancing human rights on a global scale.

Diplomats and diplomatic missions play a crucial role in conflict prevention and the pursuit of peaceful solutions in critical situations.

Conflict Resolution: Diplomats work in conflict prevention and resolution, whether through mediating peace negotiations, promoting diplomatic agreements, or facilitating discussions between parties in conflict. Diplomacy contributes to de-escalating tensions and preventing armed conflicts.

Conflict resolution is one of the central roles of diplomacy in the contemporary world. Diplomats play an essential role in conflict prevention and resolution, contributing to the reduction of tensions and the maintenance of peace.

Mediation in Peace Negotiations: Diplomats often act as mediators in peace negotiations between conflicting parties. This role involves facilitating dialogue between the parties in conflict, helping identify areas of compromise, and working toward the development of sustainable peace agreements. Diplomatic mediation can be crucial in preventing armed conflicts and promoting peaceful resolution.

Promotion of Diplomatic Agreements: Diplomats work on negotiating and promoting diplomatic agreements and treaties that can help resolve conflicts. These agreements can address a wide range of issues, from border delineation and trade to security cooperation. Diplomatic treaties and agreements often lay the foundation for long-term peace and cooperation.

Facilitation of Conversations: In conflict situations, diplomats often act as facilitators of conversations between conflicting parties. This role involves creating a conducive environment for dialogue and ensuring that the parties feel heard and respected. Diplomacy facilitates communication and bridge-building between conflicting parties.

Prevention of Escalation: Diplomacy also plays an important role in preventing the escalation of tensions. Diplomats can intervene early in conflict situations to calm the waters and prevent the situation from worsening. Preventive diplomacy focuses on identifying and addressing the underlying causes of conflicts before they turn into major crises.

Peace Diplomacy: In some cases, diplomatic peace missions are established, where diplomats are sent to conflict zones to promote reconciliation, disarmament, and stabilization. These missions aim to build bridges between conflicting parties and pave the way for a peaceful resolution.

Diplomacy contributes significantly to conflict prevention and resolution, helping to prevent armed conflicts and promote peace. Diplomats, through their crisis management expertise and their ability to facilitate dialogue, are key actors in building a more peaceful and stable world.

Promotion of Human Rights: Diplomacy plays a crucial role in promoting human rights on the international stage. Diplomats advocate for justice, equality, and the respect of fundamental rights in their bilateral relations and in international forums.

Human Rights Diplomacy: States send diplomats to international missions and intergovernmental organizations dedicated to promoting and protecting human rights, such as the United Nations and the International Court of Justice. These diplomats work to influence the development of policies, resolutions, and treaties that defend human rights globally.

Bilateral Diplomacy: In their bilateral relations with other countries, diplomats advocate for human rights, discuss issues of concern, and promote policies and practices that respect fundamental rights. This may include discussions on specific cases of human rights abuses or cooperation in projects and programs to improve the human rights situation.

Women's Rights Diplomacy: Diplomacy has been instrumental in the promotion of women's rights, gender equality, and the fight against gender-based violence. Diplomats advocate for policies and international agreements that promote gender equality and work to influence laws and practices in this area.

Peace and Human Rights Diplomacy: In conflict situations, peace diplomacy is often combined with the promotion of human rights. Diplomats work to ensure that the rights of individuals in conflict areas are respected and protected and seek justice and accountability for human rights abuses.

Public Diplomacy and Human Rights: Public diplomacy involves interacting with civil society, the media, and public opinion to promote policies that respect human rights. Diplomats often engage in human rights promotion through speeches, press releases, and public education programs.

Promoting Rights in Agreements and Treaties: In treaty and agreement negotiations, diplomats can ensure that human rights are an integral part of these agreements. This may include provisions related to labor rights, minority rights, refugee protection, and more.

Promoting human rights through diplomacy is essential to ensure that states fulfill their obligations under international human rights treaties and respect universal human rights principles. Diplomats play a vital role in building a world where all individuals enjoy their fundamental rights and live with dignity.

International Cooperation: Diplomacy fosters cooperation between nations on a wide range of issues, from combating poverty and climate change to managing health crises and collaborating on security.

International cooperation is a central component of modern diplomacy, and diplomats work tirelessly to promote collaboration between nations on a wide range of issues that affect the global community.

Poverty and Development: Diplomacy plays an essential role in promoting cooperation to address poverty and promote sustainable development worldwide. Diplomats negotiate assistance agreements and collaborate on development programs aimed at improving the living conditions of vulnerable populations.

Climate Change and the Environment: International cooperation is essential in the fight against climate change and environmental protection. Diplomats participate in international agreements and treaties, such as the Paris Agreement, to address global environmental issues and promote sustainable practices.

Health Crises: In global health crises, such as pandemics, diplomats work to coordinate international responses. This includes collaboration on the distribution of medical resources, the promotion of scientific research, and the implementation of measures to contain the spread of diseases.

Security Collaboration: Diplomacy plays a fundamental role in promoting international security. Diplomats work to negotiate arms control treaties, prevent conflicts, and promote stability in crisis areas.

International Trade: Diplomacy is essential in international trade negotiations. Diplomats negotiate bilateral and multilateral trade agreements that promote market openness, economic growth, and job creation.

Human Rights and Justice: International cooperation on human rights and justice matters is critical. Diplomats work to establish standards and treaties that promote justice, equality, and accountability for human rights violations.

Education and Culture: Diplomacy also promotes collaboration in educational and cultural areas. This includes student exchange programs, the promotion of cultural diversity, and the protection of cultural heritage.

Humanitarian Assistance: Diplomats play a crucial role in coordinating humanitarian assistance efforts in crisis situations, such as natural disasters and conflicts. This includes mobilizing resources and delivering aid to affected populations.

International cooperation through diplomacy is essential to address global challenges and promote a safer, sustainable, and fair world. Diplomats play a key role in building bridges between nations and finding solutions to issues affecting humanity as a whole.

Negotiating Agreements and Treaties: Diplomats are responsible for negotiating and agreeing upon bilateral and multilateral treaties and agreements that address globally significant issues such as trade, the environment, security, and science and technology.

The negotiation of agreements and treaties is a central role of diplomats and a fundamental part of international diplomacy. Diplomats work to negotiate, agree upon, and promote a wide variety of treaties and agreements addressing globally significant issues.

International Trade: Diplomats often negotiate important trade agreements. They negotiate free trade treaties, investment agreements, and other trade-related agreements to promote market openness and facilitate the exchange of goods and services between countries.

Environment: Diplomats work on negotiating treaties and agreements related to the environment, such as the Paris Agreement on climate change.

These agreements seek to address global environmental issues and promote sustainable practices.

Security and Disarmament: Diplomats participate in arms control treaties and disarmament agreements to promote international security and reduce the proliferation of nuclear and conventional weapons.

Science and Technology: International cooperation in science and technology is another area where diplomats work to foster global collaboration. This can include agreements for joint research, knowledge and technology exchange, and cooperation in areas such as space exploration.

Human Rights: Diplomats can be involved in negotiating treaties and agreements that promote human rights and aim to establish standards and principles for ensuring justice, equality, and the protection of fundamental rights.

International Security: Security agreements, such as mutual defense treaties, are negotiated by diplomats to promote international stability and cooperation in the field of international security.

Arms Trade and Nuclear Non-Proliferation: Diplomats also work on agreements related to the arms trade and nuclear non-proliferation, seeking to control the transfer of arms and prevent the spread of nuclear weapons.

Bilateral Assistance and Cooperation: In addition to multilateral treaties, diplomats also negotiate bilateral agreements between countries on various topics, from economic assistance to education cooperation and security collaboration.

The negotiation of agreements and treaties is essential for international cooperation and for establishing legal frameworks and standards governing relations between nations. Diplomats play a crucial role in building these agreements, which often have a significant impact on peace, security, trade, the environment, and other aspects of international policy.

Public Diplomacy: Public diplomacy involves direct interaction with civil society, the media, and public opinion to explain and promote a country's policies and objectives. Diplomats play a significant role in building bridges and creating understanding between nations and their citizens.

Public diplomacy is an essential tool of modern diplomacy that focuses on direct interaction with civil society, the media, and public opinion, both in the home country and abroad. Diplomats play a crucial role in building bridges and promoting understanding between nations and their citizens through various strategies and activities. Below are key aspects of public diplomacy:

Communication and Promotion: Diplomats serve as spokespersons for their country abroad, explaining their government's policies and objectives to foreign audiences. This may include delivering speeches, issuing press releases, giving interviews, and promoting initiatives and programs.

Culture and Education: Promoting culture and education is an important part of public diplomacy. Diplomats can organize cultural events, exhibitions, concerts, and educational activities to enhance intercultural understanding and knowledge exchange.

Academic and Student Exchange: Academic and student exchange programs, such as the Fulbright scholarships, are a significant aspect of public diplomacy. They facilitate the exchange of students, scholars, and professionals between countries, promoting mutual understanding and learning.

International Visitor Programs: Diplomats can coordinate programs that bring foreign leaders and professionals to their home country for knowledge and idea exchange. This fosters collaboration and dialogue between nations.

Digital Diplomacy: Social media and online communication are powerful tools in public diplomacy. Diplomats can use platforms like Twitter, Facebook, and Instagram to reach wider audiences and promote messages and policies.

Promotion of Investment and Trade: Public diplomacy efforts may include promoting investments and trade opportunities in the home country. This can involve organizing business events and highlighting economic advantages.

Citizen Diplomacy: Diplomats also interact with citizens of their own country abroad and expatriate communities to maintain cultural ties, provide consular assistance, and promote cooperation among nationals living abroad.

Crisis Management and Emergency Communication: In crisis situations, such as natural disasters or medical emergencies, diplomats play an important role in emergency communication and assisting citizens abroad.

Public diplomacy is essential for building a country's image and influence abroad, promoting mutual understanding, and strengthening bilateral relations. Through various strategies, diplomats work to create bridges and establish strong relationships between nations and their citizens, contributing to international peace and cooperation.

3.Basic Principles of Negotiation:

The fundamental principles of negotiation are essential for achieving effective and constructive agreements in a wide variety of situations.

Seeking Mutually Beneficial Solutions: Negotiation should not be seen as a competition in which one party wins at the expense of the other. Instead, the goal should be to find solutions that are mutually beneficial. This involves identifying shared interests and seeking agreements that satisfy the needs and desires of both parties. When both parties benefit, the agreement tends to be more enduring and less prone to future conflicts.

Effective Communication: Communication is crucial in any negotiation process. This includes the ability to actively listen to the other party to understand their needs, interests, and concerns. Communication also involves the clear presentation of your own ideas and proposals. Transparency and empathy are key to building a trust relationship in negotiation.

Preparation and Knowledge: Preparation is fundamental for a successful negotiation. Before entering the negotiation table, it's important to research and be knowledgeable about relevant facts, goals, and positions of both parties, as well as any relevant information about the context. Solid preparation allows you to formulate effective strategies and tactics.

In addition to these three fundamental principles, negotiation also benefits from principles like flexibility, patience, the ability to compromise on minor points to achieve an agreement on key issues, and emotion management. Ultimately, successful negotiation involves a balance between advocating for your interests and being willing to find solutions that satisfy both parties, contributing to the building of long-term relationships and effective dispute resolution.

Hostage negotiation is a delicate and critical task that involves a set of specific basic principles to ensure the safety of the hostages and the peaceful resolution of the situation.

Priority: Safeguarding Human Lives: The primary priority in hostage negotiation is the preservation of human lives. This means that the lives and safety of the hostages are the most important consideration, and any action must take into account this fundamental principle. The priority of safeguarding human lives is the most fundamental principle in hostage negotiation. The safety and well-being of the hostages must take precedence over any other goal or consideration. This involves a series of actions and decisions:

Not putting hostages at risk: Any action taken during negotiations must carefully consider the impact on the lives and safety of the hostages. This includes planning rescue operations or handling demands and conditions from the captors.

Seeking peaceful solutions: The priority should always be to find a peaceful solution that allows the safe release of the hostages. This may require concessions and compromises, but the lives of the hostages should not be endangered.

Maintaining calm and avoiding provocations: Negotiators must avoid actions that could provoke the captors and endanger the hostages. Calmness and patience are essential in these situations.

Providing medical care and psychological support: Hostages often experience high-stress conditions and may require medical care and psychological support. This should be provided in a timely and appropriate manner.

Coordination with authorities: Hostage negotiation teams must work closely with authorities and security forces to ensure the safety of the hostages and make informed decisions.

Emphasis on confidentiality: Sensitive information related to negotiations and the safety of the hostages must be handled with the utmost confidentiality to prevent captors from gaining an advantage or feeling provoked.

This principle underscores the importance of negotiations focusing on the safety and lives of the individuals involved and not on other secondary objectives. Hostages' lives are invaluable, and any action taken should be in line with the priority of preserving them.

Direct and Open Communication: Effective communication with captors is essential. Negotiators must establish direct and open channels of communication with the captors to facilitate dialogue and understand their demands and concerns.

Direct and open communication is an essential principle in hostage negotiation as it lays the foundation for effective dialogue with captors.

Establishment of Communication Channels: Negotiators must take steps to establish reliable and secure communication channels with the captors. This may include the use of phones, radios, or other agreed-upon means. Active Listening: Negotiators must practice active listening to understand the demands, concerns, and needs of the captors. This involves paying attention to what is said and asking questions to clarify information. Maintaining Constructive Dialogue: It is essential to maintain a constructive and respectful dialogue with captors. This involves avoiding provocations and arguments that can increase tension. Communication of Proposals and Conditions: Negotiators must present proposals and conditions clearly and directly. This includes explaining proposed agreements and how they will be fulfilled. Managing Expectations: Negotiators must also be realistic about what they can offer and what they cannot. Managing expectations is key to avoiding misunderstandings and conflicts. Communication Security: The security of communication channels is critical. Negotiators must take measures to ensure that conversations are not intercepted and that the location of the hostages is not revealed. Flexibility in Communication Approach: Negotiators must be willing to adapt their communication approach based on the circumstances. This may include changes in the frequency of conversations or interlocutors. Mediation and Facilitation of Conversations: In some cases, negotiators may also act as mediators or facilitators between captors and authorities to facilitate more effective dialogue.

Direct and open communication is essential for understanding the demands and concerns of captors, which in turn facilitates the search for peaceful solutions and the safe release of hostages. Without effective dialogue, hostage negotiation would be much more challenging and risky.

Negotiation Professionals: Hostage negotiation must be conducted by professionals experienced in such situations. Negotiators must be well-trained in hostage negotiation techniques and crisis management.

The involvement of highly trained professionals in hostage negotiation is crucial to ensure the safety of the hostages and achieve a successful resolution. Here are some important considerations related to this principle:

Specialized Training: Hostage negotiators must receive specialized training in hostage negotiation techniques and crisis management. This training includes the development of communication skills, risk assessment, and persuasion techniques.

Understanding Psychology: Hostage negotiation professionals must understand the psychology of captors and hostages. This allows them to adapt their communication and negotiation approach to the specific dynamics of the situation.

Preparation for Crisis Scenarios: Negotiators must be prepared to face extremely stressful and dangerous situations. This includes the ability to stay calm and make rational decisions in moments of high tension.

Risk Assessment and Scenario Planning: Hostage negotiation professionals must be experts in risk assessment and scenario planning. This allows them to anticipate possible turns in the situation and take preventive measures.

Coordination with Security Forces: Negotiators must work closely with security forces and other relevant agencies. This ensures a coordinated and effective response in case a rescue operation becomes necessary.

Confidentiality and Security: Negotiators must handle information with the utmost confidentiality to avoid endangering the safety of the hostages. This includes protecting the identity of negotiators and any sources of information.

Adaptability: Every hostage situation is unique. Negotiation professionals must be flexible and capable of adapting to changing circumstances.

Psychological Support: Negotiators may also require psychological support after facing traumatic situations. Attention to mental health is important for their long-term well-being.

Hostage negotiators must be highly trained and well-prepared experts who can approach situations calmly, professionally, and empathetically. Their experience and training are essential for the safety of the hostages and for achieving a peaceful resolution of the crisis.

Building Trust: Trust is fundamental in hostage negotiation. Negotiators must work to build a trust relationship with the captors, which can help achieve a peaceful resolution.

Building trust is a critical aspect of hostage negotiation since a trust relationship between negotiators and captors can aid in achieving a peaceful resolution and ensuring the safety of the hostages.

Active Listening and Empathy: Negotiators must practice active listening and demonstrate empathy toward captors. This involves understanding and validating their concerns and demands, even if they do not agree with them.

Commitment to Agreements: Fulfilling agreed-upon commitments is essential for building trust. When captors see negotiators keeping their promises, they are more likely to trust them in the future.

Transparency: Negotiators must be transparent about their intentions and actions. Lack of transparency can undermine trust and generate suspicion.

Establishing Ongoing Communication: Maintaining continuous and regular communication with captors can help build trust over time. This includes providing updates on the progress of negotiations and addressing captors' questions or concerns.

Willingness to Listen: Negotiators must show a genuine willingness to listen and understand captors, even when the situation is tense. This may require patience and tolerance.

Crisis Management and De-escalation: Building trust also involves the ability to manage the crisis in a way that minimizes tension and violence. Negotiators must work to de-escalate the situation whenever possible.

Offering Constructive Solutions: Negotiators can offer constructive solutions that benefit both parties. This may include compromises and concessions that demonstrate a willingness to find common ground.

Recognition of Human Dignity: Recognizing the human dignity of all involved, including captors, is important for building trust. Showing respect and treating all parties with dignity is fundamental.

Building trust is a gradual and often challenging process in hostage negotiation, but it is essential to establish a solid foundation for crisis resolution. When captors trust negotiators and their willingness to address demands constructively, the likelihood of achieving a peaceful release of hostages increases significantly.

Maintaining Calm and Patience: Patience is essential in hostage negotiation. Negotiators must remain calm, even in high-tension situations, and avoid making hasty decisions that could endanger the hostages.

Maintaining calm and patience is crucial in hostage negotiation, as situations are often extremely tense and dangerous.

Thoughtful Decision-Making: Negotiators must avoid making impulsive or rushed decisions that could jeopardize the hostages. Careful reflection and evaluation of implications are essential before taking any action.

Emotion Control: The ability to control emotions is fundamental. Negotiators must remain calm, even in high-tension situations, to prevent increasing hostility or stress in the situation.

Managing Frustration and Stress: Hostage negotiations are often lengthy and frustrating. Negotiators must develop strategies to effectively manage their own stress and frustration.

Avoiding Provocations: Provocations and hostility can increase the risk to hostages. Negotiators must avoid any actions or words that could exacerbate the situation.

Controlled Communication: Communication with captors must be controlled and measured. Negotiators must avoid impulsive emotional responses and focus on effective communication.

Team Support: Negotiators work in teams, and mutual support is essential for maintaining calm and patience. Emotional support can be provided, and the negotiation burden can be shared.

Planning and Strategy: Careful planning and strategy implementation are ways to maintain control of the situation and avoid hasty decisions. Negotiators must be prepared for different scenarios and have a clear action plan.

Pressure Management: The pressure from captors, authorities, the media, and public opinion can be intense. Negotiators must know how to handle this pressure and keep their focus on the safety of the hostages.

Patience and composure are essential qualities for hostage negotiators, as their ability to maintain control of the situation and make rational decisions in critical moments can make a difference in the safety of the hostages and the outcome of the negotiation.

Situation Assessment: Negotiators must continuously assess the situation to understand changes in captors' demands, the hostages' conditions, and any other relevant factors. This ongoing assessment helps adapt negotiation strategies.

Continuous Monitoring: Negotiators must maintain constant monitoring of the situation, which involves closely following events, captors' communications, and any changes in demands or conditions.

Risk Assessment: Risk assessment is essential to understand potential threats to the hostages and identify possible opportunities for a peaceful resolution of the situation.

Intelligence Updates: Negotiators must have up-to-date information about the captors, their motivations, and other relevant factors. This may require cooperation from intelligence agencies or other sources.

Interviews with Hostages: Speaking with the hostages can provide valuable information about their health, safety, and captors' actions. This feedback can help tailor negotiation strategies.

Demand Assessment: Captors' demands can change over time. Negotiators must assess new demands and their feasibility.

Communication with Authorities: Negotiation teams must maintain constant communication with authorities and security forces to share information and coordinate actions.

Crisis Scenarios: Negotiators must be prepared for different crisis scenarios and assess how these could affect the safety of the hostages and negotiation strategies.

Adaptation of Strategies: Based on the situation assessment, negotiators must be willing to adapt their negotiation strategies. This may involve changes in concessions, communication with captors, or planning rescue operations.

Continuous situation assessment is essential for making informed decisions in hostage negotiation and for adjusting strategies as circumstances evolve. This contributes to the safety of the hostages and the pursuit of a peaceful and successful crisis resolution.

Establishing Clear Limits and Guidelines: Negotiators must set clear limits and guidelines for the negotiations. This includes defining what is negotiable and what is not, as well as complying with applicable laws and regulations. Establishing clear limits and guidelines is essential in hostage negotiation to maintain the security and integrity of the process.

Definition of Negotiable Items: Negotiators must clearly define what is negotiable and what is not. This includes identifying limits in terms of possible concessions, demands that cannot be met, and areas of compromise.

Compliance with Laws and Regulations: Negotiators must act in compliance with applicable laws and regulations, which may include legal restrictions on certain types of concessions or interactions with captors.

Protection of National Security: In some cases, negotiators may face limitations due to national security interests. It is important that negotiations do not jeopardize national security.

Ethics and Values: Negotiators must act ethically and in accordance with the values of society and the institution they represent. This may involve not compromising on issues that go against fundamental ethical principles.

Good Negotiation Practices: Negotiators must follow guidelines of good negotiation practices, which include promoting peaceful solutions and protecting the lives of the hostages.

Communication of Limits to Captors: Effectively communicating limits to the captors is important. This can help avoid misunderstandings and reduce unrealistic expectations.

Maintaining Hostage Safety: Limits must be set in a way that ensures the safety of the hostages. Negotiators should not take actions that increase the risk to the hostages.

Coordination with Authorities: Limits and guidelines must be coordinated with authorities and security forces to ensure a unified and safe response.

Establishing clear limits and guidelines is fundamental to ensure that negotiations are conducted safely and effectively. By doing so, the integrity of the negotiation process is protected, and decisions that could jeopardize the hostages or national security are avoided.

Support and Coordination: Hostage negotiation teams often work closely with security forces, crisis response teams, and other relevant agencies. Coordination is essential to ensure the safety of all involved.

Support and coordination are essential in hostage negotiation, as it involves the collaboration of multiple parties with different responsibilities and skills.

Teamwork: Hostage negotiation teams are often composed of professionals with different roles and responsibilities. Effective communication and teamwork are essential for success.

Coordination with Security Forces: Negotiators must coordinate their efforts with security forces responsible for maintaining safety at the hostage site. This coordination may include establishing secure zones, perimeter protection, and rescue operation planning.

Effective Communication: Seamless communication between negotiation teams and security forces is crucial to ensure the synchronization of efforts and avoid misunderstandings.

Sharing Relevant Information: Up-to-date and relevant information must be shared among all involved parties. This includes data about the captors, the hostages' situation, and any changes in demands or conditions.

Clear Role Definition: Each team should have clearly defined roles and responsibilities. This prevents duplicated efforts and ensures that each team focuses on its specific tasks.

Joint Risk Assessment: Risk assessments should be conducted jointly to understand the situation in its entirety and determine the best strategies to ensure hostage safety.

Respect for Skills and Experience: Each team should respect the skills and experience of the others. This contributes to a collaborative and efficient working environment.

Emotional Support: In hostage situations, emotional support among team members is important to maintain morale and resilience.

Captors' Communication Channel: Coordination may also include the transmission of messages and communications between the captors and negotiation teams.

Information Security: Sensitive information must be handled with the utmost security to prevent it from falling into the hands of the captors.

Planning and Strategy: Careful planning and strategy implementation are ways to maintain control of the situation and avoid hasty decisions. Negotiators must be prepared for different scenarios and have a clear action plan.

Pressure Management: The pressure from captors, authorities, the media, and public opinion can be intense. Negotiators must know how to handle this pressure and keep their focus on the safety of the hostages.

Patience and composure are essential qualities for hostage negotiators, as their ability to maintain control of the situation and make rational decisions in critical moments can make a difference in the safety of the hostages and the outcome of the negotiation.

Situation Assessment: Negotiators must continuously assess the situation to understand changes in captors' demands, the hostages' conditions, and any other relevant factors. This ongoing assessment helps adapt negotiation strategies.

Continuous Monitoring: Negotiators must maintain constant monitoring of the situation, which involves closely following events, captors' communications, and any changes in demands or conditions.

Risk Assessment: Risk assessment is essential to understand potential threats to the hostages and identify possible opportunities for a peaceful resolution of the situation.

Intelligence Updates: Negotiators must have up-to-date information about the captors, their motivations, and other relevant factors. This may require cooperation from intelligence agencies or other sources.

Interviews with Hostages: Speaking with the hostages can provide valuable information about their health, safety, and captors' actions. This feedback can help tailor negotiation strategies.

Demand Assessment: Captors' demands can change over time. Negotiators must assess new demands and their feasibility.

Communication with Authorities: Negotiation teams must maintain constant communication with authorities and security forces to share information and coordinate actions.

Crisis Scenarios: Negotiators must be prepared for different crisis scenarios and assess how these could affect the safety of the hostages and negotiation strategies.

Adaptation of Strategies: Based on the situation assessment, negotiators must be willing to adapt their negotiation strategies. This may involve changes in concessions, communication with captors, or planning rescue operations.

Continuous situation assessment is essential for making informed decisions in hostage negotiation and for adjusting strategies as circumstances evolve. This contributes to the safety of the hostages and the pursuit of a peaceful and successful crisis resolution.

Establishing Clear Limits and Guidelines: Negotiators must set clear limits and guidelines for the negotiations. This includes defining what is negotiable and what is not, as well as complying with applicable laws and regulations. Establishing clear limits and guidelines is essential in hostage negotiation to maintain the security and integrity of the process.

Definition of Negotiable Items: Negotiators must clearly define what is negotiable and what is not. This includes identifying limits in terms of possible concessions, demands that cannot be met, and areas of compromise.

Compliance with Laws and Regulations: Negotiators must act in compliance with applicable laws and regulations, which may include legal restrictions on certain types of concessions or interactions with captors.

Protection of National Security: In some cases, negotiators may face limitations due to national security interests. It is important that negotiations do not jeopardize national security.

Ethics and Values: Negotiators must act ethically and in accordance with the values of society and the institution they represent. This may involve not compromising on issues that go against fundamental ethical principles.

Good Negotiation Practices: Negotiators must follow guidelines of good negotiation practices, which include promoting peaceful solutions and protecting the lives of the hostages.

Communication of Limits to Captors: Effectively communicating limits to the captors is important. This can help avoid misunderstandings and reduce unrealistic expectations.

Maintaining Hostage Safety: Limits must be set in a way that ensures the safety of the hostages. Negotiators should not take actions that increase the risk to the hostages.

Coordination with Authorities: Limits and guidelines must be coordinated with authorities and security forces to ensure a unified and safe response.

Establishing clear limits and guidelines is fundamental to ensure that negotiations are conducted safely and effectively. By doing so, the integrity of the negotiation process is protected, and decisions that could jeopardize the hostages or national security are avoided.

Support and Coordination: Hostage negotiation teams often work closely with security forces, crisis response teams, and other relevant agencies. Coordination is essential to ensure the safety of all involved.

Support and coordination are essential in hostage negotiation, as it involves the collaboration of multiple parties with different responsibilities and skills.

Teamwork: Hostage negotiation teams are often composed of professionals with different roles and responsibilities. Effective communication and teamwork are essential for success.

Coordination with Security Forces: Negotiators must coordinate their efforts with security forces responsible for maintaining safety at the hostage site. This coordination may include establishing secure zones, perimeter protection, and rescue operation planning.

Effective Communication: Seamless communication between negotiation teams and security forces is crucial to ensure the synchronization of efforts and avoid misunderstandings.

Sharing Relevant Information: Up-to-date and relevant information must be shared among all involved parties. This includes data about the captors, the hostages' situation, and any changes in demands or conditions.

Clear Role Definition: Each team should have clearly defined roles and responsibilities. This prevents duplicated efforts and ensures that each team focuses on its specific tasks.

Joint Risk Assessment: Risk assessments should be conducted jointly to understand the situation in its entirety and determine the best strategies to ensure hostage safety.

Respect for Skills and Experience: Each team should respect the skills and experience of the others. This contributes to a collaborative and efficient working environment.

Emotional Support: In hostage situations, emotional support among team members is important to maintain morale and resilience.

Captors' Communication Channel: Coordination may also include the transmission of messages and communications between the captors and negotiation teams.

Information Security: Sensitive information must be handled with the utmost security to prevent it from falling into the hands of the captors.

4-Profile of a Hostage Negotiator.

The profile of a hostage negotiator is crucial in kidnapping or hostage situations, as it plays a vital role in crisis management and the pursuit of a peaceful solution. A good hostage negotiator should possess a set of skills, traits, and specific training to perform their role effectively. Here is a general profile of what is expected of a hostage negotiator:

Calm and Patience: Hostage negotiators must remain calm in extremely stressful situations. Patience is essential as negotiations can take time.

Calmness and patience are essential qualities for hostage negotiators. In hostage situations, stress and tension are often very high, and negotiators must be able to maintain composure in the midst of this crisis.

Hostility Reduction: Maintaining calm and patience can help reduce hostility and the risk of escalating violence by captors. Negotiators must avoid impulsive emotional reactions.

Building Trust: Calmness and patience can contribute to building trust between captors and negotiators. When captors feel they are dealing with rational and controlled individuals, they are more likely to be willing to negotiate.

Effective Negotiations: Negotiations in hostage situations can be time-consuming as agreements can be complex and sensitive. Patience is essential for working through details and reaching an agreement that benefits all parties involved.

Maintaining Safety: Calmness and patience are also crucial for ensuring the safety of the hostages. Negotiators must avoid any actions that could jeopardize the hostages or themselves.

Stress Management: Stress can cloud judgment and hinder effective decision-making. Calmness and patience help negotiators manage stress and make rational decisions in critical moments.

Resistance to Manipulation: Captors may try to manipulate negotiators through emotional tactics. Calmness and patience help negotiators resist manipulation and maintain control of the situation.

Calmness and patience are essential traits that enable hostage negotiators to perform their role effectively and safely in crisis situations. These qualities contribute to building trust, reducing hostility, and the ability to make rational decisions in extremely stressful circumstances.

Empathy: They must be able to understand and empathize with the emotions and concerns of both captors and hostages. Empathy can help establish a bond of trust.

Empathy is a crucial skill for hostage negotiators in hostage or kidnapping situations.

Building a Trusting Relationship: Empathy can help establish a trusting relationship with captors and hostages. When negotiators demonstrate an understanding of the emotions and concerns of the parties involved, they are more likely to feel heard and respected.

Facilitating Communication: Empathy creates an environment in which people are more willing to communicate openly. Captors and hostages may be more inclined to share important information if they feel that negotiators understand them and do not judge them.

Effective Negotiations: By understanding the concerns and motivations of captors, negotiators can adapt their negotiation strategies more effectively. Empathy allows them to identify possible points of agreement and solutions that benefit both parties.

Reduction of Hostility: Empathy can contribute to reducing hostility and aggression on the part of captors. When captors feel that negotiators care about their concerns, they may be less inclined to resort to violence.

Emotional Support for Hostages: Hostages may be experiencing significant emotional distress during a hostage situation. Empathetic negotiators can provide emotional support to hostages, which can help alleviate their anxiety and fear.

Avoiding a Rigid Approach: Empathy enables negotiators to avoid a rigid and authoritarian approach that could exacerbate the situation. Instead, they can adapt to the changing needs and emotions of the parties involved.

Building Bridges: Empathy can also help build bridges toward a peaceful resolution. By understanding the perspectives of all parties, negotiators can identify solutions that meet the fundamental needs of each.

Empathy does not imply supporting or justifying the actions of captors but rather demonstrating a genuine understanding of their emotions and concerns. Hostage negotiators are trained to balance empathy with firmness in the pursuit of a peaceful and safe resolution.

Communication Skills: Hostage negotiators must be experts in verbal and non-verbal communication. They must be able to convey their messages effectively and listen attentively.

Communication skills are essential for hostage negotiators in crisis situations, as effective communication can make a difference in achieving a peaceful and safe resolution.

Verbal Communication: Clarity: Negotiators must be clear and concise in expressing their messages. Using simple and direct language is fundamental, as confusion can lead to misunderstandings.

Effective Negotiation: They should be skilled in verbal negotiation, presenting strong arguments and seeking compromises that benefit all parties.

Emotional Control: Maintaining calm when speaking is essential. Negotiators must avoid emotional or provocative responses that could exacerbate the situation.

Empathy: Empathetic verbal communication involves actively listening to the parties involved, validating their emotions and concerns, and responding in a compassionate manner.

Non-Verbal Communication: Body Language: Negotiators must pay attention to their own body language, ensuring that it is consistent with their verbal message. An open and relaxed posture can convey confidence.

Active Listening: Non-verbal communication also applies to the ability to actively listen. Negotiators must show attention and interest through gestures such as nodding and maintaining eye contact.

Gestural Control: Avoiding gestures that can be interpreted as threatening or challenging is essential. Inappropriate gestures can trigger negative reactions.

Caution in Emotional Expression: Negotiators must be aware of how their facial expressions can influence the perception of the parties involved.

Showing empathy and understanding through appropriate facial expressions can be beneficial.

Active Listening: The ability to actively listen is crucial. Negotiators must pay full attention to what captors and hostages are saying to understand their concerns and needs.

Asking clear and relevant questions can help gather important information and maintain the conversation.

Active listening involves not only paying attention to the words but also to the emotions behind them. Negotiators must be sensitive to the emotional signals being conveyed.

Verbal and non-verbal communication skills are fundamental for hostage negotiators as they enable effective communication, the maintenance of composure, and the building of trust in crisis situations. These skills are an integral part of situation management and the pursuit of a peaceful resolution.

Decision-Making: In crisis situations, negotiators must make rapid and well-founded decisions. They must continuously assess the situation and adjust their approach accordingly.

Effective decision-making is one of the key competencies that hostage negotiators must possess, especially in high-stress and crisis situations.

Speed and Accuracy: In hostage situations, time is critical. Negotiators must make quick and accurate decisions to effectively manage the crisis and minimize risks to both hostages and themselves.

Continuous Assessment: The situation can change rapidly, so negotiators must constantly evaluate available information and the dynamics of the crisis. This involves keeping track of the actions of the captors, the reactions of the hostages, and any other significant developments.

Goal Prioritization: Negotiators must set clear goals and prioritize them. The safety of the hostages should be the top priority, followed by the pursuit of a peaceful resolution and the minimization of any harm.

Identifying Areas of Agreement: Effective decision-making involves seeking areas where the involved parties may be willing to compromise. This may require identifying points of agreement and presenting proposals that benefit all parties.

Contingency Planning: Negotiators must have contingency plans in case the situation deteriorates or unexpected problems arise. These plans should be well-thought-out and prepared in advance.

Collaboration with Support Teams: Negotiators work closely with other professionals, such as the police, psychologists, and security experts. They must make decisions that align with the overall team strategy and take into account the areas of expertise of team members.

Effective Communication: Decision-making is not limited to actions but also involves effective communication with the involved parties. Negotiators must clearly and persuasively communicate their decisions, explaining how they contribute to a peaceful resolution.

Adaptability: Circumstances can change rapidly in hostage situations. Negotiators must be flexible and prepared to adjust their approaches and decisions as the situation evolves.

Ethics and Values: Decisions made by negotiators must align with ethical principles and fundamental values, such as the preservation of life and respect for human rights. They should avoid actions that compromise the ethical integrity of their work.

Decision-making in hostage situations is an extremely challenging task that requires a delicate balance between speed and accuracy, empathy and firmness, and adaptability. Negotiators are trained to face these situations with a professional and safety-oriented approach to ensure a peaceful resolution.

Crisis Management Training: Hostage negotiators typically receive specialized training in crisis management and negotiation techniques. This includes learning strategies for dealing with high-risk situations.

Crisis management training is a fundamental component of preparing hostage negotiators. This specialized training provides them with the skills, knowledge, and techniques necessary to deal with high-risk situations and make effective decisions in the midst of a crisis.

Negotiation Techniques: Negotiators receive training in advanced negotiation techniques specific to hostage situations. This includes strategies for establishing and maintaining communication with captors, identifying areas of agreement, managing the negotiation process, and achieving a peaceful resolution.

Situation Awareness: Negotiators must be well-informed about the current situation, including the backgrounds of the captors, their motivations, and any demands they may have raised. This helps them better understand the context in which they are working and adapt their strategies accordingly.

Simulations and Training Scenarios: Hostage negotiation teams often conduct drills and training exercises to simulate crisis situations. This allows them to practice their skills in a controlled environment and develop effective teamwork.

Risk Assessment: Crisis management training includes the ability to assess and manage risk. Negotiators must be able to determine the level of risk in a given situation and make decisions that minimize the threat to hostages and response personnel.

Strategic Communication: Negotiators learn to use strategic communication to influence captor behavior and encourage a peaceful resolution. This may include using persuasion tactics and strategies to buy time.

Crisis Psychology: Training also addresses crisis psychology, helping negotiators understand the impact of stress and emotions on individuals involved in the crisis. This enables them to adapt their approach and strategies based on the emotional dynamics at play.

Human Rights and Ethics: Negotiators receive training in human rights and ethics to ensure that their actions and decisions adhere to fundamental principles, such as the preservation of life and respect for the rights of all individuals involved.

Interdisciplinary Collaboration: Negotiation teams work closely with other professionals, such as the police, psychologists, and security experts. Training promotes interdisciplinary collaboration and effective coordination among team members.

Crisis management training is essential to ensure that negotiators are prepared to address hostage situations in a professional and safe manner. This specialized training equips them with the tools needed to manage the crisis, communicate effectively, and seek a peaceful resolution in extremely challenging circumstances.

Situation Awareness: They should be well-informed about the current situation, including the backgrounds of the captors, their motivations, and any demands they may have made. The more information they have, the better they can negotiate.

Situation awareness is crucial for hostage negotiators, as it allows them to better understand the context in which they are working and adapt their negotiation strategies effectively.

Captors' Backgrounds: Knowing the backgrounds of the captors, their identities, their history, and any relevant information about who they are can be crucial. This can help negotiators understand the possible motivations behind the kidnapping and anticipate how they might react in different situations.

Motives for Kidnapping: Understanding the motives behind the kidnapping is essential. It could be for political, economic, personal, or other reasons. The better negotiators understand the motives of the captors, the more effective their strategies can be in addressing their demands and concerns.

Information about Hostages: Knowing the hostages, their number, their identity, their health status, and any relevant information about them is important. This allows negotiators to develop strategies to ensure their safety and well-being.

Site or Situation History: If possible, it is useful to know the history of the location where the hostage-taking occurs. This may include details about previous incidents, security issues, or any other factors that could affect crisis management.

Political and Social Context: Knowledge of the political and social context in which the kidnapping occurs can be valuable. Broader political or social events may influence the motivations and demands of the captors.

Technology and Communication: Understanding available technological capabilities and communication options can be crucial. This includes knowing how to establish and maintain communication with the captors, as well as using technology to gather information or monitor the situation.

Interagency Collaboration: Negotiators often work in collaboration with security agencies, police forces, and other professionals. Knowledge of the capabilities and resources of these institutions is important to coordinate efforts and ensure a comprehensive response.

Detailed Situation Awareness allows negotiators to make informed decisions, adapt their negotiation strategies, and maintain effective communication with the captors. The more information they have, the better prepared they will be to manage the crisis and seek a peaceful and safe resolution.

Teamwork: In most cases, hostage negotiators work as part of a team with other professionals, such as the police, psychologists, and security experts. They must be able to collaborate effectively.

Teamwork is essential in managing hostage situations because it involves the collaboration of various professionals with different roles and areas of expertise.

Effort Coordination: Managing a hostage crisis requires the collaboration of multiple agencies and professionals, such as the police, negotiators, psychologists, security experts, and others. Working as a team allows for efficient coordination of available efforts and resources.

Specialization: Each team member brings their specialized expertise and knowledge. Negotiators focus on communication and negotiation, while the police handle security and logistics. Psychologists can provide emotional support to the hostages. Collaboration allows for leveraging each individual's expertise.

Effective Communication: Teamwork requires effective communication among members. Information must flow consistently and accurately to make informed decisions and adapt strategies as needed.

Coordinated Planning: Planning the response to a hostage situation must be coordinated. Teams must work together to develop contingency plans, negotiation strategies, and rescue strategies, if necessary.

Mutual Support: Hostage situations can be extremely stressful and emotionally challenging. Working as a team allows members to provide mutual support and share the emotional burden.

Risk Assessment: Different team members can contribute to risk assessment from their specialized perspectives. This helps make informed decisions about how to address the situation as safely as possible.

Flexibility and Adaptability: Teamwork allows for flexibility and adaptability as the situation evolves. Teams can adjust their strategies and tactics based on changes in the crisis dynamics.

Shared Ethics and Values: Working as a team ensures that all members share fundamental ethical values, such as the preservation of life and respect for human rights. This is crucial in decision-making and crisis management.

Accountability: Team collaboration also involves mutual accountability. Each member is responsible for their role and making decisions that benefit the safety of the hostages and the success of the operation.

Teamwork is essential for effectively addressing hostage situations because it combines the skills and expertise of various professionals to achieve comprehensive and safe crisis management. Coordinated collaboration and effective communication are fundamental to success in these situations.

Building Trust: Negotiators must be able to establish a trusting relationship with the captors. This involves demonstrating respect and understanding without necessarily endorsing their actions.

The ability to build trust is a critical aspect of the work of hostage negotiators in crisis situations. Trust is essential for establishing effective communication with captors and for progressing toward a peaceful resolution.

Open and Respectful Communication: Negotiators must communicate openly and respectfully with captors. This includes actively listening to their concerns and demands, even if not in agreement. Respectful communication helps establish a trusting environment.

Empathy and Understanding: Showing empathy and understanding towards the emotions and concerns of captors is crucial. This doesn't imply endorsing their actions but rather acknowledging and validating their emotions. Empathy can help build a trusting bond.

Long-Term Relationship Building: In some hostage situations, negotiation may take time. Negotiators must be willing to build long-term relationships with captors, which requires gradually building trust.

Promise of Safety: Negotiators can gain the trust of captors by letting them know that their primary concern is the safety of the hostages. Ensuring that hostages will not be harmed is a key component of building trust.

Transparency in Negotiations: Negotiators must be transparent in negotiations, avoiding promises they cannot fulfill. Honesty and integrity are crucial for maintaining the captors' trust.

Credibility and Professionalism: The credibility and professionalism of negotiators are important for building trust. Captors must perceive negotiators as competent and reliable professionals.

Time-Gaining: Sometimes, gaining time can be an effective strategy for building trust and allowing emotions to calm down. Negotiators can use this time for negotiation and peacefully resolving the situation.

Expectation Management: Negotiators must be realistic about what they can achieve. Managing expectations helps prevent the loss of trust if all the captors' demands cannot be met.

It's important to note that building trust with captors does not mean negotiators agree with their actions or demands. Their primary goal is to ensure the safety of the hostages and seek a peaceful and safe resolution. The ability to build trust is an integral part of their professional approach to hostage crisis management.

Strategy and Planning: Hostage negotiators develop strategies and negotiation plans before addressing the situation. These plans must be flexible and adapt as the crisis unfolds.

Strategy and planning are critical aspects of the work of hostage negotiators. Before addressing a hostage situation, negotiators must develop detailed strategies and plans that allow them to manage the crisis effectively.

Situation Assessment: Before approaching the crisis, negotiators must conduct a thorough assessment of the situation. This includes gathering information about the captors, hostages, the location of the hostage-taking, and any other relevant information.

Goal Setting: Negotiators must clearly define their goals. The top priority is the safety of the hostages, followed by the pursuit of a peaceful resolution and the minimization of harm. Setting clear goals helps guide the strategy and planning.

Development of Strategies: Specific strategies must be developed to address the situation. This includes how to establish communication with the captors, how to address their demands and concerns, and how to progress toward a peaceful resolution.

Contingency Planning: Negotiators must have contingency plans in case the situation deteriorates or unexpected problems arise. These plans should be flexible and prepared in advance.

Coordination with Other Teams: Hostage negotiation teams often collaborate with the police, psychologists, security experts, and other professionals. Strategy and planning must be coordinated with these teams to ensure a comprehensive response.

Internal Communication: Effective communication within the negotiation team is essential. They must ensure that all team members are aware of the strategy and plans and can coordinate their efforts effectively.

Flexibility: As the crisis unfolds, changes in the situation's dynamics are likely to occur. Negotiators must be flexible and prepared to adjust their strategies and plans as the crisis evolves.

Negotiation Skills: The strategy should include specific negotiation techniques to address the captors' demands and achieve a peaceful resolution. This may include identifying points of agreement and building trust.

Time Management: Time management is crucial in hostage situations, as time can be a critical factor. Negotiators must plan how to use time effectively to achieve their goals.

Review and Update: The strategy and planning should be reviewed and updated periodically as the situation evolves. This ensures that negotiators are working with the most up-to-date information.

Strategy and planning are essential for addressing hostage situations professionally and safely. Plans must be flexible and adapt as the crisis unfolds, requiring effective communication and constant situation assessment. The top priority is always the safety of the hostages and the pursuit of a peaceful resolution.

Security Maintenance: The safety of the hostages and the negotiation team is a top priority. Negotiators must be able to ensure that their actions do not endanger anyone.

Risk Assessment: Negotiators must be experts in risk assessment. This involves identifying and analyzing potential threats and hazards, both stemming from the captors' actions and decisions made by the negotiation team.

Secure Communication: Establishing and maintaining secure communication with the captors is crucial. Negotiators must avoid unnecessary exposure and ensure that communication does not reveal information that could compromise the safety of the hostages or the team.

Action Restrictions: Negotiators must ensure that their actions do not trigger a violent reaction from the captors. This may require restricting certain actions or communications that could increase the risk.

Rescue Planning: In high-risk situations, negotiators must be prepared to coordinate efforts with law enforcement or other rescue teams. Rescue planning must be done with extreme care to ensure the safety of the hostages and everyone involved.

Knowledge of Security Procedures: Negotiators must be aware of security procedures and protocols and follow them rigorously. This includes the use of physical and technological security measures.

Personal Defense Training: In extreme situations, negotiators may require personal defense training to protect themselves and the hostages in the event of an imminent threat.

Environment Management: Security also involves managing the environment of the hostage-taking. Negotiators must consider how to address security in areas such as the evacuation of civilians, facility protection, or the implementation of secure zones.

Collaboration with Other Professionals: Negotiators work closely with the police, security experts, and other professionals. Coordination with these teams is essential to ensure the safety of everyone involved.

Safety is an integral component of negotiation strategy and planning. Negotiators are trained to balance the pursuit of a peaceful resolution with the top priority of maintaining the safety of all individuals involved and making decisions that minimize potential risks.

Ethics and Values: Hostage negotiators must act ethically and uphold fundamental values, such as human life and human rights.

Ethics and values are fundamental in the work of hostage negotiators. Respect for human life and human rights is essential at all stages of hostage crisis management. Here are some key aspects related to ethics and values in this context:

Preservation of Life: Human life is sacred, and the safety and well-being of the hostages are the highest priority. Negotiators must make decisions that seek to preserve the lives of the hostages and minimize the risk of harm.

Respect for Human Rights: Human rights are universal and inalienable. Negotiators must respect and protect the rights of all individuals involved in the situation, including the captors. This includes the right to life, personal integrity, freedom, and dignity.

Compliance with the Law: Negotiators must operate within legal frameworks and ethical standards. They should avoid taking actions that conflict with the law, and their focus should be on seeking a peaceful and legal resolution to the crisis.

No Endorsement of Illegal Actions: While negotiators may seek to understand the motivations of the captors, they must not endorse or justify their illegal actions. Their goal is to resolve the crisis peacefully and legally.

Respectful Communication: Communication with the captors and other individuals involved must be respectful and non-provocative. Negotiators should avoid actions or words that may increase tension or the risk of violence.

Transparency and Honesty: Transparency and honesty are essential in communication with the captors. Negotiators should be truthful about what they can and cannot do and avoid making promises they cannot keep.

Emotional Support for Hostages: Negotiators can provide emotional support to hostages, who may be experiencing a high level of stress and anxiety. This should be done in a respectful and understanding manner.

Managing the Relationship with Captors: Negotiators must aim to establish a trusting relationship with the captors without endorsing their actions. This is a delicate balance that requires negotiation skills and strong ethics.

Cooperation with Other Professionals: Negotiators must work in collaboration with the police, psychologists, and other crisis experts. This cooperation should be based on shared ethical principles.

Ethics and values play a fundamental role in the work of hostage negotiators. Their focus is on safety, the preservation of life, and the pursuit of a peaceful and legal resolution of the crisis, while respecting the fundamental human rights of all individuals involved.

Hostage negotiators must be highly trained professionals who work closely with law enforcement and other experts to achieve a peaceful resolution in crisis situations. Their primary goal is the safety of the hostages and the secure resolution of the incident.

5.Types of Hostages and Hostage Situations

There are several types of hostages and hostage-taking situations, each presenting specific challenges for response and negotiation teams.

Civil Hostages: Civil hostages are individuals who are abducted for various reasons, such as common crime, family disputes, personal vendettas, or accidental incidents. These situations can vary in severity and complexity, and crisis management may require the intervention of the police or negotiation teams.

Civil hostages are individuals who become hostages in situations unrelated to political or terrorist motivations. These situations can vary in terms of their causes and severity, often resulting from common crime, family disputes, personal vendettas, or other factors.

Varied Motivations: Kidnappers in civil hostage situations may have a wide range of motivations. These can include obtaining money, goods, or other material benefits; resolving personal, family, or workplace disputes; or taking hostages as a result of accidental events or common crimes, such as robberies or assaults.

Nature of the Crisis: The severity and complexity of the crisis can vary considerably. In some cases, civil hostages may be taken as collateral in financial or legal disputes, while in others, the situations can be more dangerous and threatening.

Police Intervention: In most civil hostage situations, the police are the first responders. Tactical response and negotiation teams may be called in to manage the crisis and ensure the safety of the hostages and a peaceful resolution.

Negotiation and Resolution: Managing a civil hostage crisis often involves negotiation. Hostage negotiation teams can communicate with the kidnappers, listen to their demands, and work toward a peaceful resolution. The priority remains ensuring the safety of the hostages.

Escalation of Response: If the situation becomes more dangerous or if the kidnappers turn violent, an escalation of the response may be necessary, which can include rescue tactics or the intervention of specialized teams.

Emotional Support for Hostages: Civil hostages may experience a high level of stress and anxiety during the crisis. Professionals can provide emotional support to help them cope with the situation.

Focus on Safety and Peaceful Resolution: The primary priority in all civil hostage situations is the safety of the hostages. Crisis management focuses on seeking a peaceful resolution and ensuring that the hostages are not harmed.

Long-Term Effects: Civil hostage situations can have long-term effects on the victims and their families. Post-crisis attention may include psychological support and counseling to help individuals recover from the traumatic experience.

Civil hostage situations are diverse and require a professional and coordinated response to ensure the safety of those involved and achieve a peaceful resolution to the crisis. Police intervention and hostage negotiation teams are essential for handling these situations effectively.

Hostages in Bank Heists: Bank heists often involve hostages as criminals attempt to use them as human shields or as collateral to escape with money or other assets. The police and negotiation teams' response is essential to ensure the safety of hostages and a peaceful resolution of the situation.

Hostages in bank heists are a particular type of hostage-taking situation that presents specific challenges. These situations can be extremely dangerous due to the possibility of criminals using hostages as human shields or to pressure authorities.

Criminal Motivation: In bank heists, criminals aim to obtain money or other material resources. They may enter the bank with the intention of stealing cash, jewelry, documents, or other valuable items.

Use of Hostages: Criminals may take bank employees or customers as hostages to ensure their own safety and to escape from the crime scene. Hostages may be used as human shields to avoid confrontation with the police.

Police Response: The police response to a bank heist is swift and highly coordinated. Tactical response teams and hostage negotiators are mobilized to manage the crisis. The priority is to ensure the safety of the hostages and the general public.

Negotiation: Hostage negotiation teams can be deployed to communicate with the criminals and work toward a peaceful resolution. This may involve negotiating demands and ensuring that the hostages are not harmed.

Delicate Decision-Making: Decision-making is delicate in these situations. Authorities must balance the need to ensure the safety of the hostages with the need to apprehend the criminals. Rescue tactics may be employed if deemed necessary, but efforts are always made to avoid a violent confrontation.

Training and Professionalism: Hostage response and negotiation teams are highly trained and prepared to handle high-risk situations like bank heists. Professionalism and composure are essential for managing these situations.

Emotional Support for Hostages: During and after the crisis, emotional support is provided to the hostages, as the experience can be highly stressful and traumatic.

Investigation and Prosecution: After the crisis is resolved, an investigation is initiated to bring the criminals to justice and recover any stolen property.

Bank heists are high-risk hostage-taking situations that require a rapid and professional response. Collaboration between the police, hostage negotiation teams, and other security professionals is essential to ensure the safety of the hostages and a peaceful resolution of the situation.

Political Hostages: Political hostages are kidnapped for political reasons, either to pressure the government to take specific actions or to convey a political message. These situations can be highly complex and may require the involvement of government agencies, international diplomacy, and specialized negotiators with political expertise.

Political hostages are individuals kidnapped with the purpose of achieving political goals or conveying a specific political message. These situations are highly complex and can involve a wide range of actors, from rebel groups to extremist organizations. Here are some key aspects related to political hostages:

Political Motivations: Political kidnappers often have a political agenda, which can include promoting a change in government policies, the release of political prisoners, raising awareness of a cause, or spreading a specific political message.

International Context: Political hostage situations often involve an international context. Kidnappers can be rebel groups, extremist organizations, or even state actors. This can complicate the crisis resolution and require the intervention of international diplomacy.

Diplomatic Intervention: Resolving political hostage situations often involves the intervention of government agencies, international diplomacy, and political negotiations. Governments may be brought to the negotiating table to discuss the kidnappers' demands.

Specialized Negotiation: Negotiation teams in political hostage situations must be highly specialized and trained in political and diplomatic matters. Negotiation can be complex and protracted.

Hostage Protection: The safety of the hostages is the top priority, and response teams must work to ensure they are not harmed. Managing security in political hostage situations can be particularly challenging due to political circumstances and international pressure.

Communication with Kidnappers: Communication with political kidnappers is crucial, and negotiations may involve discussing specific demands or the exchange of prisoners. The ability to establish constructive dialogue is essential.

Support for Hostages' Families: Hostages' families often experience a high level of distress and anxiety. Providing emotional support and counseling to families is an important part of crisis management.

Long-Term Effects: Political hostage situations can have long-term effects on victims, their families, and international relations. Post-crisis attention may include psychological support and efforts to address the political and diplomatic implications of the situation.

Managing political hostage situations is highly complex and requires the collaboration of government and diplomatic actors. The priority is to ensure the safety of the hostages and seek a peaceful and ultimately political resolution to the crisis.

Hostages in Multiple Hostage Incidents: In multiple hostage incidents, a group of people is taken hostage in a public place, such as a school, shopping mall, or industrial facility. Managing these crises involves coordination between the police, tactical response teams, and hostage negotiators.

Multiple hostage incidents, where a significant group of people is taken hostage in a public place, are particularly delicate crisis situations. These crises can involve a wide variety of factors and present unique challenges.

Varied Locations: Multiple hostage incidents can occur in places such as schools, shopping malls, industrial facilities, places of worship, or any other public location. The choice of location can influence the complexity of crisis management.

Number of Hostages: In these incidents, a significant number of people may be taken hostage. Crisis management must consider the safety of all individuals involved.

Diverse Motivations: The motivations behind these incidents can vary. They may be related to personal issues, political, ideological reasons, or simply acts of violence without an apparent motive. Determining motivations is essential for addressing the situation.

Response Coordination: Responding to multiple hostage incidents requires careful coordination among law enforcement, tactical response teams, hostage negotiators, medical professionals, and other experts. Communication and coordination are crucial.

Communication with Kidnappers: In some cases, the kidnappers may have specific demands. Hostage negotiation teams can be deployed to establish communication with the kidnappers and seek a peaceful resolution.

Negotiation and Rescue Tactics: The decision to negotiate or carry out rescue tactics depends on the assessment of the situation and threats to the safety of the hostages. Safety remains the top priority.

Emotional Support for Hostages: People taken as hostages may be experiencing a high level of stress and anxiety. Emotional and psychological support is important to help them cope with the situation.

Environment Management: Managing the environment is essential to ensure the safety of individuals and restrict unauthorized entry into the crisis area.

Duration of the Crisis: The duration of the crisis can vary widely, from issues resolved in hours to protracted situations that can last for days. Long-term management is a challenge.

Long-Term Effects: Multiple hostage incidents can have lasting effects on victims, hostages, and the community at large. Post-crisis attention may include psychological support and efforts for recovery and prevention.

Managing multiple hostage incidents is a highly complex task and will require a coordinated and professional response from law enforcement and other professionals. The top priority in all these situations is to ensure the safety of the hostages and the general public, seeking a peaceful and secure resolution to the crisis.

Hostages by Terrorist Groups: Terrorist groups can take hostages to advance their political agenda, obtain ransoms, or other purposes. These situations are extremely delicate and may require the intervention of specialized response teams and international security efforts.

Hostages taken by terrorist groups are individuals abducted by terrorist organizations or groups to promote their political agenda, obtain ransoms, or achieve other objectives. These situations are highly delicate and dangerous, often involving a wide range of factors, including international politics.

Terrorist Motivations: Terrorist groups have political, ideological, or religious goals they seek to advance through violence and coercion. Hostage kidnappings can be part of their strategy to draw attention to their causes or demand concessions.

International Context: Hostage situations involving terrorist groups often have an international context. Kidnappers and hostages may come from different countries, complicating crisis management and requiring international diplomacy.

Delicate Negotiation: Negotiating with terrorist groups is extremely delicate and may involve discussing specific demands, such as the release of prisoners or ransom payments. Hostage safety is the top concern, and negotiation teams must seek a peaceful resolution without endangering the hostages.

Specialized Response Teams: Managing hostage situations involving terrorist groups requires the intervention of highly specialized response teams, which may include special forces units, security experts, diplomats, and experienced negotiators.

International Coordination: International coordination is essential to address hostage situations involving terrorist groups. Governments of affected countries, as well as international organizations, can play a significant role in crisis resolution.

Long-Term Security: The long-term security and reintegration of hostages into society are ongoing concerns. After their release, hostages may need psychological support and counseling to recover from the traumatic experience.

Political and Diplomatic Effects: Hostage situations involving terrorist groups can have significant political and diplomatic implications. They can influence relations between countries and international politics.

Prevention and Security: Prevention and security are key aspects to prevent future abductions by terrorist groups. This may include efforts to counter radicalization and the funding of terrorist organizations.

Managing hostage situations involving terrorist groups is a highly complex task that requires an internationally coordinated response and the application of a variety of strategies to ensure the safety of the hostages and seek a peaceful resolution to the crisis.

Hostages in Correctional Settings: Some individuals may be taken as hostages in correctional settings, such as prisons or jails. In such cases, hostages may include other inmates or correctional staff, and crisis management can be complicated due to the specific dynamics and constraints of the prison environment.

Hostage situations in correctional settings, such as jails or prisons, present unique challenges due to the dynamics and specific constraints of those environments. These situations may involve inmates taking other inmates, correctional staff, or other individuals present in the prison as hostages.

Diverse Motivations: Motivations behind hostage takings in correctional settings may vary. They can include demands related to the conditions of confinement, the release of specific inmates, disagreements with correctional staff, or disputes among inmates.

Inmates as Hostages: In some situations, inmates may take other inmates as hostages. This can occur due to internal conflicts, attempts to gain advantages, or even as part of escape attempts.

Correctional Staff as Hostages: In other cases, correctional staff, such as guards or officials, may be taken as hostages. This may be part of an escape attempt, an act of violence directed at staff, or in response to specific demands.

Environmental Constraints: Prisons and jails have security and access restrictions that complicate the management of hostage situations. Security procedures and physical structures of the facilities can hinder the intervention of security forces.

Communication and Negotiation: Communication and negotiation with the hostage-takers can be particularly challenging in correctional settings. Hostages may be under constant surveillance, making discreet communication difficult.

Professional Intervention: Managing hostage situations in correctional environments requires the intervention of highly trained professionals, including tactical response teams and negotiators experienced in correctional settings.

Effects on Inmate Population: Hostage situations in correctional settings can have a significant impact on the inmate population and the overall atmosphere of the facility. They can cause additional tensions and safety concerns.

Peaceful Resolution: Despite the difficulties, a peaceful resolution of the crisis is sought, with the safety of the hostages and the restoration of order in the facility being priorities.

Investigation and Prosecution: After the crisis is resolved, an investigation is conducted to determine responsibilities, and charges may be filed against those responsible.

Managing hostage situations in correctional settings is highly complex and requires a professional and coordinated response to ensure the safety of all individuals involved and seek a peaceful resolution to the crisis, while addressing the specific concerns of the correctional environment.

Hostages in Domestic Hostage-Taking Situations: Domestic hostage-taking situations often involve family members or close individuals. Motives can stem from family disputes, relationship issues, or disputes over child custody. These situations can be emotionally charged and may require the intervention of response teams and negotiators specializing in family conflicts.

Domestic hostage-taking situations are particularly delicate and emotionally charged, as they involve close individuals, such as family members or partners. Motivations behind these situations often relate to family disputes, relationship issues, or disputes over child custody. Here are key aspects related to hostages in domestic hostage-taking situations:

Personal or Family Motivations: Domestic hostage-taking situations often originate from personal or family issues, such as conflicts between partners, divorces, disputes over child custody, family debts, or other family disagreements.

Emotional Nature: Due to the emotional nature of these conflicts, domestic hostage-taking situations can be particularly volatile and dangerous. Hostage-takers may be emotionally disturbed or desperate.

Family Hostages: Hostages in these situations are often family members, including spouses, children, or other close relatives. This can increase the complexity of the situation due to the personal relationships involved.

Specialized Negotiation: Negotiating in domestic hostage-taking situations requires specific skills since it may be necessary to address highly charged conflicts and emotions. Negotiation teams must be experts in handling family disputes and relationship conflicts.

Prevention and Early Response: Prevention and early response to warning signs of family conflicts are essential to prevent situations from escalating into hostage-taking incidents. Mediation and counseling can be valuable resources in cases of family disputes.

Emotional Support: People taken as hostages in domestic situations may experience a high level of stress and anxiety. Emotional support and counseling are essential to help victims and hostages cope with the situation.

Peaceful Resolution: Despite the intense emotions involved, a peaceful resolution to the crisis is sought, with the safety of all involved as the top priority.

Long-Term Protection: After the crisis is resolved, long-term protection measures may be required to ensure the safety of the hostages and prevent future episodes of domestic violence.

Managing domestic hostage-taking situations requires a professional and coordinated response that takes into account the emotional and personal nature of the crisis. The top priority is to ensure the safety of all involved and seek a peaceful resolution. Prevention and early intervention in family disputes can play a crucial role in mitigating these crises.

Hostages in Workplace or Business Hostage-Taking Situations: Occasionally, employees may be taken as hostages in the workplace or commercial facilities. These situations can arise from labor disputes, financial problems, or even criminal actions. Crisis management may involve workplace security teams and hostage negotiators.

Workplace or business hostage-taking situations involve employees who are taken as hostages in their workplace or commercial facilities. These situations can stem from a variety of reasons, including labor disputes, financial problems, or even criminal actions.

Diverse Motivations: Motivations behind workplace hostage takings can vary. They may be related to labor disputes, layoffs, financial issues within the company, personal vendettas, workplace safety issues, or even criminal actions such as robberies.

Workplace Hostages: Hostages in these situations are typically employees who are present in the workplace when the crisis unfolds. Hostage-takers can be disgruntled employees, former employees, suppliers, or even individuals external to the company.

Workplace Security: Companies should have workplace security measures in place to prevent or respond to hostage-taking situations. This includes training staff in crisis management and cooperation with local authorities.

Workplace Security Response: Companies often have workplace security teams and emergency plans to respond to hostage-taking situations. These teams are trained to manage workplace security and collaborate with external law enforcement.

Negotiation and Resolution: In workplace hostage-taking situations, security teams may work to negotiate with hostage-takers and seek a peaceful resolution. Hostage safety is the top priority.

Coordination with Authorities: In hostage-taking cases, the intervention of local law enforcement is required to ensure the safety of the hostages and resolve the crisis.

Emotional Support: Employees involved in hostage-taking situations may experience a high level of stress and anxiety. The company should provide emotional support and counseling to affected employees.

Effects on the Company: Hostage-taking situations can have a significant impact on the company, including reputation, employee morale, and business operations. The company may need guidance on crisis management and recovery.

Long-Term Security: After the crisis is resolved, it's important to consider long-term workplace security and take measures to prevent future similar situations.

Managing workplace or business hostage-taking situations requires a professional and coordinated response involving workplace security teams, local law enforcement, and hostage negotiators. The top priority is to ensure the safety of the hostages and seek a peaceful resolution while addressing implications for the company and its employees.

Each type of hostage situation presents unique challenges, and the proper management of these crises requires coordination among law enforcement, tactical response teams, hostage negotiation professionals, and, in some cases, government and diplomatic agencies.

6.Preparation for Hostage Negotiation

Preparation for a hostage negotiation is crucial as it can make a difference in the safe resolution of the crisis. Below are the key steps and elements for preparing a hostage negotiation:

Information Gathering:

Obtain information about the current situation, including the number of kidnappers, hostages, and the exact location.

Gather background information on the kidnappers, such as their identities, motivations, and possible demands.

Collect information about the hostages, including their health status and specific needs.

Information gathering is the first essential step in preparing for a hostage negotiation. Here are the key aspects of this step:

Obtaining information about the current situation:

Identify and confirm the exact location of the hostage situation.

Determine the number of kidnappers involved and, to the extent possible, ascertain their location and weaponry.

Gather information about the hostages, such as their number, location within the facility, and physical condition.

Background information on the kidnappers:

Identify the kidnappers and obtain information about their backgrounds, criminal records, or known affiliations.

Understand their motivations and objectives, if possible, through prior investigations and witness statements.

Establish secure communication channels to interact with the kidnappers and gather additional information.

Collecting information about the hostages:

Identify the hostages and confirm their location and health status.

Obtain information about the specific needs of the hostages, such as medications, medical assistance, or emotional concerns.

Evaluate any information about personal relationships between the hostages and the kidnappers that may influence the crisis dynamics.

Information gathering is fundamental for making informed decisions and developing effective negotiation strategies. Having a solid understanding of the situation and the individuals involved is essential to ensure the safety of the hostages and seek a peaceful resolution of the crisis.

Background information on the kidnappers is a critical step in preparing for a hostage negotiation.

Identifying the kidnappers:

Obtain information enabling precise identification of the kidnappers, including names, physical descriptions, and available photographs.

Gather details about their location, movements, and possible accomplices if feasible.

Criminal backgrounds and known affiliations:

Investigate the kidnappers' criminal backgrounds to understand their criminal history, if any.

Determine if the kidnappers have known affiliations with criminal groups, terrorists, or similar organizations. This can provide insight into their possible motivations.

Understanding motivations and objectives:

Collect information about the kidnappers' potential motivations through prior investigations, witness testimonies, and public statements, if available.

Try to comprehend their short-term and long-term objectives, which can assist in designing an effective negotiation strategy.

Establishing secure communication channels:

Set up confidential and secure communication channels with the kidnappers. This may include phone numbers, emails, or encrypted messaging platforms.

Appoint a negotiation team or communication specialists trained in managing effective and secure communication with the kidnappers.

Collecting additional information:

Continue gathering information about the kidnappers as the situation unfolds. This may include details about their demands, behavior, and any changes in the crisis dynamics.

Obtaining background information on the kidnappers is essential for establishing effective communication, understanding their motivations and objectives, and designing a strong negotiation strategy. The safety of the hostages and the peaceful resolution of the crisis heavily depend on the information gathered about the kidnappers.

Background information on the kidnappers is a critical step in preparing for a hostage negotiation. Here are the key aspects of this process:

Identifying the kidnappers:

Obtain information that allows for accurate identification of the kidnappers, including names, physical descriptions, and photographs if available.

Gather details about their location, movements, and potential accomplices if possible.

Criminal backgrounds and known affiliations:

Investigate the kidnappers' criminal histories to understand their criminal records, if any.

Determine if the kidnappers have known affiliations with criminal groups, terrorists, or similar organizations. This information can provide insights into their potential motivations.

Understanding motivations and objectives:

Collect information about the potential motivations of the kidnappers through prior investigations, witness statements, and any public statements, if available.

Seek to comprehend their short-term and long-term objectives, which can help in designing an effective negotiation strategy.

Establishing secure communication channels:

Set up confidential and secure communication channels with the kidnappers. This may involve phone numbers, email addresses, or encrypted messaging platforms.

Appoint a negotiation team or communication specialists who are trained to effectively and safely manage communication with the kidnappers.

Gathering additional information:

Continue collecting information about the kidnappers as the situation unfolds. This may include details about their demands, their behavior, and any changes in the dynamics of the crisis.

Obtaining background information on the kidnappers is essential for establishing effective communication, understanding their motivations and objectives, and designing a strong negotiation strategy. The safety of the hostages and the peaceful resolution of the crisis heavily depend on the information gathered about the kidnappers.

Training and Education:

Ensure that negotiators are properly trained in negotiation techniques, crisis management, and effective communication.

Familiarizing with negotiation strategies and tactics specific to different types of hostage situations, such as political hostages, domestic situations, workplace situations, etc.

Practicing hostage situation management in training exercises and drills.

Training and education for hostage negotiators are fundamental steps in preparing to face hostage situations. Here are the key aspects of this process:

Training in negotiation techniques, crisis management, and effective communication:

Provide negotiators with robust training in negotiation techniques, including how to build trust with kidnappers and how to manage demands and conversations effectively.

Train negotiators in crisis management, which involves the ability to remain calm and make decisions under pressure.

Enhance communication skills, both verbal and non-verbal, to convey messages clearly and effectively.

Getting familiar with specific strategies and tactics:

Understand negotiation strategies specific to different types of hostage situations. This may include political, domestic, workplace, and more.

Study tactics that are effective in crisis management, including how to identify potential areas of agreement with kidnappers and how to maintain the safety of the hostages.

Practice in training exercises and drills:

Conduct training exercises and drills involving hostage situations to allow negotiators to gain practical experience.

Repeat realistic scenarios to improve decision-making and adaptability in high-pressure situations.

Evaluate negotiators' performance in exercises and provide constructive feedback.

Development of observation and listening skills:

Teach negotiators to observe non-verbal signals from both kidnappers and hostages, which can provide clues about their emotional state and intentions.

Emphasize the importance of active listening during conversations with kidnappers to detect changes in their demands or behavior.

Training in managing emotional crises:

Prepare negotiators to face highly stressful and emotional situations and equip them with tools to maintain calm and empathy in such circumstances.

Develop skills to manage anxiety and stress, both in negotiators and hostages.

Ongoing training and education are essential for negotiators to effectively deal with hostage situations and seek a peaceful resolution. Practice and proper preparation are fundamental for success in managing such crises.

Establishment of a negotiation team:

Appoint an experienced negotiation leader and a team of negotiators who can work together in a coordinated manner.

Include experts in communication, psychologists, and subject matter experts on the team as needed.

Set up protocols for internal communication and coordination with other teams, such as law enforcement.

Establishing a negotiation team is a fundamental step in preparing for hostage negotiation. Here are the key aspects of this process:

Appointment of an experienced negotiation leader:

Select a negotiation leader with experience in hostage situations and strong leadership skills.

The negotiation leader will assume the primary responsibility for directing the negotiation process and making strategic decisions.

Formation of a coordinated team of negotiators:

Choose a team of negotiators who can work together in a coordinated manner under the leadership of the negotiation leader.

Team members should be experts in negotiation techniques, communication, and crisis management.

Inclusion of additional experts as needed:

Identify if additional experts, such as psychologists or specialists in hostage situations, are required on the team to address specific aspects of the situation.

Psychologists can be essential in understanding and managing the emotions and dynamics of the crisis, both for kidnappers and hostages.

Establishment of internal communication protocols:

Define clear protocols for internal communication within the negotiation team to ensure effective coordination.

Establish secure communication channels and procedures for sharing information quickly and efficiently.

Coordination with other teams and law enforcement:

Collaborate with other teams that may be involved in managing the crisis, such as local law enforcement, tactical teams, medical services, and other specialists.

Set up coordination protocols to ensure an efficient and safe response to any contingencies.

Clear roles and responsibilities:

Assign specific roles and responsibilities within the negotiation team to ensure an efficient distribution of tasks.

This includes designating a primary negotiator to interact with kidnappers and assigning secondary functions, such as note-taking, tracking demands, and managing logistics.

Team training and exercises:

Conduct regular team training and exercises to foster team cohesion, improve internal communication, and rehearse simulated crisis situations.

Establishing a strong and coordinated negotiation team is essential for successfully managing a hostage situation. Effective collaboration and clear role assignments allow for a more efficient and secure response throughout the crisis.

Development of a negotiation plan:

Create a detailed plan that includes negotiation strategies, communication lines, potential concessions, and limits.

Establish a protocol for collecting and verifying key information during the negotiation.

Identify points of contact and communication procedures with the kidnappers.

Developing a negotiation plan is essential for addressing a hostage situation successfully. Here are the key aspects of this process:

Creation of a detailed plan:

Develop a comprehensive negotiation plan that outlines the strategies and tactics to be employed during the crisis.

The plan should include a strategic approach to addressing the demands of the kidnappers and ensuring that negotiations are conducted effectively.

Communication Lines: Establish clear and secure communication channels with the kidnappers. This may include phone numbers, emails, or secure messaging platforms. Determine who will be the primary negotiator interacting with the kidnappers and how communication within the team will be managed.

Possible Concessions and Limits: Identify potential concessions that can be offered to the kidnappers based on the identified demands and objectives. Set clear limits on the maximum concessions that can be granted and specify which demands are unacceptable.

Protocol for Information Collection and Verification: Design a protocol for the collection and verification of key information during negotiations. This may include how the authenticity of demands and information provided by the kidnappers will be assessed. Establish procedures for verifying the validity of information, such as requesting proof of life from the hostages.

Identification of Points of Contact and Communication Procedures: Designate a point of contact with the kidnappers, which can be the negotiation leader or the primary negotiator. Establish procedures for communication with the kidnappers, including the frequency of conversations, the language to be used, and strategies for maintaining effective dialogue.

Contingency Plan: Develop a contingency plan that includes scenarios and actions to be taken if negotiations do not progress or in case of emergency situations. Prepare strategies to manage potential threats and make quick decisions if necessary.

Regular Review and Update: Regularly review and update the negotiation plan, taking into account any changes in the situation or the kidnappers' demands. Ensure that the team is always aware of updated procedures and strategies.

A detailed negotiation plan provides a solid framework for managing a hostage crisis. It helps ensure that negotiations are conducted strategically, with a focus on safety and peaceful resolution.

Coordination with Law Enforcement:

Work closely with local law enforcement and other relevant agencies to ensure the security of the area and the individuals involved. Establish coordination protocols for tactical actions and the use of force if necessary.

Effective communication: Establish effective communication channels between the negotiation team and law enforcement to ensure a coordinated and rapid response in emergency situations. Share key information about the dynamics of the crisis and any relevant developments.

Joint Planning: Collaborate on joint planning of strategies and tactics to ensure the safety of the hostages, negotiators, and law enforcement. Evaluate possible courses of action and prepare strategies for various contingencies.

Clear Roles and Responsibilities: Ensure a clear understanding of the roles and responsibilities of each team, both the negotiation team and law enforcement. Define the circumstances under which the use of force may be authorized and who has the authority to make that decision.

Emergency Preparedness: Develop a contingency plan for emergency situations, such as the need for a tactical rescue or responding to an attempted escape by the kidnappers. Ensure that law enforcement is prepared to act quickly and decisively in critical situations.

Continuous Evaluation: Continuously evaluate the collaboration between the negotiation team and law enforcement throughout the crisis. Make adjustments as needed to address changes in the situation or the kidnappers' demands.

Effective coordination with law enforcement is essential to ensure the safety of people involved in a hostage situation. Working as a team and maintaining constant and open communication is crucial for a successful response.

Communication and Information Management:

Establish communication protocols with the kidnappers, with a focus on building a trust bond. Determine what information will be shared with the kidnappers and what will be kept confidential. Monitor and record all conversations and messages for future reference.

Communication and information management are critical aspects of hostage negotiation. Here are the key elements of this process:

Establishment of communication protocols with the kidnappers: Create clear and secure protocols for communication with the kidnappers. Set up confidential communication channels, such as secure phone numbers or encrypted emails. Designate a primary negotiator or a point of contact with the kidnappers to lead effective conversations and maintain constructive dialogue.

Building a trust bond: Maintain a focus on building a trust bond with the kidnappers. Empathy, active listening, and respectful communication can contribute to stronger relationships during negotiations. Show understanding of the kidnappers' concerns without necessarily endorsing their actions.

Determination of what information to share: Clearly define what information will be shared with the kidnappers and what will be kept confidential. This includes details about negotiations, demands, or any other relevant information. Exercise caution when disclosing sensitive information, and carefully consider the potential consequences of sharing specific details.

Management and documentation of communication: Keep comprehensive records of all communication with the kidnappers. This includes written transcripts, audio recordings, or other documentation. Maintain organized records to ensure accuracy and facilitate ongoing negotiations. Effective communication and information management are critical in hostage negotiation situations. Building trust, managing information, and keeping accurate records contribute to successful negotiations and the safety of all parties involved.

Evaluate carefully what information will be shared with the kidnappers. This may include responses to specific demands, information about the hostages' status, or details about the progress of the negotiation. Establish clear boundaries on what information is confidential and cannot be shared.

Control and Recording of Conversations: Thoroughly record and document all conversations and messages with the kidnappers. This provides a detailed record of the negotiation and can be useful for future reference. Recording of conversations or written documentation should be done discreetly and securely to maintain confidentiality.

Protection of Sensitive Information: Ensure that confidential information is safeguarded against unauthorized access and handled with extreme caution. Consider cybersecurity measures to protect electronic communications from potential interception attempts. Continuous

Communication with the Team: Maintain ongoing communication with the negotiation team, security forces, and other involved teams to share pertinent information and coordinate efforts. Keep the team updated on the progress of the negotiation and any changes in the situation.

Proper management of communication and information is crucial to maintain the safety of the hostages, understand the kidnappers' demands, and work toward a peaceful resolution of the crisis. Careful communication and recording protocols are essential to ensure the effectiveness of negotiations and the safety of all parties involved.

Preparation for Specific Demands: Carefully evaluate potential demands from the kidnappers and develop strategies to address them effectively. Prepare potential concessions and define the boundaries within which negotiations can take place.

Preparation for specific demands is a critical step in hostage negotiation. Here are the key components of this process:

Assessment of Potential Demands from Kidnappers: Thoroughly evaluate the specific demands made by the kidnappers, which may include the release of prisoners, ransom payments, meeting certain humanitarian or political needs, among others. Gain a deep understanding of the motivations behind these demands and their significance to the kidnappers.

Development of Strategies to Address Demands: Establish robust strategies to address the kidnappers' demands effectively. This includes determining how to handle the demands in a manner that aligns with negotiation objectives. Consider flexibility in responding to demands without compromising the safety of the hostages.

Preparation of Potential Concessions: Identify potential concessions that can be offered to the kidnappers based on specific demands. Evaluate the risks and benefits of each concession, taking into account their impact on the safety of the hostages and the ability to meet the demands.

Establishment of Negotiation Limits: Set clear boundaries within which negotiations can take place. Define the maximum concessions that can be granted and determine which demands are unacceptable. Defining limits is essential to prevent negotiations from becoming an endless series of concessions.

Assessment of Long-Term Implications: Consider the long-term implications of concessions and compliance with demands. This may include the impact on public safety, government policy, and future hostage situations. Balance immediate needs with long-term consequences.

Communication of Decisions to Involved Parties: Communicate decisions regarding demands and concessions to both the kidnappers and the negotiation team and security forces. Maintain clear and consistent communication with all involved parties to avoid misunderstandings and ensure a coherent response.

Preparation for specific demands involves careful and strategic planning to address the kidnappers' demands while prioritizing the safety of the hostages. Decisions should be made wisely and based on a comprehensive assessment of the risks and benefits involved.

Maintenance of Security: Implement measures to ensure the safety of negotiators and hostages during the negotiation. Continuously assess threats and risks to make informed decisions.

Maintenance of security is of utmost importance during hostage negotiation. Here are the key elements of this process:

Establishment of Security Measures: Implement security measures for both negotiators and hostages, which may include physical protection, facility security, and access management. Ensure precautions are taken to prevent risky situations during the negotiation.

Continuous Assessment of Threats and Risks: Continuously evaluate threats and risks present in the hostage situation. This may include analyzing changes in the kidnappers' behavior or the dynamics of the crisis. Use the collected information to make informed decisions regarding security.

Planning of Additional Security Measures: Prepare additional security measures in case the situation becomes more dangerous. This may include hostage evacuation, the use of tactical teams, or the activation of rescue protocols. Maintain a contingency plan that includes strategies to address emergency situations.

Coordination with Security Forces: Work closely with security forces to ensure the safety of the area and the individuals involved. Communicate any changes in risk assessment to enable a rapid and effective response.

Effective Communication About Security Measures: Maintain effective communication with the negotiation team, hostages, and security forces regarding the security measures in place. Ensure that everyone is aware of the precautions and security procedures to follow.

Flexibility and Adaptation: Be flexible and prepared to adapt to changes in security based on the evolving situation.

Constantly reassess security measures and adjust them as needed. Maintaining security is a constant priority during a hostage negotiation. Continuous evaluation of threats and risks, effective coordination with security forces, and planning additional security measures are crucial to ensure the safety of all individuals involved.

Establishment of Emergency Communication Channels: Prepare emergency communication channels to request tactical or medical support if necessary. Ensure that response teams are ready to act immediately. Establishing emergency communication channels is critical in hostage negotiation to ensure a swift and effective response in critical situations. Here are the key aspects of this process:

Preparation of Emergency Communication Channels: Establish emergency communication channels that allow for requesting immediate support, such as tactical, medical, or any other type of assistance in critical situations. Ensure that these channels are secure and available at all times.

Coordination with Response Teams: Coordinate with response teams, including tactical teams and emergency medical services, to ensure they are prepared to act immediately if their assistance is requested. Define procedures and protocols for emergency response situations.

Testing and Preparedness Exercises: Conduct regular testing and preparedness exercises involving response teams to ensure their familiarity with emergency procedures and their ability to respond effectively. Practice simulated crisis scenarios to assess coordination and response capabilities.

Availability of Emergency Resources: Ensure that the necessary resources for emergency response, such as tactical equipment, vehicles, medical equipment, and qualified personnel, are available and ready for immediate deployment. Maintain these resources on standby for activation if necessary.

Establishment of Criteria for Emergency Activation: Set clear criteria for activating response teams in emergency situations. Determine when and under what circumstances emergency assistance should be requested.

Constant Communication: Maintain constant communication with response teams and security forces to ensure they are aware of the evolving situation and ready to act if necessary.

Establishing emergency communication channels and coordinating with response teams are essential to ensure the safety of hostages and the negotiation team in crisis situations. Proper preparation and immediate responsiveness are critical for effectively addressing emergencies.

Emotional and Psychological Support: Provide emotional support to hostages before, during, and after the crisis, as well as to their families. Have counselors or psychologists available to offer support in high-stress situations.

Emotional and psychological support is essential for both hostages and their families during a hostage situation. Here are the key components of this process:

Emotional Support for Hostages: Offer emotional support to hostages to help them cope with the stress, anxiety, and trauma of the situation. Actively listen to hostages, show empathy, and provide words of encouragement and comfort.

Professional Psychological Support: Make trained crisis and trauma management counselors or psychologists available to provide psychological support to hostages. These professionals can assist hostages in dealing with the emotional impact of the experience and developing strategies to address trauma.

Communication with Hostages' Families: Establish communication channels with the families of hostages to keep them informed about the situation and provide emotional support. Offer families a point of contact with the negotiation team to address their questions and concerns.

Assessment of Psychological Needs: Continuously assess the psychological needs of hostages and their families. Each individual may react differently to the crisis and may require personalized support.

Post-Crisis Support: Continue to provide emotional and psychological support to hostages and their families even after the crisis has ended. Recognize that the emotional impact of the experience can persist in the long term and be willing to provide long-term support if necessary.

Confidentiality and Privacy Respect: Maintain confidentiality and respect the privacy of hostages and their families at all times. Provide a safe, non-judgmental environment for them to express their emotions and concerns.

Emotional and psychological support is essential to mitigate the emotional impact of a hostage situation on both the hostages and their loved ones. Providing this type of support can help individuals emotionally recover from the traumatic experience.

Proper preparation is crucial for successfully managing a hostage negotiation. Thorough planning and coordination between security teams and negotiators are essential to ensure the safety of the hostages and seek a peaceful resolution to the situation.

7.Effective Communication in Hostage Situations

Effective communication plays a central role in hostage negotiation. In extremely tense and dangerous situations, how negotiators communicate with the kidnappers can make a difference in the safety of the hostages and the success of a peaceful crisis resolution. Here are some key guidelines for effective communication in hostage situations:

Establishing Communication Channels: The first step is to establish communication channels with the kidnappers. This may involve using phones, radios, written messages, or any other secure means. Communication should be confidential and secure.

Security of Communications: Communication channels must be secure and confidential to prevent kidnappers from intercepting conversations or accessing sensitive information.

Selection of Appropriate Media: Depending on the situation, communication channels may vary. They may include secure phones, radios, written messages, secure email, or even human intermediaries acting as messengers.

Security Protocols: Negotiation teams must follow strict security protocols when establishing communication channels. This may include encrypting communications and protecting the negotiators' location.

Identification and Authentication: Negotiation teams and kidnappers must establish methods of identification and authentication to ensure that both parties are certain of each other's identity.

Proof of Life: Initial communication may include requesting a "proof of life" to confirm that the hostages are alive and reasonably safe.

Setting Schedules: Negotiation teams and kidnappers can agree on specific schedules for communications, which helps maintain predictability and the safety of conversations.

Records and Documentation: All conversations and agreements must be carefully documented. This is important for monitoring negotiations and ensuring that commitments are met.

Coordination with Authorities: Coordination with authorities and security forces is essential to ensure that communications are not compromised and to establish a response plan in case of a rescue operation.

Risk Assessment: Negotiation teams must assess the risks associated with communication and take measures to mitigate any potential threats.

Maintaining Confidentiality: Details about communication channels must be kept secret to prevent kidnappers from using this information to their advantage.

Establishing secure communication channels is a crucial step in initiating hostage negotiations and maintaining the safety of hostages and negotiators. Confidentiality and communication security are of utmost importance in these critical situations.

Direct and Open Communication: Negotiators must establish direct and open communication with the kidnappers. This involves speaking clearly and respectfully, actively listening, and responding to the kidnappers' concerns and demands.

Direct and open communication is essential in hostage negotiation, as it lays the groundwork for effective dialogue and trust-building between negotiators and kidnappers.

Clarity in Language: Negotiators should communicate clearly and without ambiguity. They should avoid using confusing or technical language that may lead to misunderstandings.

Respect and Empathy: Communication should be respectful and empathetic. Negotiators should show understanding of the concerns and demands of the kidnappers, even if they do not agree with them.

Active Listening: Active listening is crucial. Negotiators must pay attention to what the kidnappers are saying and ask questions to clarify any points of confusion.

Response to Demands: Negotiators must be able to respond effectively to the demands of the kidnappers. This involves assessing whether it is possible to meet those demands and, if not, offering clear alternatives or explanations.

Constructive Negotiation: Communication should focus on finding constructive solutions and reducing the escalation of tensions. Negotiators should be able to propose reasonable concessions and compromises.

Maintaining Calm: Calmness is essential in high-pressure situations. Negotiators must remain calm even when facing challenges and pressures.

Avoiding Provocations: Negotiators should avoid any language or actions that may provoke the kidnappers or increase tension. Communication should be non-confrontational.

Handling Hostage Communication: Negotiators must be sensitive to the fact that hostages may be used as messengers or intermediaries by the kidnappers. They should carefully assess any communication from the hostages and consider their safety.

Regular Communication: Communication should be regular and predictable to the extent possible. This helps establish a routine and maintain trust.

Conflict Resolution Effectiveness: Negotiation teams should be well-trained in conflict resolution and negotiation techniques. This allows them to address differences and demands constructively.

Direct and open communication is a fundamental part of the hostage negotiation strategy and is essential for building a trusting relationship with the kidnappers. When done effectively, it can contribute to reducing tensions and achieving a peaceful resolution to the situation.

Calmness and Empathy: Negotiators must maintain calmness at all times, even in high-tension situations. Empathy is essential for understanding the concerns and motivations of the kidnappers.

Calmness and empathy are two critical qualities that hostage negotiators must maintain in high-tension situations. These qualities help establish effective communication and build trust with the kidnappers.

Maintaining Calm: Calmness is essential for making rational decisions and avoiding impulsive responses in crisis situations. Negotiators must be able to handle pressure and stress without showing signs of panic or frustration.

Conveying Confidence: Negotiators' calm demeanor can influence the kidnappers' perception of the seriousness and credibility of the negotiations. Kidnappers are more likely to trust individuals who remain composed in critical situations.

Tension Reduction: Negotiators' calmness can help reduce tension in the situation. When kidnappers see that negotiators are committed to a peaceful resolution and not seeking confrontation, they may be more willing to cooperate.

Avoiding Provocations: Maintaining calmness involves avoiding provocations or language that could escalate hostility from the kidnappers. Negotiators should be aware of words and actions that could be interpreted negatively.

Empathy: Empathy involves the ability to understand and share the concerns and emotions of the kidnappers. Negotiators must be able to put themselves in the kidnappers' shoes and understand their motivations and needs.

Active Listening: Empathy also relates to active listening. Negotiators must actively listen to the kidnappers and show genuine interest in their concerns. This can help establish a trusting relationship.

Building Bridges: Empathy is a tool for building bridges between negotiators and kidnappers. When kidnappers feel that their concerns are understood and respected, they are more likely to seek a peaceful solution.

Focus on Resolution: Calmness and empathy help maintain a focus on conflict resolution rather than confrontation. Negotiators should work to find solutions that meet the needs of both parties.

Calmness and empathy are essential components of the hostage negotiation strategy and contribute to building trust in extremely delicate situations. These qualities can help reduce tension and work towards a peaceful and secure crisis resolution.

Clarity and Transparency: Communication must be clear and unambiguous. Both negotiators and kidnappers must fully understand the terms and conditions of any agreement.

Clarity in communication is essential in hostage negotiation to avoid misunderstandings, reduce tension, and ensure that all parties are on the same page. Here are some key guidelines related to clarity in communication:

Definition of Terms: The terms and conditions of any agreement must be defined precisely. This includes clear definitions of what is being negotiated, when agreed-upon actions will take place, and any other relevant details.

Written Documentation: It is advisable to document all agreements in writing so that all parties have a clear reference. This may include a memorandum of understanding or a formal agreement.

Questions and Clarifications: Negotiators should encourage kidnappers to ask questions and seek clarifications if something is unclear. It's important that kidnappers fully understand what is expected of them and what they can expect in return.

Simple Language: Avoiding the use of technical or ambiguous language is important. Communication should be simple and direct to be understandable by all involved parties.

Mutual Confirmation: After each significant communication, it's helpful for both parties to mutually confirm their understanding of the terms and conditions. This can help prevent misunderstandings.

Transparency in Limitations: If there are limitations or restrictions on what can be agreed upon, these should be communicated transparently. For example, if certain demands are non-negotiable, kidnappers should be made aware of this.

Avoiding Ambiguities: Avoid the use of ambiguous words or phrases that can be interpreted in different ways. Ambiguity can lead to misunderstandings and distrust.

Fulfillment of Commitments: Negotiators must ensure that agreed-upon commitments are fulfilled in a timely and complete manner. Failure to do so can undermine trust.

Review and Update: As negotiations progress, it may be necessary to review and update the terms and conditions to reflect changes in the situation or kidnappers' demands.

Respecting Confidentiality: While communication should be clear, sensitive information related to negotiations must be handled with the utmost confidentiality.

Clarity in communication is essential to avoid conflicts and misunderstandings in hostage situations. It helps ensure that all parties are on the same page and that agreements are effectively fulfilled, which is crucial for the safety of hostages and the success of negotiations.

Non-Threatening Language: Negotiators must avoid any threatening or hostile language that could increase tension. Communication should be respectful and non-confrontational.

The use of non-threatening and respectful language is fundamental in hostage negotiation, as it can help reduce tension and build a trusting relationship with the kidnappers.

Respect and Courtesy: Negotiators must show respect and courtesy in their communication with the kidnappers. This involves using a calm and respectful tone of voice and treating kidnappers as legitimate interlocutors.

Avoiding Verbal Threats: At no time should negotiators employ verbal threats, intimidation, or hostile language. Threats can increase the hostility of the kidnappers and endanger the safety of the hostages.

Non-Confrontational Communication: Communication should be non-confrontational and focused on peaceful conflict resolution. Negotiators should avoid arguing or confronting the kidnappers.

Active Listening: Active listening is important. Negotiators must pay attention to the concerns of the kidnappers and respond empathetically, rather than taking a defensive or confrontational stance.

Maintaining Calm: Negotiators must remain calm even if they face provocations or hostilities from the kidnappers. Calmness can help reduce tension in the situation.

Building Bridges: Communication should focus on building bridges and finding common ground for resolving the situation. Negotiators should seek opportunities to work together rather than to confront.

Offering Alternatives: When kidnappers raise demands that cannot be met, negotiators can offer alternatives that address their concerns differently.

Reinforcing Commitment to Peaceful Resolution: Negotiators should continually reinforce their commitment to a peaceful resolution of the crisis and the safety of the hostages. This can help maintain the kidnappers' trust.

Promoting Constructive Communication: Negotiation teams should promote constructive communication that focuses on solutions rather than problems. This can help advance toward a peaceful resolution.

Transparency in Limitations: If certain demands of the kidnappers are non-negotiable, negotiators should explain these limitations clearly and without confrontation.

Adopting a non-threatening and respectful communication approach is essential for maintaining an environment conducive to peaceful resolution of the crisis. It helps reduce hostility and establishes a strong foundation for cooperation between negotiators and kidnappers.

Handling Demands and Concessions: Negotiators must be skilled in handling kidnappers' demands and evaluating which concessions are reasonable. This involves the ability to persuade and negotiate.

Handling demands and concessions is an essential skill in hostage negotiation. Negotiators must be able to carefully evaluate the kidnappers' demands, determine which concessions are reasonable, and negotiate effectively.

Evaluation of Demands: Negotiators must carefully assess kidnappers' demands to understand their motivations and needs. This includes considering both immediate and underlying demands.

Determining Feasibility: Negotiators must determine whether it is feasible to fulfill some or all of the demands. This may include legal, ethical, or practical considerations that must be taken into account.

Prioritizing Safety: The safety of the hostages is the top priority. Any concession or agreement must ensure their well-being and not endanger their lives.

Offering Reasonable Concessions: When appropriate, negotiators can offer reasonable concessions to meet some of the kidnappers' demands. These concessions should be fair and equitable.

Persuasive Negotiation: Negotiators must be persuasive and convincing in their arguments. They can use logical reasoning and arguments to explain why certain demands cannot be met or why alternative solutions are preferable.

Avoiding Yielding to Unreasonable Demands: While it's important to be flexible, negotiators should not yield to demands that are clearly unreasonable or endanger the safety of the hostages.

Maintaining Open Communication: Negotiators must maintain open communication with the kidnappers, which includes explaining the status of the negotiations and a willingness to consider their demands.

Focus on Creative Solutions: Negotiators can seek creative solutions that address the concerns of the kidnappers without compromising the safety of the hostages. This may include exploring alternatives that are acceptable to both parties.

No Promise What Cannot Be Delivered: Negotiators must be honest and refrain from promising what they cannot deliver. The reliability of negotiators is crucial for the credibility of the negotiations.

Reinforce Commitment to Peaceful Resolution: Negotiation teams must continually reinforce their commitment to the peaceful resolution of the crisis and the safety of the hostages to maintain the kidnappers' trust.

Effective handling of demands and concessions requires advanced negotiation skills as well as a strategic and equitable approach. Negotiators must be capable of finding solutions that meet the needs of both parties without jeopardizing the safety of the hostages.

Constructive Negotiation: Communication should focus on seeking constructive solutions and reducing tension escalation. Negotiators should offer alternatives and compromises whenever possible.

Constructive negotiation is essential in resolving hostage situations because it emphasizes peaceful solutions and the reduction of tension escalation. By focusing on collaboration and solutions, negotiators can contribute to a conducive environment for the safe and peaceful resolution of hostage situations.

Focus on Solutions: Negotiators must concentrate on finding solutions that satisfy the needs of both parties. This entails seeking common ground and working together to reach mutually acceptable agreements.

Tension Reduction: Constructive negotiation seeks to reduce tension and avoid confrontation. Negotiators should employ a calm and respectful approach instead of adopting a confrontational attitude.

Offer Alternatives: When it's not possible to meet all of the kidnappers' demands, negotiators can offer alternatives to address their concerns differently. This may involve creative solutions.

Reasonable Commitment: Negotiators must be willing to compromise reasonably. This entails conceding on certain aspects to progress towards a peaceful resolution.

Risk and Benefit Assessment: Negotiation teams must carefully assess the risks and benefits of any proposed agreement. This includes considering how the agreement will impact the safety of the hostages and the long-term implications.

Building Bridges: Communication should focus on building bridges and finding common ground. Negotiators should seek opportunities to collaborate rather than create further divisions.

Transparency in Limitations: If there are non-negotiable demands due to legal, ethical, or security limitations, negotiators should transparently explain these limitations.

Avoid Polarization: Constructive negotiation avoids polarization and seeks collaboration. Negotiation teams should avoid further dividing the parties involved.

Maintain Open Dialogue: Negotiators must maintain an open dialogue with the kidnappers and be willing to consider their viewpoints and needs.

Reinforce Commitment to Peaceful Resolution: Negotiation teams must continually reinforce their commitment to the peaceful resolution of the crisis and the safety of the hostages to maintain the kidnappers' trust.

Constructive negotiation is based on the premise that peaceful resolution is the most desirable goal, and effective dialogue is the path to that resolution. By focusing on solutions and collaboration, negotiators can contribute to a conducive environment for the safe and peaceful resolution of hostage situations.

Maintain Records: Detailed records of all conversations and agreements should be kept. This is important to ensure that commitments are upheld and to document the progress of the negotiations.

Maintaining accurate and detailed records of all conversations and agreements is a fundamental practice in hostage negotiation. These records serve several important roles in the negotiation process:

Documentation of Agreements: Records are an important reference for documenting all agreements reached between negotiators and kidnappers. This includes specific details of what was agreed upon, when, and how commitments will be fulfilled.

Clarity and Transparency: Records provide clarity and transparency in negotiations. They help prevent misunderstandings and post-negotiation disagreements by offering detailed documentation of what was discussed and agreed upon.

Support in Case of Disagreements: In case disagreements or disputes arise between the parties, records can serve as objective evidence of the agreed-upon terms and conditions. This can be especially useful if third-party mediation or intervention is required.

Progress Tracking: Records allow for clear tracking of negotiation progress. This is important to ensure that deadlines are met and progress is being made toward a resolution.

Legal and Ethical Protection: Records can be used to demonstrate that negotiators have acted legally and ethically in the negotiation process. This is important in situations where the actions of negotiators may come under scrutiny.

Internal Communication: Records are also useful for internal communication within the negotiation team and with relevant authorities. They help keep all parties informed about the negotiation status.

Historical Reference: In hostage situations, records can be important for future legal proceedings or investigations. They provide a complete and verifiable history of the negotiations.

It's important to securely and confidentially maintain records, as they may contain sensitive information. Additionally, they should be regularly updated to reflect the latest developments in negotiations. The accuracy and integrity of these records are essential to ensure an effective and secure negotiation process in hostage situations.

Respect for Confidentiality: Sensitive information must be handled with the utmost confidentiality and should not be disclosed to the public or in the media.

Respect for confidentiality is a critical principle in hostage negotiation, as the disclosure of sensitive information can jeopardize the safety of hostages and undermine the effectiveness of negotiations.

Protection of Hostage Safety: Confidentiality is essential for protecting the safety of hostages. The disclosure of information about negotiations, security force movements, or hostage details can be used against them by the kidnappers.

Building Trust: Kidnappers expect negotiators to maintain confidentiality regarding conversations and agreements. Unauthorized disclosure can undermine the kidnappers' trust in negotiators and hinder a peaceful resolution.

Media and Public Opinion: Unauthorized disclosure of information about negotiations can result in widespread media coverage and may increase pressure on the kidnappers, which can be detrimental.

Secure Internal Communication: Negotiation teams must establish secure internal communication protocols to ensure that confidential information is not leaked. This includes protecting electronic communications and limiting access to sensitive information.

Compliance with Laws and Regulations: Confidentiality is also subject to laws and regulations, and negotiation teams must adhere to these legal standards. This may include restrictions on disclosing classified or sensitive information.

Information Control: Negotiation teams must have strict control over information and limit access to it only to those who need it to conduct negotiations.

Ethical Conduct: Confidentiality is a key component of ethical conduct in hostage negotiation. Negotiators must adhere to high ethical standards and not use confidential information for personal gain.

Individual Responsibility: Each member of the negotiation team is responsible for protecting the confidentiality of the information they have access to and not disclosing it without authorization.

In hostage situations, confidentiality is essential to maintain the integrity of negotiations and the safety of hostages. Negotiation teams must be diligent in safeguarding confidential information and follow strict protocols to prevent unauthorized leaks.

Coordination with Authorities: Communication between negotiation teams and authorities must be smooth and effective to ensure a unified and secure response.

Effective coordination between negotiation teams and authorities is crucial in hostage negotiation. This ensures a unified and secure response in crisis situations. Here are some key considerations related to this principle:

Constant Communication: Negotiation teams must maintain constant and fluid communication with relevant authorities, which may include the police, security forces, intelligence services, and other government agencies.

Sharing Relevant Information: Negotiation teams must share relevant information with authorities so that they can make informed decisions. This includes details about the kidnappers' demands, the hostage situation, and any changes in the negotiation dynamics.

Response Coordination: Authorities should be prepared to intervene if necessary, and this response should be coordinated with negotiation teams. This involves planning rescue operations, securing surrounding areas, and other contingency measures.

Clear Roles and Responsibilities: It's important to clearly define the roles and responsibilities of negotiation teams and authorities. This prevents duplication of efforts and ensures concerted action.

Coordination Meetings: Negotiation teams and authorities can hold regular coordination meetings to stay informed about developments and ensure that everyone is on the same page.

Risk Assessment: Authorities must assess the risks associated with any actions they may undertake, taking into account the safety of the hostages and all involved parties.

Coordinated External Communication: Communication with the media and the public should be coordinated. Authorities and negotiation teams must agree on a single, clear message to avoid confusion.

Simulation Exercises: Negotiation teams and authorities can conduct simulation exercises to practice and refine their coordination procedures in crisis situations.

Respect for Roles: Negotiation teams and authorities must respect each group's functions and expertise and work together in a complementary manner.

Compliance with Laws and Regulations: Any action taken by authorities must comply with applicable laws and regulations.

Effective coordination between negotiation teams and authorities is crucial to ensure the safety of hostages and the success of negotiations. Both groups must work collaboratively and be well-prepared to address hostage situations in a unified and secure manner.

Effective communication is essential to build a trusting relationship with the kidnappers, reduce tension, and work towards a peaceful resolution of the crisis. Negotiators must be skilled in managing communication in high-stress situations and maintain a constant focus on the safety of the hostages.

8.Communication Strategies

Communication strategies play a fundamental role in hostage negotiation. These strategies are designed to facilitate effective dialogue, reduce tension, and move towards a peaceful resolution.

Establishing Secure and Confidential Communication Channels: The first step is to establish secure and confidential communication channels with the kidnappers. This can include the use of phones, radios, written messages, or any other means that ensures privacy.

Establishing secure and confidential communication channels with the kidnappers is one of the initial critical tasks in hostage negotiation. Here are some additional considerations on how to achieve this effectively:

Absolute Confidentiality: Communication channels must ensure absolute confidentiality. This involves using encrypted and secure communication systems to prevent third parties from accessing the conversations.

Identity Verification: Before establishing communication, it's important to verify the identity of the kidnappers to ensure you're negotiating with the correct party. This can be done through the exchange of pre-agreed passwords or specific information.

Continuous Availability: Communication channels must be continuously available. Kidnappers may reach out at any time, so negotiators must be prepared to respond at any moment.

Alternative Means: It's useful to have multiple communication channels available in case one fails. This can include backup phone lines, communication radios, secure online messaging, and other methods.

Security Protocols: Negotiation teams should follow established security protocols when using communication channels. This can include security testing to detect potential vulnerabilities.

Recording Conversations: Conversations with the kidnappers should be recorded and documented rigorously. This provides a record of what was discussed and agreed upon.

Setting Contact Times: It's helpful to establish regular schedules and frequencies for contact with the kidnappers. This helps maintain open and predictable communication.

Designated Negotiators: Negotiation teams should designate specific individuals as points of contact for conversations with the kidnappers. This prevents confusion and ensures consistent communication.

Training in Communication Channel Use: Negotiators should be well-trained in using communication channels and maintaining the security of conversations.

Assessment of Potential Risks: Negotiation teams should constantly assess potential risks associated with communication, such as the possibility of kidnappers tracing calls or identifying locations.

Maintaining a Focus on Safety: The safety of the hostages and negotiators must be the primary consideration in communication. If a threat to safety is perceived at any point, security protocols should be activated immediately.

Establishing secure and confidential communication channels is essential for effective dialogue with kidnappers and progress toward a peaceful resolution in hostage situations. Safety and confidentiality must be priorities at all times.

Direct and Open Communication: Negotiators should establish direct and open communication with the kidnappers. This involves speaking clearly and respectfully, actively listening, and responding to the concerns and demands of the kidnappers.

Direct and open communication with kidnappers is crucial in hostage negotiation. Here's more information on how to implement this strategy effectively:

Speaking Clearly and Respectfully: Negotiators should speak clearly and respectfully. Avoiding ambiguous or threatening language is essential to establish a positive tone of communication. Courtesy and respect are key to building trust.

Active Listening: Effective communication is not just about talking but also about listening. Negotiators should actively listen to the kidnappers to understand their concerns and demands. Asking open-ended questions and encouraging conversation can be helpful.

Responding to Concerns and Demands: Kidnappers may have legitimate concerns, and it's important for negotiators to respond to these concerns comprehensively. Demonstrating a willingness to address demands seriously can pave the way for potential agreements.

Avoiding Confrontation: Communication should not be confrontational. Negotiators should avoid the use of threatening or challenging language, as it can increase hostility and tension in the situation.

Clarity in Terms and Conditions: Ensuring that both negotiators and kidnappers fully understand the terms and conditions of any agreement is crucial. Clarity prevents misunderstandings and future disagreements.

Flexibility and Seeking Solutions: In some situations, negotiators may need to be flexible and seek creative solutions. If kidnappers make demands that cannot be met in full, negotiators can offer alternatives that address their concerns differently.

Explaining Limitations: If there are legal or policy restrictions that prevent the fulfillment of certain demands, negotiators should explain these limitations honestly and respectfully. This can help kidnappers understand why certain demands cannot be met.

Reinforcing Commitment to Peaceful Resolution: Negotiation teams should continuously reinforce their commitment to a peaceful resolution of the crisis and the safety of the hostages. This may include reminding kidnappers that violence is not the solution, and all efforts are focused on preventing harm to those involved.

Direct and open communication is an essential component of hostage negotiation, as it establishes a foundation for dialogue and trust-building. By maintaining a respectful and understanding approach, negotiators can increase the chances of reaching a peaceful resolution in hostage situations.

Setting a Tone of Respect: Negotiators should maintain a tone of respect and courtesy in all interactions with the kidnappers. Mutual respect is essential for building trust.

Avoiding Excessive Emotional Reactions: Negotiators should refrain from excessive emotional reactions, such as anger or frustration, that can escalate tension.

Active Listening: Actively listening to the kidnappers and demonstrating that their concerns are important is a way to show respect. Asking questions to gain a deeper understanding of their perspectives is also valuable.

Recognition of Human Rights: Negotiators should emphasize that they respect the fundamental human rights of both the hostages and the kidnappers. This may include mentioning the importance of the physical and emotional well-being of all involved.

Treating Kidnappers as Valid Interlocutors: Negotiators should consider kidnappers as valid interlocutors, meaning that their concerns and demands are legitimate within the context of the negotiation.

Respecting Cultural Differences: In international situations, it's crucial to respect cultural and religious differences that may influence the perceptions and expectations of the kidnappers. Sensitivity to these differences can be crucial.

Empathetic Communication: Empathy is a key component of respect. Negotiators should strive to understand the emotions and perspectives of the kidnappers, even if they do not agree with them.

Avoiding Derogatory Comments or Insults: Negotiators should refrain from making derogatory or insulting comments towards the kidnappers, as this can increase hostility and hinder negotiations.

Reinforcing the Importance of Peaceful Resolution: Negotiation teams must repeatedly emphasize that peaceful resolution is the primary goal and that violence is not the solution.

Maintaining Team Composition and Communication: Negotiators must ensure that all team members maintain a tone of respect in all their interactions and communications. This helps ensure consistent and unified communication.

Mutual respect is essential for building a solid foundation in hostage negotiation and for moving toward a peaceful resolution. By maintaining a tone of respect in all interactions, negotiators can enhance the chances of reaching an agreement and ensuring the safety of all involved parties.

Clarity and Transparency: Communication should be clear and unambiguous. Both negotiators and kidnappers should fully understand the terms and conditions of any agreement.

Clarity and transparency in communication are fundamental in hostage negotiation, as they prevent misunderstandings and ensure that all involved parties are on the same page. Here are some additional guidelines on how to achieve clear and transparent communication:

Defining Terms and Conditions: Negotiators should clearly define the terms and conditions of any proposed agreement. This includes specifying what is expected of both parties and what the obligations and responsibilities are.

Avoiding Technical Jargon: Communication should be understandable to all parties. Avoiding the use of technical or legal jargon that may be confusing to the kidnappers is essential.

Mutual Confirmation: After discussing the terms and conditions, it is useful to ask kidnappers to confirm their understanding. This can be done by requesting them to repeat what has been agreed upon.

Written Documentation: If possible, important agreements and commitments should be documented in writing. A written agreement can serve as a reference and prevent future disagreements.

Clarifying Specific Conditions: If kidnappers have questions or concerns about any aspect of the agreement, negotiators should be willing to clarify and provide additional information.

Emphasizing Commitments: Negotiators should emphasize the importance of fulfilling agreed-upon commitments. This helps ensure that both parties are motivated to adhere to the agreement.

Transparency about Limitations: If there are legal or policy restrictions that limit negotiators' ability to fulfill certain demands, it's important to communicate these limitations honestly and transparently.

Joint Review: Before reaching a final agreement, it is beneficial to jointly review the terms and conditions to ensure that all parties are in agreement and there are no misunderstandings.

Educating Kidnappers: Negotiators can take steps to educate kidnappers about legal and political aspects that may influence the resolution of the crisis.

Keeping Records: Detailed records of all conversations and agreements should be maintained. This provides backup documentation and accurate reference for both parties.

Clarity and transparency are key to preventing misunderstandings and building a strong foundation in hostage negotiation. Ensuring that everyone fully understands the terms and conditions is essential for moving toward a peaceful resolution and ensuring the safety of the hostages.

Non-Threatening Language: Negotiators should avoid any threatening or hostile language that may increase tension. Communication should be respectful and non-confrontational.

The use of non-threatening language is crucial in hostage negotiation as it contributes to reducing tension and maintaining an environment conducive to a peaceful resolution of the crisis. Here are some additional guidelines on how to maintain respectful and non-confrontational communication:

Avoiding Direct or Implicit Threats: Negotiators should refrain from making threats, whether they are direct or implied, during conversations with the kidnappers. The use of threats can increase hostility and endanger the safety of the hostages.

Fostering Constructive Dialogue: Instead of adopting a confrontational approach, negotiators should encourage constructive dialogue that focuses on finding solutions and reducing escalation of tensions.

Maintaining a Calm and Respectful Tone: Communication should be kept in a calm and respectful tone at all times. Keeping calm is essential to avoid emotional reactions that may worsen the situation.

Using Non-Provocative Words and Phrases: The words and phrases used in communication should be carefully chosen to avoid provocations. Avoiding aggressive or inflammatory language is essential.

Listening with Empathy: When listening to the concerns and demands of the kidnappers, negotiators should do so with empathy and understanding, rather than taking a confrontational or critical stance.

Acknowledging Emotions: It is important to acknowledge the emotions of the kidnappers and validate their feelings, even if you do not agree with them. This can help calm the situation.

Avoiding Verbal Provocations: Negotiators should avoid responding to verbal provocations from the kidnappers. Instead, they can use diversion techniques or simply remain silent if necessary.

Reinforcing the Commitment to Peaceful Resolution: During conversations, negotiation teams should continuously reinforce their commitment to the peaceful resolution of the crisis and the safety of the hostages.

Maintaining Team Composition: All team members should be trained to maintain non-threatening and respectful language in their communications with the kidnappers.

Seeking Constructive Solutions: Instead of focusing on problems or conflicts, negotiators should strive to find constructive solutions that address the concerns of both parties.

Maintaining non-threatening and respectful language is essential for establishing a communication environment that promotes a peaceful resolution of the crisis and ensures the safety of the hostages.

Active Listening: Active listening is crucial. Negotiators should pay full attention to the concerns of the kidnappers and respond empathetically, rather than adopting a defensive or confrontational posture.

Active listening plays a crucial role in hostage negotiation, as it allows negotiators to understand the concerns and demands of the kidnappers and build a solid foundation for effective communication. Here are some additional guidelines on how to carry out active listening effectively:

Giving Full Attention: When communicating with kidnappers, negotiators should give their full attention to the dialogue. This means avoiding distractions and focusing entirely on the conversation.

Showing Genuine Interest: Negotiators should demonstrate genuine interest in understanding the concerns of the kidnappers. This can be achieved through gestures, facial expressions, and body language that show empathy and concern.

Asking Open-Ended Questions: Asking open-ended questions that encourage deeper conversation is a way to show interest and gain additional insights into the kidnappers' perspectives.

Reflecting and Summarizing: Negotiators can reflect and summarize what they have heard from the kidnappers to confirm that they have understood their concerns correctly. This can also help the kidnappers feel heard.

Avoiding Interruptions: Interruptions should be avoided as much as possible. Allowing the kidnappers to fully express themselves before responding is important.

Managing One's Emotions: Negotiators must manage their own emotions during the conversation. Maintaining calm and composure is essential to sustain an effective communication environment.

Avoiding Judgment or Criticism: Negotiators should refrain from judging or criticizing the kidnappers for their opinions or demands. Instead, they should adopt a non-critical and understanding attitude.

Validating Emotions: Recognizing the emotions of the kidnappers and validating their feelings is an effective way to show empathy and understanding.

Avoiding Defensiveness: Negotiators should steer clear of a defensive or justificatory stance during the conversation. Instead, they should focus on understanding and responding to the kidnappers' concerns.

Reinforcing the Commitment to Peaceful Resolution: During the conversation, negotiation teams must continuously reaffirm their commitment to a peaceful resolution of the crisis and the safety of the hostages.

Active listening is an essential component of effective communication in hostage situations. It enables negotiators to comprehend the kidnappers' perspectives and needs, which, in turn, contributes to building a trusting relationship and seeking peaceful solutions.

Empathy: Negotiators should display empathy toward the kidnappers. This involves understanding their concerns, motivations, and perspectives, which can help establish a human connection.

Empathy plays a crucial role in hostage negotiation as it enables negotiators to understand and connect with the kidnappers on a human level. Here are some additional guidelines on how to effectively display empathy in these situations:

Listening with Intent: Listening with the intent to understand the emotions and perspectives of the kidnappers is an important first step in showing empathy. This entails paying attention to the emotional nuances behind their words.

Validating Emotions: Recognizing and validating the emotions of the kidnappers is essential for displaying empathy. You can say things like, "I understand that you're feeling a lot of frustration in this situation."

Avoiding Criticism or Judgment: Negotiators should refrain from criticizing or judging the kidnappers for their demands, actions, or perspectives. Instead, they should adopt a non-critical attitude.

Adopting a "We" Perspective: Instead of seeing themselves as adversaries, negotiators can adopt a "we" perspective by acknowledging that everyone shares the goal of a peaceful resolution and the safety of the hostages.

Showing Understanding: Making comments that demonstrate a deep understanding of the kidnappers' concerns is an effective way to display empathy. For example, "I can see why this is so important to you."

Avoiding Offensive Language: Negotiators should avoid any offensive or provocative language that might hurt the feelings of the kidnappers.

Finding Common Ground: Identifying areas of agreement or mutual interest can help build a human connection. These commonalities can be used as a basis for seeking solutions.

Providing Emotional Support: In high-stress situations, kidnappers may benefit from some emotional support. Negotiators can express their understanding of how difficult the situation can be and offer words of encouragement.

Reinforcing the Commitment to Peaceful Resolution: During the conversation, negotiation teams must continuously reaffirm their commitment to a peaceful resolution of the crisis and the safety of the hostages, demonstrating genuine empathy for the situation.

Maintaining Calm and Patience: Empathy is also expressed through maintaining calm and patience, even in high-tension situations.

Empathy is an essential element in building a trusting relationship with the kidnappers and moving toward a peaceful resolution of the crisis. Showing understanding and consideration for the emotions and perspectives of the kidnappers can be a determining factor in the success of the negotiation.

Offering Constructive Alternatives: When kidnappers present demands that cannot be met directly, negotiators can offer alternatives that address their concerns differently. This demonstrates flexibility and a willingness to seek solutions.

Offering constructive alternatives is an effective strategy in hostage negotiation to address demands that cannot be met directly. Here are some additional guidelines on how to offer alternatives effectively:

Identifying Underlying Demands: Before offering alternatives, negotiators should work to understand the underlying demands of the kidnappers. What are they trying to achieve with their demands? This understanding is crucial for proposing suitable alternatives.

Exploring Creative Solutions: Negotiation teams can conduct brainstorming sessions to explore creative solutions that address the kidnappers' concerns differently from the initial proposals.

Consulting with Experts or Advisors: In complex situations, negotiators can consult with external experts or advisors to assess and develop viable alternatives.

Highlighting Mutual Benefits: When presenting alternatives, it is helpful to emphasize the mutual benefits that can arise from these solutions. This can persuade kidnappers that the alternatives are in their interest.

Ensuring Legal Compliance: The proposed alternatives must comply with applicable laws and regulations. Negotiators should not make commitments that violate the law.

Maintaining an Open Dialogue: Negotiation teams should maintain an open and receptive dialogue with the kidnappers to discuss alternatives constructively.

Offering Reasonable Compromises: Alternatives should be reasonable and fair compromises that take into account both the kidnappers' concerns and the negotiators' limitations.

Setting Realistic Deadlines: When proposing alternatives, it is useful to set realistic deadlines for their implementation. This can help maintain steady progress in the negotiations.

Clarifying Expectations: Negotiators should clarify the expectations of both parties regarding the proposed alternatives. This includes details on how they will be carried out and what is expected from each side.

Reinforcing the Commitment to Peaceful Resolution: During the conversations, negotiation teams must continuously reaffirm their commitment to a peaceful resolution of the crisis and the safety of the hostages, even when offering alternatives.

Offering constructive alternatives can play an important role in finding solutions that satisfy both parties and in reducing the escalation of tensions in hostage situations. By showing flexibility and a willingness to seek solutions, negotiators can move toward a peaceful resolution.

Reinforcing the Importance of Peaceful Resolution: Negotiation teams must continuously reaffirm their commitment to a peaceful resolution of the crisis and the safety of the hostages.

Reinforcing the importance of peaceful resolution is a fundamental principle in hostage negotiation. Here are some additional guidelines on how to maintain and communicate this commitment effectively:

Constant Communication: Throughout all stages of negotiation, negotiation teams must consistently remind and reinforce their commitment to peaceful resolution and the safety of the hostages. This can be achieved through repeated statements of the intention to avoid violence and reach a peaceful agreement.

Emphasizing Mutual Benefit: Negotiators can highlight how a peaceful resolution benefits both parties. This can include ensuring that the kidnappers achieve their goals non-violently and that the hostages are safely released.

Remembering the Risks of Violence: It is useful to remind the kidnappers of the risks associated with resorting to violence, including potential legal and political repercussions. This can serve as an additional incentive to seek a peaceful solution.

Maintaining a Positive Language: Negotiators should use positive language that promotes peace and cooperation rather than fostering hostility or confrontation.

Emphasizing the Priority of Hostage Safety: The safety of the hostages should always be the top priority. Negotiators can stress that any violent action endangers the hostages and is unacceptable.

Keeping Calm and Composure: Negotiation teams should maintain calm and composure at all times, reinforcing the message that they are committed to a peaceful resolution.

Clarifying Dialogue Channels: Ensuring that dialogue channels are open and that conversations continue is a way to demonstrate a commitment to peaceful resolution.

Consulting with Leaders or Higher Authorities: In some situations, negotiation teams may consult with leaders or higher authorities to ensure that their commitment to peaceful resolution is supported at all decision-making levels.

Offering Constructive Alternatives: By providing constructive alternatives to address the kidnappers' demands, negotiation teams demonstrate their commitment to finding peaceful and viable solutions.

Placing Humanity at the Center: Remembering that all those involved in the negotiation are human beings and that violence can have devastating consequences is an effective way to maintain a commitment to peaceful resolution.

Peaceful resolution of the crisis and the safety of the hostages should be the number one priority in hostage negotiation. By continually reinforcing this commitment, negotiation teams can contribute to creating a conducive environment for a peaceful resolution of the situation.

Maintaining Calm: Patience and composure are essential. Negotiators must remain composed even in high-tension situations and avoid making hasty decisions.

Maintaining calm is a fundamental principle in hostage negotiation, as decisions made in high-tension situations can have significant consequences. Here are some additional guidelines on how to maintain composure effectively:

Stress Management Training: Hostage negotiation teams often receive specific training in stress management to be prepared for extremely tense situations. This training provides them with techniques to maintain composure under pressure.

Effective Internal Communication: Maintaining composure involves effective internal communication among team members. They must be in sync, share information efficiently, and support each other.

Breathing and Relaxation: Practicing breathing and relaxation techniques can help maintain composure in high-stress situations. Negotiators can use these techniques when they feel the pressure is increasing.

Long-Term Thinking: Maintaining composure involves maintaining a long-term perspective and focusing on the ultimate goal: a peaceful resolution of the crisis and the safety of the hostages.

Avoiding Hasty Decisions: Making hasty decisions can be harmful. Negotiators should resist the pressure to make impulsive decisions and instead carefully consider the implications of each step.

Consulting with the Team: In times of uncertainty, negotiators can consult with other team members to gain different perspectives and make informed decisions.

Constant Assessment: Constantly assessing the situation is key to maintaining composure. Negotiators must gather information and adapt their strategies as necessary.

Keeping Communication Open: Open communication with the kidnappers is essential to avoid misunderstandings that could lead to an escalation of tension. Negotiators must communicate clearly and respectfully.

Firm yet Calm Leadership: Team leaders must demonstrate firm yet calm leadership. This sends a message of authority and control.

Support Resources: Negotiators can access support resources, such as psychologists or advisors, to help them maintain composure and deal with stress.

Maintaining composure is essential for effective decision-making and for maintaining an environment conducive to a peaceful resolution in hostage situations. The negotiators' serenity can influence the behavior of the kidnappers and the outcome of the negotiations.

Promoting Trust: Negotiation teams must work to build and maintain a trusting relationship with the kidnappers. Trust can facilitate the negotiation process.

Maintaining Integrity: Negotiators must maintain integrity in all their interactions with the kidnappers. This includes fulfilling commitments and promises made during negotiations.

Honesty in Communications: Honesty is essential. Negotiators must be honest about what they can and cannot do and must not give false hopes.

Showing Respect: Showing respect to the kidnappers is fundamental to building trust. This includes using respectful language and behavior in all interactions.

Meeting Commitments: Once an agreement is reached, it is essential to meet the agreed-upon commitments. Non-compliance can erode trust.

Displaying Empathy: Showing empathy for the concerns and perspectives of the kidnappers is an effective way to build trust. This demonstrates a genuine understanding of their situation.

Setting Clear Expectations: Negotiation teams must set clear expectations regarding deadlines, actions, and commitments to avoid misunderstandings.

Supporting the Process: Negotiators can demonstrate their commitment to the negotiation process by offering emotional support to the kidnappers during moments of tension.

Promoting Mutual Benefits: Highlighting the mutual benefits of a peaceful resolution can foster trust by showing that both parties have an interest in reaching an agreement.

Offering Security Guarantees: Negotiators can offer security guarantees to the kidnappers as part of an agreement, which can help build trust.

Being Prepared to Compromise on Some Points: Showing a willingness to compromise on some points can demonstrate to the kidnappers that negotiators are committed to finding a mutually acceptable solution.

Consulting with Experts: In complex situations, negotiation teams can consult with experts in psychology, anthropology, or other fields to better understand the mindset and motivations of the kidnappers.

Reinforcing the Commitment to Peaceful Resolution: At every stage of negotiation, negotiation teams must reaffirm their commitment to a peaceful resolution of the crisis and the safety of the hostages.

Promoting trust is an ongoing process and may require time and effort. However, a strong trusting relationship can be a determining factor in the success of hostage negotiation.

Avoiding Provocations: Negotiators must avoid provoking or confronting the kidnappers, as this can increase hostility and endanger the safety of the hostages.

Avoiding provocations is essential in hostage negotiation because any action that increases hostility can be detrimental and jeopardize the safety of the hostages. Here are some additional guidelines on how to avoid provocations effectively:

Maintaining a Respectful Language and Tone: Communication with the kidnappers should always be respectful and non-confrontational. Avoid using threatening or provocative language.

Not Blaming or Judging: Negotiators should refrain from blaming or judging the kidnappers for their actions. Instead, they should focus on seeking constructive solutions.

Not Making Threats: Negotiators should not make threats, as this can trigger an escalation of hostility by the kidnappers.

Avoid Discussing Sensitive Topics: In some cases, certain topics can be sensitive and provoke an emotional response from the kidnappers. Negotiators should exercise caution when addressing these issues.

Avoid Ridicule or Disdain: Ridiculing or showing disdain toward the kidnappers will only increase hostility. Negotiators should show respect at all times.

Not Giving Unreasonable Ultimatums: Unreasonable ultimatums can provoke a negative response from the kidnappers. Negotiators should avoid setting unrealistic or unacceptable deadlines.

Listening Actively and Empathetically: Actively listening to the kidnappers, showing empathy, and understanding their concerns can help avoid provocations.

Being Prepared for Temporary Withdrawal: If the situation becomes too tense, negotiators may consider the possibility of temporarily withdrawing to avoid further provocations.

Consulting with Psychology Experts: In particularly delicate situations, negotiation teams can consult with psychology experts or advisors who can provide guidance on how to avoid provocations.

Clear and Transparent Communication: Communication must be clear and transparent at all times to prevent misunderstandings that can lead to tensions.

Highlighting Mutual Benefits: Demonstrating how a peaceful resolution benefits both parties can reduce hostility and promote cooperation.

Reinforcing the Commitment to Peaceful Resolution: At every stage of negotiation, negotiation teams must reaffirm their commitment to a peaceful resolution of the crisis and the safety of the hostages.

Avoiding provocations is essential to maintain a negotiation environment that favors the safety of the hostages and a peaceful resolution of the crisis. Patience and careful communication management are key to avoiding potentially dangerous situations.

Communication strategies must be tailored to the specific situation and the dynamics of the kidnappers. Effective communication is essential.

9.Hostage Situation Assessment.

Hostage situation assessment is a crucial process carried out by security forces and response teams in hostage-taking scenarios. The primary objective is to gather information about the ongoing situation and make informed decisions to ensure the safety of the hostages and a peaceful resolution of the crisis.

Communication: Establishing communication with the kidnappers is essential. This can be done through negotiators or specialized response teams. Communication allows for obtaining information about the kidnappers' demands and objectives, as well as the condition of the hostages.

Negotiators: Negotiators are crisis management professionals who act as intermediaries between the authorities and the kidnappers. Their primary goal is to establish a channel of communication with the kidnappers, keep them calm, and gather information about their demands and objectives. Negotiators try to persuade the kidnappers to release the hostages peacefully and safely.

Secure communication: Communication must be conducted securely to prevent the kidnappers from locating or identifying the security forces. Encrypted communication devices or secure channels are often used to ensure confidentiality.

Understanding demands: Communication allows authorities to understand the kidnappers' demands and concerns. This is essential to determine whether the demands are reasonable or negotiable. By understanding the motivations of the kidnappers, negotiators can adapt their approach to seek a peaceful solution.

Maintaining composure: Negotiators are trained to remain calm and handle the situation with empathy. They can help reduce tension and hostility among the parties, increasing the chances of a peaceful resolution.

Setting deadlines: In some cases, deadlines can be established for resolving the situation. This is done carefully, as it can increase pressure on the kidnappers but may also jeopardize the safety of the hostages. Communication can be useful for negotiating and extending deadlines if necessary.

Communication with hostages: In addition to communicating with the kidnappers, authorities must also maintain a line of communication with the hostages to ensure their safety and receive information about their health and well-being.

Communication is a strategic tool in the management of hostage situations and is part of a comprehensive approach to achieving a peaceful and secure resolution. However, it is important to remember that each situation is unique, and the communication strategy must be adapted accordingly. The safety of the hostages is always the top priority.

Location assessment: Determining the exact location of the kidnappers and hostages is vital for planning an effective response. This may involve the use of surveillance equipment, maps, or tracking technology.

Surveillance teams: The use of surveillance equipment, such as security cameras or drones, can provide valuable information about the location of the kidnappers and hostages. This allows authorities to have an overview of the situation and how the people involved are moving.

Maps and blueprints: Using maps and blueprints of the location where the hostage-taking is taking place is important. These documents can help identify escape routes, shelter areas, and entry and exit points. Maps can also be useful for planning tactics and strategies.

Tracking technology: In some situations, security forces may use tracking technology to trace the location of the kidnappers and hostages. This may include the use of GPS devices or satellite tracking systems. However, it is important to do this discreetly to prevent the kidnappers from discovering the technology.

Information from witnesses and hostages: People who have witnessed the hostage-taking and the hostages themselves can provide information about the location and conditions on-site. This may include details about the building's structure or the features of the surrounding area.

Communication with kidnappers: Through communication with the kidnappers, information about the location can be obtained. Specific questions about where the hostages are and the conditions in which they are held may be part of the conversations with the kidnappers.

Coordination of response teams: The location assessment information is shared and coordinated among the response teams, including the police, special forces, and other professionals involved in crisis management. This ensures that everyone is aware of the situation and can work together effectively.

Location assessment is crucial for planning an effective and safe response in hostage situations. This information provides a solid foundation for decision-making and the implementation of tactical strategies that minimize the risk to the hostages and allow for a safe resolution of the crisis.

Hostage identification: Determining how many hostages there are, their ages, gender, and health status is essential. This helps prioritize medical care if necessary and establish a strategy for their safe release.

Number of hostages: Accurately determining the number of hostages is fundamental. This allows authorities to know how many lives are at risk and plan their response accordingly. In some situations, the number of hostages can be confusing due to chaos or lack of information, so a careful count is important.

Ages and gender: Knowing the ages and genders of the hostages is important for adapting the response and assistance appropriately. For example, if there are children or vulnerable individuals among the hostages, this may require special attention and additional consideration of their well-being.

Health status: Evaluating the health status of the hostages is critical. Some hostages may need immediate medical attention due to injuries, illnesses, or pre-existing medical conditions. This information is crucial to ensure that emergency medical care is provided when necessary.

Prioritizing medical care: Information about the health status of the hostages helps authorities prioritize medical care. Serious injuries or urgent medical conditions should be addressed before any other considerations.

Safe release strategy: Knowing the characteristics of the hostages can influence the strategy for their safe release. For example, if there are hostages with special medical needs, authorities may consider releasing them first to receive appropriate medical care.

Communication with hostages: Maintaining an open line of communication with the hostages is also important to assess their health and well-being.

They can provide information about their needs and concerns, which can guide the authorities' response.

Accurate identification of the hostages is essential for making informed decisions and ensuring their safety. This information helps design a crisis resolution strategy that takes into account the needs and health of the hostages and prioritizes their safe release. The protection and well-being of the hostages are the top priority in these situations.

Physical and emotional conditions: Evaluating the physical and emotional conditions of the hostages is important for their well-being. This may require the involvement of mental health professionals and medical personnel.

Physical conditions:

Injuries and medical needs: Assessing whether the hostages have suffered physical injuries during the hostage-taking is fundamental. Authorities must provide emergency medical care if necessary. The presence of medical professionals or paramedics on-site may be crucial for attending to injured hostages.

Basic needs: Ensuring that the hostages have access to basic necessities such as water, food, and medical care is essential for their physical well-being. Response teams should coordinate the safe delivery of these supplies.

Emotional and psychological conditions:

Trauma assessment: The experience of being a hostage can be profoundly traumatic. Mental health professionals can assess the emotional state of the hostages and provide psychological support to help them cope with the trauma.

Calming and reassuring: Hostages may be anxious, scared, or stressed. Negotiators and mental health professionals can help calm the hostages, provide emotional support, and establish positive communication to maintain their morale.

Communication with family members: In many cases, hostages may be concerned about their family members. Authorities can facilitate communication between the hostages and their loved ones to reduce emotional distress.

Negotiation with kidnappers: Evaluating the emotional conditions of the hostages can provide valuable information for negotiators. Understanding how the hostages feel and what their emotional needs are can influence negotiation tactics and the strategy to ensure the hostages' safety.

Attending to the physical and emotional conditions of the hostages is essential to ensure their well-being during the crisis. In addition to mental health and medical professionals, social workers and crisis management experts may also be involved to provide comprehensive support to the hostages. Protecting their mental and emotional health is as important as their physical safety.

Threats and weapons: Determining whether the kidnappers are armed and what their intentions are is crucial for designing an appropriate resolution approach. It is also important to identify any potential threats to the hostages.

Determining the presence of weapons: Identifying whether the kidnappers are armed and what type of weapons they possess is essential. This influences the response strategy since firearms, explosives, or other weapons can pose a significantly higher risk.

Intentions of the kidnappers: Understanding the intentions of the kidnappers is fundamental. Some kidnappers may seek a peaceful way out, while others may have more violent objectives. Evaluating their demands and communication can provide clues about their intentions.

Potential threats to the hostages: Identifying any threats or risks that the kidnappers may pose to the hostages is crucial. This includes assessing whether the kidnappers have harmed the hostages, threatened to do so, or used violence.

Improvised weapons: In addition to conventional firearms, it is important to identify any improvised weapons or explosive devices that may be present in the situation. These can be extremely dangerous and require special attention from explosive ordnance disposal teams.

Designing an appropriate resolution strategy: Information about threats and weapons will influence the resolution strategy. In situations with armed kidnappers, the planning of assault tactics or specific negotiation strategies will be based on this assessment.

Prioritizing hostage safety: The top priority in managing hostage situations is the safety of the hostages. The assessment of threats and weapons is essential for making decisions that minimize the risk to the hostages and ensure their safe release.

Assessment of threats and weapons is an integral part of the response planning in hostage situations. The information collected during this assessment helps authorities make informed and strategic decisions to address the crisis safely and effectively.

Internal communication: Maintaining effective communication among response teams, negotiators, and other authorities is essential for coordinating actions and making joint decisions.

Effective internal communication is a critical element in managing hostage situations. Here are some key points about the importance of maintaining smooth communication among response teams, negotiators, and other authorities:

Coordination of efforts: In hostage situations, it is crucial for all response teams to work in a coordinated manner and be aware of real-time developments. Internal communication enables effective coordination among security forces, negotiators, medical teams, and other professionals involved.

Exchange of information: Information is essential for making informed decisions. Internal communication ensures that relevant information is shared in a timely manner, and all teams have access to key details about the situation, the kidnappers' demands, and the hostages' condition.

Joint decision-making: Managing hostage situations often involves critical real-time decision-making. Internal communication facilitates collaboration among experts and team leaders, allowing them to make joint decisions that prioritize the safety of the hostages and response personnel.

Adjusting strategies: Hostage situations can evolve rapidly. Internal communication allows teams to adjust their strategies and tactics as needed based on new developments, such as changes in the kidnappers' demands or the hostages' condition.

Personnel safety: Keeping response personnel safe is an important consideration. Internal communication can help ensure that teams are aware of potential threats and risks, enabling them to take measures to protect themselves.

Coordination with other agencies: In some situations, coordination with other agencies, such as local police, violent incident response teams, emergency medical services, and other organizations, may be necessary. Internal communication facilitates this inter-agency coordination.

Communication with negotiators: Internal communication also involves coordination with negotiators who are in direct contact with the kidnappers. Information shared between negotiators and response teams is vital for an effective resolution strategy.

In summary, effective internal communication is essential to ensure a coordinated and safe response in hostage situations. Collaboration among all teams and agencies involved is crucial for protecting hostages and achieving a peaceful resolution of the crisis.

Formation of a crisis team: Establishing a crisis team composed of experts in hostage response tactics, negotiators, psychologists, and other professionals is crucial to guide the assessment and resolution strategy.

Hostage response tactics experts: These professionals are trained in tactics and strategies to respond to hostage situations. They are responsible for planning and executing tactical operations, such as assaults or releases, if necessary.

Negotiators: Negotiators are experts in crisis management and communication with kidnappers. Their goal is to establish a dialogue with the kidnappers, maintain calm, and gather information about their demands and objectives, with the hope of achieving a peaceful resolution.

Psychologists and mental health professionals: Psychologists and mental health professionals play a crucial role in providing emotional support to hostages and assessing their psychological well-being. They can also provide guidance to response teams on how to deal with traumatized hostages.

Communication and public relations specialists: These professionals are responsible for managing communication with the media and the families of the hostages, ensuring that information is disseminated in a controlled and accurate manner.

Coordinators and team leaders: These individuals are responsible for directing and coordinating the operations of the crisis team as a whole. They organize and oversee all activities and decisions made during the crisis.

Security experts: It is essential to have security experts to assess threats and risks, as well as to develop security strategies for response personnel and hostages.

Lawyers and legal experts: In some situations, legal or juridical issues may arise. Lawyers and legal experts can provide guidance on legal aspects and processes that need to be followed.

Technology and Communications Experts: In the digital age, having experts in technology and communications is essential to ensure that communication with the kidnappers is conducted securely and that advanced technologies are used to monitor the situation.

The collaborative work of these professionals in a crisis team is essential to guide the situation assessment and resolution strategy. Decision-making in hostage situations is complex, and having a multidisciplinary team allows for addressing a wide range of challenges and maximizing the chances of a peaceful and safe resolution.

Strategic Planning: Once sufficient information has been gathered, a resolution strategy must be developed that takes into account the safety of the hostages and the objectives of the kidnappers. This may include negotiation tactics, assault, or a mixed approach, depending on the situation.

Assessment of the Current Situation: Strategic planning begins with a detailed review of all the information collected during the initial assessment of the situation. This includes data about the kidnappers, the hostages, the demands, weaponry, and the conditions on-site.

Definition of Objectives: It is important to establish clear objectives for the operation. The primary goal is the safety of the hostages. Additionally, objectives may include the apprehension of the kidnappers, evidence gathering, and a peaceful resolution of the situation, depending on the circumstances.

Selection of the Resolution Strategy: Depending on the situation and objectives, a decision is made regarding whether to use a negotiation, assault, or mixed strategy. The choice of strategy is based on factors such as the kidnappers' demands, the assessment of threats and weapons, and the potential for a peaceful resolution.

Tactical Planning: Once the strategy is selected, a detailed tactical plan is developed, which includes team coordination, identification of entry and exit points, the use of lethal or non-lethal force (in the case of assault), event sequencing, and assignment of specific tasks.

Communication and Negotiation: If a negotiation strategy is chosen, guidelines for communication with the kidnappers are established. This may include the appointment of a negotiation team and the creation of a communication protocol.

Contingency Preparation: Strategic planning must include measures to address contingencies, such as unexpected changes in the situation, the unpredictable reaction of the kidnappers, or the need for emergency medical assistance.

Team and Agency Coordination: All involved teams, including security forces, tactical response teams, negotiators, and medical professionals, must coordinate their efforts according to the strategic plan.

Ongoing Review and Update: Strategic planning is a dynamic process that is reviewed and updated as the situation evolves. It is essential to adapt to real-time changes and reevaluate the plan as needed.

Strategic planning is fundamental to ensuring an effective and safe response in hostage situations. It provides a framework for coordinating all actions and efforts, maximizing the chances of a successful resolution that protects the hostages and minimizes risks.

Continuous Assessment: Situation assessment must be continuous as the crisis unfolds. New and updated information can change the resolution strategy.

Adaptation to Changes: As the crisis develops, it is crucial to adapt the strategy and tactics as necessary. Changes in the kidnappers' demands, the hostages' condition, weaponry, or the kidnappers' behavior may require adjustments to the resolution strategy.

Informed Decision-Making: Continuous assessment provides updated information for making informed real-time decisions. This is essential to ensure that actions taken are consistent with the safety objectives of the hostages.

Risk Management: Ongoing assessment allows for the identification and management of risks as they arise. It can help avoid dangerous situations or take measures to protect hostages and response personnel.

Team Coordination: Communication and coordination between response teams, negotiators, and other authorities must be continuous to ensure that everyone is aware of the latest developments and can adjust their actions accordingly.

Intelligence Information Updates: The intelligence information collected during ongoing assessment can help anticipate future actions by the kidnappers and provide clues on how to proceed.

Contingency Preparedness: Continuous assessment allows for preparedness for unexpected contingencies. In hostage situations, it is crucial to anticipate different scenarios and be ready to act if they arise.

Maintaining Hostage Safety: The top priority at all times is to ensure the safety of the hostages. Continuous assessment ensures that this priority remains the central focus.

Peaceful Resolution: Whenever possible, a peaceful resolution should be sought. Continuous assessment can identify opportunities for negotiation and the safe release of hostages.

Continuous assessment is crucial to ensuring that the resolution strategy is flexible and adaptable as the crisis unfolds. Quick responsiveness and informed decision-making are essential to protect hostages and achieve a successful resolution.

Training and Preparation: It is essential for response teams to be well-trained and prepared for hostage situations. Simulation and training are crucial to ensure an effective and safe response.

Skill Development: Training provides members of response teams with the skills and knowledge needed to address hostage situations. This includes tactical, negotiation, communication, and crisis management skills.

Familiarity with Procedures: Response teams must be familiar with the procedures and protocols established for hostage situations. This includes strategic planning, team coordination, communication, and security.

Simulation and Training Scenarios: Simulating hostage situations is a critical part of training. Training scenarios provide a practical experience that allows teams to practice decision-making and response in a controlled environment.

Development of Strategies and Tactics: During training, specific strategies and tactics are developed for addressing hostage situations. This includes how to negotiate with kidnappers, conduct tactical operations, and assess and manage threats and weapons.

Team Testing: Training also allows for testing the coordination and effectiveness of response teams. This includes evaluating how teams work together and identifying areas for improvement.

Knowledge Updates: Training must be ongoing and updated to stay current with best practices and new techniques. Tactics and strategies can evolve over time, and teams must stay informed of these changes.

Remaining Calm Under Pressure: Training also helps teams develop skills to remain calm and make effective decisions under pressure, which is essential in hostage situations.

Assessment and Feedback: After simulation and training, it is important to conduct a detailed assessment and provide feedback to team members. This allows for learning from experiences and improving skills.

Preparation and training are crucial to ensure that response teams are ready to handle hostage situations safely and effectively. Regular practice and ongoing training are essential to maintain high levels of readiness and improve response capabilities in these high-risk situations.

In hostage situations, the top priority is the safety of the hostages, and situation assessment is a critical component for achieving this goal. The peaceful resolution of the crisis is always the desired outcome, but in some cases, more assertive tactics may be necessary to protect the hostages and eliminate the threat.

10.Establishing a Hostage Negotiation Team

Establishing a hostage negotiation team is an important step in managing hostage situations. Below are the steps for setting up a hostage negotiation team:

Selection of Team Members: Choose individuals with exceptional communication skills, empathy, and the ability to remain calm under pressure. Include individuals with experience in crisis management and high-stress situations. Ensure that team members have a deep understanding of negotiation protocols and strategies.

Exceptional Communication Skills: Negotiators must be able to communicate effectively, clearly, and calmly, even in high-stress situations. They should be experts in listening and expressing themselves in a conciliatory and persuasive manner.

Empathy and Understanding: Team members should be capable of understanding and showing empathy towards the concerns and demands of the kidnappers. Empathy is essential for establishing a trusting relationship with both the kidnappers and the hostages.

Emotional Control: The ability to remain calm under pressure is crucial. Negotiators must be able to control their own emotions and emotional reactions, even when facing extremely stressful situations.

Crisis Management Experience: Previous experience in crisis management is a valuable asset. This may include experience in security, psychology, social work, or related fields.

Teamwork Skills: Hostage negotiation team members should be collaborative and capable of working closely with other response teams, such as law enforcement and tactical assault teams.

Knowledge of Protocols and Procedures: Negotiators should be thoroughly familiar with the protocols and procedures established for hostage situations. They should be experts in the use of specific negotiation techniques.

Training and Education: Team members should have received specific training in hostage negotiation, including communication techniques, negotiation tactics, and training in hostage simulation scenarios.

Conflict Resolution Skills: The ability to resolve conflicts peacefully and reach compromises is essential in hostage negotiation. Negotiators must be capable of finding solutions that satisfy both the kidnappers' demands and the needs of the hostages and public safety.

Background and Credibility: The credibility of negotiators with the kidnappers is important. In some cases, having relevant backgrounds or knowledge (such as cultural or regional politics) can be beneficial.

Medical and Emotional Conditions: Team members should be in good physical and emotional condition, as facing hostage situations can be extremely stressful. Regular medical examinations and psychological assessments should be conducted.

The selection of hostage negotiation team members should be careful and based on the combination of skills needed to address hostage situations safely and effectively. The team should be diverse in skills and backgrounds to handle a wide range of situations and challenges.

Training and Preparation:

Provide training in hostage negotiation and crisis management. This includes effective communication techniques, empathy, emotional control, and conflict management. Conduct simulation exercises and training scenarios to allow team members to practice their skills in simulated hostage situations. Provide training in early warning sign identification and situation assessment. Design a Training Program:

Develop a training program that covers the essential aspects of hostage negotiation. The program should be comprehensive and based on best practices and proven strategies. Incorporate Expert Trainers:

Hire or invite expert trainers in hostage negotiation and crisis management to lead the training. The experience and knowledge of experts are invaluable. Training in Communication Techniques:

Provide training in effective communication techniques, such as active listening, empathy, and clear expression. Negotiators must be experts in establishing and maintaining open and productive communication. Simulation Scenarios:

Organize simulation scenarios of hostage situations. Training scenarios allow team members to practice their skills in a controlled environment and receive feedback. Emotional Management Training:

Training should include the development of skills to stay calm and control emotions, both one's own and those of the kidnappers and hostages. Knowledge of Protocols and Procedures:

Ensure that team members are fully familiar with the protocols and procedures established for hostage situations. They should be experts in the use of specific negotiation techniques.

Assessment and Feedback:

Provide regular assessments of team members' performance in training scenarios. Feedback is essential for continuous improvement. Training in Emotional Intelligence:

Emotional intelligence is critical in hostage negotiation. Training in this area should include recognizing and managing one's own and others' emotions.

Conflict Resolution Training:

Negotiators must be experts in conflict resolution and finding solutions that satisfy the kidnappers' demands and the hostages' needs.

Security Training:

Ensure that team members receive personal security training and risk assessment training in hostage situations.

Ongoing Updates:

Training should be continuous and updated to stay current with the best practices and the latest negotiation techniques.

Training should be an ongoing process to keep hostage negotiators at the top of their skills and knowledge. Regular practice and skill refinement are essential for successfully addressing hostage situations safely and effectively.

Development of Protocols and Procedures:

Define protocols and procedures for communication with the kidnappers, information gathering, decision-making, and negotiation management.

Establish a secure communication protocol to protect the location and identity of negotiators.

Assessment of the Current Situation and Potential Risks:

Understand the nature of the hostage situation, including the number of kidnappers, hostages, their demands, and any perceived threats. Assess potential risks and possible complications.

Defining Roles and Responsibilities:

Identify and assign specific roles to team members. This may include a team leader, a communicator, a lead negotiator, a backup negotiator, an intelligence observer, among others.

Establishing Communication Channels:

Define internal and external communication channels. Ensure that communication channels are secure and resistant to interception.

Communication Plan with Kidnappers:

Establish a protocol for communication with the kidnappers. This includes how to initiate and maintain communication, the use of specific phrases and tones, and the frequency of contact.

Gathering Information and Assessing Demands:

Set procedures for gathering information about the kidnappers' demands and the status of the hostages. This may include specific questions to be asked and how to document the collected information.

Negotiation and Decision-Making:

Develop a process for decision-making and negotiation management. This includes how to address demands, how to respond to changes in the situation, and when to seek additional guidance.

Hostage and Response Personnel Safety:

Establish security measures to protect both hostages and response personnel. This may include hostage evacuation in the event of a tactical assault and safeguarding the negotiation team's location.

Handling Crisis or Emergency Situations:

Plan how the negotiation team will respond to crisis situations, such as an escalation of violence by the kidnappers or a medical emergency among the hostages.

Communication with Other Teams and Authorities:

Set procedures for communication and coordination with other response teams, such as law enforcement and tactical teams.

Training and Regular Exercises:

Include protocols for ongoing training and regular exercises to keep the team updated and ready to act.

Continuous Evaluation and Review:

Protocols and procedures should undergo continuous evaluation and review to adapt to lessons learned and changes in best practices.

Recording and Documentation:

Establish procedures for recording and documenting all communications and actions taken during the crisis. This can be crucial for future investigations or reviews.

Protocols and procedures should be clear, flexible, and adaptable to changing situations. The hostage negotiation team should be thoroughly familiar with these protocols and regularly practice their implementation through simulation exercises and training scenarios. Training and constant practice are essential to ensure the team is ready to respond effectively in hostage situations.

Coordination with Other Teams:

Ensure that the hostage negotiation team is in close coordination with other response teams, such as law enforcement and tactical assault teams.

Establish Effective Internal Communication among all involved teams.

Establish a Unified Command Center:

Coordination begins by establishing a unified command center where representatives from all involved teams can work together. This facilitates communication and joint decision-making.

Appoint an Operations Coordinator:

Assign an operations coordinator to act as the primary point of contact between the teams. This individual should be well-informed about the current situation and coordinate the actions of all teams.

Effective Communication:

Establish clear and secure communication channels among the teams. This may include radios, secure phone lines, or encrypted messaging systems. Effective communication is essential for sharing up-to-date information.

Information Sharing:

Share critical and updated information among the teams. This includes details about the kidnappers' demands, the hostages' status, the kidnappers' location, and other relevant data.

Define Roles and Responsibilities:

Ensure that each team understands its specific roles and responsibilities. This includes protecting the hostages, communicating with the kidnappers, tactical assault tactics (if necessary), medical support, coordination with authorities, and media management.

Coordination Exercises:

Conduct simulation exercises involving all teams to practice coordination. These exercises help identify potential issues and improve communication and collaboration.

Continuous Information Flow:

Maintain a constant flow of information among the teams to ensure everyone is aware of the latest developments and can adjust their actions accordingly.

Communication with Team Leaders:

Ensure that leaders of each team are in contact and are aware of the overall strategy and objectives.

Prioritize Hostage and Response Personnel Safety:

The top priority should always be the safety of the hostages and response personnel. All teams must work together to achieve this goal.

Continuous Evaluation and Strategy Updates:

As the situation evolves, teams should be prepared to adapt their strategies and tactics as needed. Continuous evaluation is essential for making informed decisions.

Communication with External Authorities:

Coordinate with local and national authorities to ensure that appropriate resources and assistance are applied. Additionally, communication with security agencies may be necessary to manage the situation.

Effective coordination between teams is essential to manage hostage situations safely and effectively. Effective communication and collaboration enable teams to work together to address all aspects of the crisis and maximize the chances of a successful resolution.

Resources and Support:

Provide the necessary resources for the negotiation team to operate effectively, including secure communication equipment, access to intelligence information, and legal counsel if needed.

Secure Communication Resources:

Provide secure communication equipment, such as encrypted radios or secure phones, to enable secure and encrypted communication between the negotiation team and other teams.

Access to Intelligence Information:

Ensure that the negotiation team has access to up-to-date intelligence information about the kidnappers, their potential locations, and other relevant data.

Legal Counsel:

Provide access to legal counsel to ensure that actions taken are in compliance with the law and proper procedures.

Medical and Healthcare Support:

Ensure that medical and healthcare professionals are available in case medical attention is needed for hostages or response personnel.

Psychological Support:

Offer psychological support and counseling for negotiation team members, as facing hostage situations can be emotionally challenging.

Tactical and Assault Teams:

Coordinate with tactical and assault teams in case a rescue operation is necessary. Provide support and coordination to ensure the safety of all involved.

Documentation and Recording:

Provide the means and training necessary for proper documentation of all communications and actions taken during the crisis. This documentation can be crucial for future investigations or reviews.

Access to Financial Resources:

Ensure that the negotiation team has access to financial resources to meet the kidnappers' demands, if necessary, or to cover other costs related to crisis management.

Equipment and Supplies:

Ensure that the negotiation team has the necessary equipment and supplies, such as recording devices, writing materials, and any other specific equipment required for their work.

Support from Top Management:

Obtain backing and authority from top management to make important and strategic decisions. This ensures that the negotiation team can act with confidence and authority.

Coordination with External Authorities:

Coordinate with local, regional, and national authorities to ensure that the necessary resources and assistance are applied based on the magnitude of the crisis.

Continuous Evaluation:

Conduct regular assessments of the negotiation team's performance and provide feedback for continuous improvement.

Keep team members updated on best practices and the latest negotiation techniques.

Collect Updated Information:

As the situation unfolds, it's essential to continue gathering updated information about the kidnappers, hostages, demands, location, and any changes in the dynamics of the crisis.

Communication Monitoring:

Constantly monitor communication with the kidnappers. This includes reviewing phone calls, emails, or other means of communication, as well as interpreting any changes in tone or demands.

Threat and Risk Assessment:

Continue evaluating potential threats to the hostages, response personnel, and public safety in general. This may include identifying weapons or explosives and considering the kidnappers' intentions.

Analysis of Demands and Objectives:

Constantly assess the kidnappers' demands and objectives to understand their motivations and find potential points of agreement.

Communication with Other Teams:

Maintain constant communication with other involved teams, such as law enforcement and tactical teams, to share information and coordinate actions.

Coordination with External Authorities:

Coordinate with local, regional, and national authorities to ensure that the necessary resources and assistance are applied based on the magnitude of the crisis.

Reevaluation of Strategies:

As new information is gathered, be flexible in adjusting strategies and tactics as needed. Strategies may need to be modified to achieve a safe resolution.

Prioritize Hostage Safety:

At all times, the top priority should be ensuring the safety of the hostages. Ensure that the actions taken are designed to protect the hostages.

Communication with Top Management:

Keep senior authorities and team leaders updated on the evolution of the situation and any changes in strategy.

Emotional and Mental Health Support:

Provide ongoing support to response team members, as facing hostage situations can be emotionally challenging.

Preparation for Contingencies:

Be prepared to face unforeseen situations and contingencies, and adjust strategies as needed.

Continuous evaluation is essential to ensure that the actions taken are informed and aligned with the safety objectives for the hostages. Flexibility and adaptability in the strategy are crucial for dealing with constantly changing hostage situations.

Communication with Kidnappers:

Develop an approach to communication with the kidnappers. This includes creating a communication protocol, identifying possible points of agreement, and managing their demands.

Designation of Negotiators:

Appoint members of your hostage negotiation team to act as primary and backup negotiators. These individuals should be experts in effective communication techniques, empathy, and conflict resolution.

Initiate Contact:

If there hasn't been initial contact from the kidnappers, you should take the initiative to establish communication. This can be done through phone calls, emails, or any other secure and appropriate means.

Maintain Calm and Empathy:

During conversations, negotiators should remain calm and empathetic. Avoid confrontations or emotional responses that could escalate tension.

Build Trust:

Work to establish a trusting relationship with the kidnappers. This can be a gradual process and may take time. Actively listening to their concerns and demonstrating understanding is essential.

Avoid Unfulfillable Promises:

Avoid making promises that cannot be kept, as this could undermine your team's credibility and worsen the situation.

Clear Communication:

Be clear and direct in your communication with the kidnappers. Use clear and precise language and avoid misunderstandings.

Listen and Inquire:

Listen attentively to what the kidnappers have to say and ask questions to gather additional information. This can help understand their demands and motivations.

Do Not Concede to Unsafe Demands:

Do not concede to demands that jeopardize the safety of the hostages or are illegal. Your top priority should be the safety of the hostages.

Negotiate in Good Faith:

Negotiate in good faith and show willingness to seek mutually acceptable solutions as long as they are safe and legal.

Keep a Record of Conversations:

Record and document all conversations with the kidnappers. This can be valuable for future investigations and reviews.

Set Time Limits:

If possible, set time limits for conversations and negotiations. This can help prevent the situation from dragging on indefinitely.

Communication with Other Teams:

Maintain constant communication with other involved teams, such as law enforcement and tactical teams, to share information and coordinate actions.

Continuous Situation Assessment:

Continuously assess the situation and potential threats. As the situation evolves, adjust the communication strategy as needed.

Communication with the kidnappers is a delicate process that requires negotiation skills, patience, and empathy. The main goal is to achieve a safe resolution of the crisis and protect the lives of the hostages.

Emotional Support for Team Members:

Provide emotional support and mental health care to negotiation team members, as facing hostage situations can be extremely stressful.

Emotional Resilience Training:

Offer emotional resilience training to team members before they face hostage situations. This training can help them develop skills to deal with stress and intense emotions.

Access to Psychological Support:

Ensure that team members have access to mental health professionals, such as psychologists or counselors, who can provide emotional support and tools to manage stress.

Debriefing After the Crisis:

Conduct debriefing sessions after the crisis to allow team members to share their experiences, emotions, and concerns. These sessions can provide a safe space for expression and reflection.

Individualized Counseling:

Offer individualized counseling for team members who may need additional support. Each person may experience the situation differently, and individualized support can be beneficial.

Awareness of Stress Signs:

Train team members to recognize signs of stress in themselves and their colleagues. This can help identify and address stress early.

Rest and Rotation:

In prolonged hostage situations, ensure that team members have opportunities to rest and recover. Personnel rotation can help prevent fatigue.

Personal Support Network:

Encourage team members to maintain a personal support network outside of work, such as friends, family, or trusted colleagues, with whom they can talk and vent.

Promotion of Self-Care:

Promote self-care among team members. This includes the importance of getting enough sleep, maintaining a balanced diet, exercising, and practicing relaxation techniques.

Open Communication with Leadership:

Ensure that leaders are available and willing to listen to team members' concerns. Open and two-way communication is essential.

Continuous Assessment of Emotional Health:

Regularly assess the emotional health of team members and provide additional support as needed.

Promotion of Group Resilience:

Foster team cohesion and group resilience. Camaraderie and support among team members can be a source of emotional strength.

Emotional support is essential to maintain the health and well-being of response team members in hostage situations. Providing resources and training in emotional resilience, as well as access to mental health professionals, can help team members cope with the stress and emotions associated with these crises.

Support from Top Management:

Ensure that the negotiation team has the necessary backing and authority from top management to make important and strategic decisions.

Authority for Key Decisions:

Top management should grant leaders of the response team the authority to make critical decisions in real-time. This includes decision-making regarding negotiation strategy, kidnappers' demands, and tactical operations.

Resource Allocation:

Ensure that the necessary resources for crisis management are allocated, such as secure communication equipment, medical and support personnel, psychological support, and financial resources to meet reasonable kidnappers' demands.

Communication with Competent Authorities:

Top management should establish and maintain communication with competent authorities at the local, regional, or national level, such as the police, military, or government. This ensures that the necessary resources and assistance are applied based on the crisis's magnitude.

Communication with Other Departments:

Coordinate with other departments and teams within the organization to ensure that everyone is aware of the situation and can provide support, resources, and collaboration as needed.

Logistical and Administrative Support:

Provide logistical and administrative support to ensure that response teams have access to the facilities, equipment, and supplies needed to effectively perform their work.

Communication with the Media and the Public:

Top management should handle communication with the media and the public in a coordinated and controlled manner, providing accurate information and limiting the dissemination of details that could endanger the hostages.

Long-Term Support:

Recognize that managing a hostage situation can have long-term repercussions on response team members and the organization as a whole. Providing long-term support, such as counseling and follow-up, is essential.

Review and Continuous Improvement:

After the crisis is resolved, top management should support the review and continuous improvement of procedures and protocols to learn from the experience and be better prepared for future similar situations.

Top management support is essential to ensure that the response team has the authority and resources needed to effectively and safely manage the situation. This collaboration and support are critical to protecting the lives of the hostages and the well-being of team members.

A well-trained and coordinated hostage negotiation team plays a crucial role in the successful management of hostage situations.

11.Hostage Negotiator Training

Hostage negotiator training is essential to ensure the safety of all individuals involved in a hostage situation. These professionals must be prepared both psychologically and tactically to address these high-risk situations.

Communication Training:

Active Listening: Negotiators must be experts in listening and understanding the concerns and demands of both the kidnappers and the hostages.

Effective Communication: Learning to communicate clearly and calmly, maintaining a calm and respectful tone.

Active Listening: Negotiators must excel in active listening, which involves paying full attention to what the kidnappers and hostages are saying. This helps better understand their concerns and needs.

Empathy: Negotiators should be capable of putting themselves in the shoes of the kidnappers and hostages, showing empathy toward their emotions and concerns. This empathy can help establish a human connection that is crucial for negotiation.

Effective Communication: Negotiators must communicate clearly, calmly, and respectfully. They should avoid confrontations and aggressive language, as this can increase tension in the situation.

Building Trust: Trust is crucial in any negotiation. Negotiators should strive to earn the trust of the kidnappers and demonstrate their commitment to seeking a peaceful solution.

Non-Verbal Communication: In addition to words, non-verbal communication is important. Negotiators should pay attention to the non-verbal cues from kidnappers and hostages, such as body language and facial expressions, to better understand their emotions and mental states.

Strategic Negotiation: Negotiators must learn to use effective negotiation strategies, such as asking open-ended questions to gather information, maintaining a calm and controlled tone, and recognizing areas of agreement when possible.

Handling Demands and Concessions: Negotiators must learn to handle the demands of kidnappers and make controlled concessions when necessary. This involves balancing the needs of the kidnappers with the safety of the hostages and the application of the law.

Crisis Communication: Negotiators must be able to handle high-tension situations and make quick decisions to maintain the safety of all involved.

Communication training for hostage negotiators involves regular practice and simulations to develop and maintain these skills. It is important that negotiators are prepared to face high-stress and high-pressure situations, and effective communication plays a fundamental role in the peaceful resolution of hostage takings.

Psychology and Profiling:

Studying the Kidnapper's Mind: Negotiators must understand the psychology behind hostage-taking to anticipate and address their needs and demands.

Hostage Profiling: Identifying different types of hostages and how they react under stress.

Studying the Kidnapper's Mind:

Kidnapper Profile: Negotiators are trained to understand the typical psychological profiles of kidnappers, including their motivations, personalities, and possible mental disorders.

Motivation: Possible reasons behind hostage-taking, such as political, economic, personal, or emotional motivations.

Assessing Threat Level: Negotiators must be able to assess the threat level posed by the kidnapper and their willingness to cause harm.

Hostage Profiling:

Identifying Types of Hostages: Negotiators learn to identify different types of hostages, from those who may be cooperating with kidnappers out of fear to those who might attempt resistance.

Behavior Under Stress: Studying how hostages may react and how their behavior changes when in a hostage situation.

Psychology-Based Communication:

Use of Persuasion Techniques: Negotiators can apply psychological principles to persuade kidnappers to make more rational and less impulsive decisions.

Emotion Management: Psychology training helps negotiators deal with the emotions of both kidnappers and hostages while maintaining an objective focus.

Risk Assessment:

Negotiators must be able to assess risk in real-time and make decisions based on this assessment to ensure the safety of everyone involved.

Training in psychology and profiling helps negotiators better understand the people involved in a hostage situation, which can be critical for making strategic decisions and for guiding negotiations effectively. Knowledge of psychology and profiling can also help predict potential reactions and needs of kidnappers and hostages, leading to a safer and more peaceful resolution of the situation.

Negotiation Techniques:

Negotiation Strategies: Learning to develop effective strategies to stay calm, gain the trust of kidnappers, and achieve agreements that benefit all parties.

Controlled Concessions: Knowing when and how to make concessions, ensuring they are controlled and do not endanger hostages or security forces.

Building Rapport: Creating a relationship of trust and empathy with kidnappers. This may include building human connections through respectful communication and acknowledging kidnappers' concerns.

Active Listening: Carefully and actively listening to what the kidnappers say, allowing them to express themselves and voice their demands. Active listening involves asking open-ended questions and reflecting what has been said to demonstrate understanding.

Recognizing and Validating Emotions: Acknowledging the emotions of kidnappers, even if you do not agree with their actions. Validating their emotions can help reduce hostility and open the door to cooperation.

Setting Clear Goals: Defining concrete objectives and goals for negotiation. This may include agreeing on what is expected to be achieved and what the non-negotiable boundaries are.

Offering Limited Choices: Presenting limited options to kidnappers to give them a sense of control and the illusion of choice, which can help avoid the feeling of being cornered.

Building Bridges: Finding common ground and areas of agreement with kidnappers to build pathways to a peaceful resolution. This can be especially useful in reducing hostility and increasing cooperation.

Buying Time: Sometimes, buying time can be critical to allow security forces to prepare and assess the situation. Negotiators can use various techniques to achieve this, such as strategically asking questions and prolonging the conversation.

Handling Demands and Concessions: Evaluating and managing kidnappers' demands carefully and in a controlled manner. Making concessions when necessary, but always with the safety of hostages as the top priority.

Non-Verbal Communication: Using non-verbal communication effectively to convey empathy, calm, and authority. Body language and facial expressions can influence kidnappers' perceptions of the negotiator.

Closing Strategies: Knowing when and how to safely close an agreement and ensuring that all parties understand the terms and agree with them.

It's important to remember that negotiation techniques can vary depending on the situation and the kidnappers' personalities, so adaptability and the ability to read and respond to the situation's dynamics are essential. Additionally, these techniques should be applied with a focus on the safety of the hostages and the peaceful resolution of the hostage situation.

Simulations and Practical Training: Hostage-Taking Drills: Negotiators must engage in practical exercises simulating hostage-taking situations to develop their negotiation skills and strategies.

Evaluation and Feedback: After each drill, a review is conducted to identify areas for improvement and receive constructive feedback. Realistic Scenarios: Drills should be designed to simulate hostage-taking situations as realistically as possible. This includes recreating the environment, situational dynamics, and roles of kidnappers and hostages.

Active Participation: Negotiators must actively participate in the drills, taking on their respective roles, whether as negotiators, kidnappers, hostages, or support personnel. This allows them to apply negotiation techniques and strategies in simulated situations.

Feedback and Assessment: After each drill, a detailed review should be conducted to evaluate the negotiators' performance. This includes identifying strengths and weaknesses and providing constructive feedback for continuous improvement.

Complexity Scaling: Drills can vary in complexity. Starting with simpler situations and gradually increasing complexity can help negotiators gain confidence and develop their skills progressively.

Variety of Scenarios: Drills should address a variety of possible scenarios, including hostage takings with political, criminal, or personal motivations. This prepares negotiators to face diverse real-world situations.

Coordination with Other Professionals: In many cases, drills involve working closely with other professionals, such as security forces, tactical teams, or psychologists. This helps improve interdisciplinary coordination and communication.

Training in Decision-Making Under Pressure: Drills can also focus on developing decision-making skills under high-stress conditions. Negotiators must learn to quickly assess situations and make informed decisions in critical moments.

Documentation and Incident Analysis: Drill results should be documented and analyzed in detail. This allows for later review and the identification of areas for improvement at both the individual and team levels.

Team Training: Hostage negotiator training often involves teamwork. Drills help teams develop the coordination and effective communication needed to deal with high-risk situations.

Continuous Training: Drills should not be a one-time event. They should be regularly scheduled to maintain and enhance negotiators' skills and ensure they are prepared to face any hostage situation that may arise.

Simulations and practical training are essential for negotiators to gain the experience and confidence necessary to effectively and safely handle hostage situations. This hands-on preparation complements the theoretical knowledge and skills acquired through training.

Stress Management Training: Emotional Control: Negotiators must learn to stay calm under pressure and deal with emotionally intense situations.

Relaxation Techniques: Use relaxation and stress management techniques to maintain focus and mental clarity.

Stress Awareness: Negotiators must understand the effects of stress on their performance and well-being. This involves recognizing the physical and emotional signs of stress, such as increased heart rate, muscle tension, and anxiety.

Relaxation Techniques: Negotiators are taught various relaxation techniques that can help reduce stress in the moment, such as deep breathing, meditation, and biofeedback.

These techniques can help maintain composure in intense situations. Emotional Control: Learning to control emotions is critical. Negotiators must be able to maintain calm and serenity, even in high-tension situations, to make rational decisions and communicate effectively.

Stress Preparedness: Negotiators must be prepared to face highly stressful situations. This includes developing coping strategies and a stress management plan before entering a hostage situation.

Psychological Support: Negotiators are provided with psychological support, including the option to consult with psychologists or mental health professionals to help cope with stress and the emotional impact of their work.

Training in Decision-Making Under Pressure: Negotiators must learn to make effective decisions in high-stress situations. This involves practicing decision-making under pressure in simulated situations.

Venting and Peer Support: Establishing a support network among colleagues is important. Negotiators can share their experiences and concerns with other team members, which can help relieve stress.

Setting Boundaries: It is important for negotiators to set clear boundaries to protect their emotional well-being and prevent burnout. This can include time management and taking regular breaks.

Physical Exercise and Health: Maintaining good physical health through regular exercise and a balanced diet can help reduce stress. Negotiators must care for their overall well-being.

Resilience Training: Resilience is the ability to bounce back from challenging situations. Negotiators must be trained to develop resilience and overcome the challenges they may face in their work.

Stress management is essential for hostage negotiators to effectively perform their job and protect their emotional well-being. The stress management methods learned in training are crucial for maintaining mental clarity and the ability to make rational decisions in high-risk situations.

Collaboration with Other Professionals: Teamwork: Hostage negotiators often work closely with other professionals, such as security forces, psychologists, experts in rescue tactics, and others.

Effort Coordination: It is essential for all parties involved to work together in a synchronized manner to ensure a safe outcome. Security Forces: Hostage negotiators typically work closely with security forces, such as the police, SWAT teams, or other specialized units.

Collaboration involves effective communication and coordination to ensure the safety of all parties involved. Psychologists and Mental Health Specialists: Psychologists and other mental health professionals can play a significant role in managing hostage situations.

They help understand the psychology of kidnappers and hostages, offer emotional support, and provide counseling on psychology-based negotiation strategies.

Communication Experts: Communication experts can provide advice on effective communication strategies with kidnappers.

This can include persuasion techniques, rhetoric management, and word choice to achieve a peaceful resolution.

Tactical Rescue Teams: In some situations, a tactical rescue team may be necessary to intervene if negotiations are unsuccessful. Collaboration involves coordination between negotiators and the tactical team to ensure the safety of hostages.

Experienced Negotiators: Hostage negotiators often collaborate with each other, especially in high-risk situations. Shared experience and feedback can be valuable for developing effective negotiation strategies.

Medical Professionals: In the case of injuries or health issues among hostages or kidnappers, collaboration with medical professionals is essential. This may include doctors, paramedics, or emergency personnel to provide medical care.

Crisis Management and Decision-Making Experts: Crisis management experts can provide guidance on decision-making in high-stress situations. This includes risk assessment and strategic planning.

Lawyers and Legal Advisors: In some situations, consulting with lawyers and legal advisors may be necessary to understand the legal implications of certain decisions or agreements.

Effective collaboration with these professionals involves open and ongoing communication, as well as coordinated efforts to achieve the goals of a peaceful and safe resolution of the hostage situation. Each professional brings their expertise and knowledge to address different aspects of the situation and ensure the best possible decisions are made for the safety of all parties involved.

Ongoing Updates: Continuous Training: Since hostage-taking tactics and situations change over time, negotiators must stay up to date and receive ongoing training.

Evolution of Threats: Threats and tactics used by kidnappers and criminals can change over time. Therefore, it is crucial for negotiators to be aware of current trends and new strategies employed in hostage situations.

Changes in Legislation and Policies: Laws and policies governing the management of hostage situations can change. Negotiators must stay updated on changes in legislation and guidelines from security and law enforcement agencies.

Technology and Communications: Technological advancements have a significant impact on hostage situation management. Negotiators must stay informed about the latest technologies and communications that can be useful in negotiation and hostage situation resolution.

Improvements in Negotiation Tactics and Techniques: Training and knowledge in the field of negotiation tactics and techniques continue to evolve.

Negotiators must stay updated with best practices and the latest research in this area.

Case Studies and Lessons Learned: Analyzing real case studies of hostage situations and lessons learned from previous incidents is essential for continuous learning.

These studies provide valuable insights into what worked and what didn't, and how to improve in the future.

Regular Exercises and Drills: Conducting regular exercises and drills is an effective way to keep skills and preparedness up to date. This allows negotiators to practice in simulated situations and learn from each experience.

Participation in Conferences and Ongoing Training: Hostage negotiators should attend conferences, workshops, and regular training in the field of security and crisis management. These events offer opportunities to learn from experts and stay updated on best practices.

Mentorship and Teamwork: Collaborating with more experienced colleagues and receiving mentorship can be a valuable way to learn and stay current in the field of hostage management.

Continuous updates are essential to ensure that hostage negotiators are prepared to handle high-stress situations and evolve with changing security dynamics. Staying informed and honing skills is crucial to ensuring an effective and safe response to hostage situations.

The training of hostage negotiators is a comprehensive process that combines communication skills, psychological knowledge, tactical strategy, and emotional control. These professionals play a crucial role in the peaceful resolution of hostage situations and the safety of all parties involved.

12.Decision-Making in Hostage Situations

Decision-Making in Hostage Situations: Decision-making in hostage situations is a critical and challenging task. Hostage negotiators must make quick and precise decisions that balance the safety of the hostages, the safety of law enforcement personnel, and the pursuit of a peaceful resolution.

Assessment of the Situation: The first stage involves a rapid but thorough assessment of the situation. Negotiators must determine the number of kidnappers and hostages, their location, the weapons or threats they pose, and any other relevant information.

Number and Location of Kidnappers and Hostages: Negotiators must determine how many kidnappers are involved in the situation, their specific location, and whether hostages are present. This helps establish a basic understanding of the situation's dynamics.

Weapons and Threats: Negotiators must identify the type and quantity of weapons the kidnappers possess, as well as any other potential threats, such as explosives. This influences the strategy and risk management.

Motivation of Kidnappers: Trying to understand the kidnappers' motivations is crucial. It may be political, economic, personal, or related to a specific cause. This understanding is fundamental to negotiation.

Physical Location and Environment: Negotiators need to know the physical location of the hostage situation, such as a building, vehicle, facility, etc. Additionally, they must consider environmental conditions and other relevant details.

Hostages and Their Status: Identifying the number of hostages and their health and well-being is important. This may include identifying injured hostages or those at immediate risk.

Communications and Initial Demands: If communication has been established with the kidnappers, it is important to record any initial demands or concerns expressed by them. This provides useful information to initiate negotiations.

Entry and Exit Routes: Negotiators must be aware of the entry and exit routes to the hostage area. This is important for the safety of law enforcement and the development of rescue strategies.

Intelligence Gathering: Intelligence information must be collected from all available sources, including witness testimonies, security camera recordings, phone calls, and other relevant data.

Ongoing Updates: Situation assessment is not static. It must be continuously updated as new information becomes available. Negotiators must be prepared to adjust their approach and strategy based on changes in the situation.

Situation assessment provides a solid foundation for making informed decisions during a hostage situation. The accuracy and thoroughness of this stage are essential for developing an effective and safe crisis management strategy.

Establishment of Goals: Negotiators must clearly define the goals of the negotiation. This may include the safe release of hostages, the peaceful surrender of kidnappers, or the acquisition of crucial information.

Precise Goal Definition: Goals must be specific and clearly defined. For example, a goal may be the safe release of all hostages, the peaceful surrender of kidnappers, or the acquisition of crucial information to ensure safety.

Prioritization of Hostage Safety: Hostage safety must be the top priority in goal definition. Any established goals must align with the protection of the lives and well-being of the hostages.

Viability Consideration: Goals must be realistic and achievable. Negotiators must evaluate whether it is possible to achieve the established goals and what actions may be necessary to accomplish them.

Flexibility in Goals: While it's important to have clear goals, negotiators must also be flexible and willing to adapt their goals based on the evolving situation and the actions of the kidnappers.

Communication of Goals to Kidnappers: Clearly and directly communicating the goals to the kidnappers is essential. This sets expectations and can help establish a foundation for negotiation.

Goal-Oriented Negotiation: During negotiation, negotiators must maintain their focus on achieving the established goals. Each concession or demand must be assessed based on whether it aids or hinders the achievement of those goals.

Secondary Goals and Intermediate Tactics: In addition to primary goals, negotiators can establish secondary goals and intermediate tactics to help progress toward resolving the situation. These may include obtaining specific information or creating bridges for cooperation.

Review and Adjustment of Goals: As the situation evolves, goals may need adjustment. Negotiators must be willing to review and adapt their goals as they gather new information.

The establishment of clear goals provides a solid framework for negotiation in hostage situations. These goals help negotiators maintain focus, make informed decisions, and work toward a resolution that prioritizes the safety and well-being of the hostages.

Strategic Communication: Communication with kidnappers must be strategic. Negotiators must establish a connection with kidnappers, earn their trust, and encourage cooperation.

Establishment of a Communication Line: The first step is to establish a communication line with the kidnappers. This may involve the use of phones, radios, or other means of communication. The goal is to establish a channel for dialogue.

Building Rapport: Negotiators must strive to build a trusting relationship with the kidnappers. This involves active listening, showing empathy and respect, and finding common ground to establish an emotional connection.

Open and Honest Communication: Negotiators must be open and honest in their communication. Sincerity is important to gain the kidnappers' trust and demonstrate a willingness to seek a solution.

Active Listening: Active listening is a crucial skill. Negotiators must pay attention to what the kidnappers are saying, ask open-ended questions to encourage conversation, and reflect what they have understood to demonstrate comprehension.

Emotion Management: Negotiators must be able to manage their own emotions and the emotions of the kidnappers. Empathy and composure can help reduce hostility and foster cooperation.

Persuasion Techniques: Negotiators can apply persuasion techniques to influence the kidnappers and encourage them to make more rational decisions. This may include logical arguments, the use of testimonials, and the presentation of options.

Establishment of Clear Boundaries: Negotiators must set clear boundaries in communication. This includes what demands are unacceptable or threats that will not be tolerated. Boundaries provide structure and security.

Building Bridges: In strategic communication, it is important to find common ground and areas of agreement with the kidnappers. These points of agreement can serve as bridges toward a peaceful resolution.

Maintaining Calm Under Pressure: Strategic communication must be maintained even in high-tension situations. Negotiators must be able to remain calm and composed to continue the dialogue.

Long-Term Communication Strategy: Negotiators must develop a long-term communication strategy that includes planning for future conversations and how to move toward a resolution.

Ongoing Assessment: Strategic communication must be continuously evaluated and adjusted based on the evolving situation and the kidnappers' responses.

Strategic communication plays a crucial role in hostage negotiation, as it can influence the final outcome and the safety of the hostages. Building relationships, empathy, and effective communication skills are fundamental in this context.

Analysis of Demands and Concessions: Negotiators must assess the demands of the kidnappers and make decisions regarding the concessions they are willing to make. These concessions must be carefully controlled to avoid endangering the safety of the hostages or giving in excessively.

Evaluation of Demands: Negotiators must carefully evaluate the kidnappers' demands. This includes understanding the nature of the demands, their feasibility, and the impact they may have on the situation. Some demands may be unacceptable due to their nature, such as the release of prisoners or the delivery of weapons.

Prioritization of Hostage Safety: Hostage safety is the top priority. Any concession made must be evaluated based on its impact on the safety of the hostages. Negotiators must avoid giving in to demands that may endanger the lives or well-being of the hostages.

Setting Clear Boundaries: Negotiators must establish clear boundaries regarding the concessions they are willing to make. This may include limits on the amount of money, the release of prisoners, the delivery of goods, or any other aspect at stake.

Communication of Boundaries to Kidnappers: It is important to communicate the boundaries clearly to the kidnappers. This sets expectations and can help prevent the escalation of unacceptable demands.

Incremental Negotiation: Negotiators may consider incremental concessions, which means they may be willing to make minor or symbolic concessions initially to gain the trust of the kidnappers and foster cooperation. However, these concessions must remain within the established limits.

Maintaining Control: Negotiators must maintain control of the situation and not allow the kidnappers to dictate the terms of the negotiation entirely. This means they must be prepared to reject unacceptable demands and, if necessary, consider other strategies, such as tactical intervention.

Recording Agreements: Any concession made must be recorded and documented. This ensures that the parties agree on the terms and minimizes ambiguity.

Coordination with Tactical Teams: Negotiators must coordinate with tactical teams in case a rescue or intervention is necessary. Tactical teams may be prepared to act if negotiation is unsuccessful.

Assessment of Long-Term Consequences: Negotiators must consider the long-term consequences of any concession they make. This may include the impact on public safety, legal implications, and political consequences.

Review and Adaptation of Strategies: As the situation evolves and new information is obtained, negotiators must review and, if necessary, adapt their strategies and concessions.

The assessment of demands and concessions is a delicate process that requires a balance between maintaining the safety of the hostages and working towards a peaceful resolution. Negotiators must make informed and strategic decisions based on the specific situation and their established objectives.

Tactical Planning: Negotiators must constantly develop and adapt a tactical strategy to achieve their goals. This may include the use of persuasive tactics, setting clear boundaries, and maintaining composure.

Development of a Tactical Strategy: Negotiators must develop a tactical strategy that outlines how they will approach the hostage situation. This strategy must be flexible and adaptable as the situation evolves.

Persuasive Tactics: Persuasive tactics are important for influencing the behavior of kidnappers and fostering cooperation. This may include presenting logical arguments, using testimonials, and effectively communicating to persuade kidnappers to reach a peaceful resolution.

Setting Clear Boundaries: Negotiators must establish clear boundaries indicating what demands or actions are unacceptable. This provides structure to the negotiation and can help prevent kidnappers from making excessive or dangerous demands.

Communication of Consequences: It is important to communicate to kidnappers the possible consequences of their actions, both negative and positive. For example, negotiators can explain the legal implications of certain actions or the impact on hostage safety.

Maintaining Calm and Composure: Negotiators must be able to remain calm and composed in high-stress situations. Serenity and emotional stability are essential for making rational decisions and avoiding impulsive reactions.

Use of Non-Verbal Communication: Non-verbal communication, such as body language and tone of voice, can play a significant role in effective communication. Negotiators must be aware of how they communicate non-verbally and how it can influence the kidnappers' perception.

Time and Patience Management: Time and patience management are crucial. Negotiators must be aware of the time and urgency but also patient to allow for an effective negotiation process to unfold.

Coordination with Tactical Teams: Negotiators must closely coordinate with tactical teams in case a rescue or intervention is necessary. Constant communication and synchronization are essential.

Risk Assessment and Short- and Long-Term Consequences: Any tactic must be assessed based on the short- and long-term risks and consequences. Negotiators must consider how their actions will impact the situation and the parties involved.

Constant assessment and adaptation: The tactical strategy must be continually reviewed and adapted as the situation evolves. Negotiators must be prepared to adjust their tactics based on the kidnappers' responses and the dynamics of the situation.

Risk Assessment: Constantly evaluating the risks of the situation is essential. Negotiators must consider the implications of their decisions on the safety of the hostages and law enforcement.

Identification of Potential Risks: Negotiators must identify and catalog potential risks associated with the situation. This includes risks to the hostages, such as physical or emotional injuries, and risks to law enforcement, such as attacks or ambushes.

Assessment of Short- and Long-Term Consequences: Decisions made during negotiation can have immediate and long-term consequences. Negotiators must consider how their actions may affect the situation and the parties involved in the present and the future.

Prioritization of Hostage Safety: Hostage safety must be the highest priority in risk assessment. Negotiators must consider how each decision could directly or indirectly impact the safety of the hostages and adjust their focus accordingly.

Assessment of Risks to Law Enforcement: Negotiators must also assess the risks to law enforcement involved in the operation. This includes considering possible ambushes, attacks, or confrontations with the kidnappers.

Determining the Need for Tactical Intervention: In high-risk situations, negotiators must consider whether tactical intervention by law enforcement is necessary. This decision must be based on a careful evaluation of risks and the likelihood of success.

Communication with Tactical Teams: Negotiators must maintain constant communication with tactical and rescue teams if they are involved. This allows for effective coordination in case an intervention is needed.

Flexibility Maintenance: Risk assessment is not static. Negotiators must be flexible and prepared to adjust their approach as the situation evolves and new information is obtained.

Assessment of Potential Threats: Negotiators must consider potential threats that may arise during the negotiation, such as changes in the behavior of the kidnappers or the disclosure of sensitive information.

Assessment of Legal and Political Risks: In addition to immediate risks, negotiators must consider the legal and political implications of their actions and decisions. This may include legal liability and the political consequences of concessions made.

Risk assessment is a critical skill in the management of hostage situations. It helps negotiators make informed decisions and balance the pursuit of a peaceful resolution with the safety of all parties involved.

Communication and Coordination: Effective communication and coordination with other professionals, such as law enforcement, psychologists, and communication experts, are essential. This ensures that all parties work together in synchrony.

Interprofessional Communication: Negotiators must establish strong lines of communication with other professionals involved, such as law enforcement, psychologists, communication experts, and medical teams. Constant and clear communication is essential for coordinating efforts and sharing relevant information.

Communication with Tactical Teams: Negotiators must maintain ongoing communication with the security and, if necessary, intervention teams. This allows for synchronized efforts and a coordinated response if the situation requires it.

Joint Communication Strategy: The communication strategy should be developed jointly with other professionals. This ensures that everyone is aligned in terms of goals and key messages.

Psychological Counseling: Psychologists play an important role in the management of hostage situations as they can provide valuable insights into the emotional state of the kidnappers and hostages. Negotiators should collaborate with psychologists to better understand the psychological dynamics of the situation.

Communication Experts: Communication experts can assist negotiators in developing effective communication strategies that are tailored to the specific situation and the profile of the kidnappers. These experts can offer advice on how to handle difficult conversations and establish an effective channel of dialogue.

Coordination of Tactical Actions and Negotiation: Communication and coordination between negotiators and tactical teams are critical. They must work together to ensure that tactical actions align with negotiation objectives and the safety of the hostages.

Communication and Safety Protocols: It is important to establish communication and safety protocols to ensure that sensitive information does not leak and that tactical operations are carried out safely.

Joint Exercises and Drills: Joint practice through exercises and drills helps improve coordination and communication among the professionals involved. These exercises can help identify potential areas for improvement and refine responses.

Constant Evaluation and Continuous Improvement: After each incident, a detailed evaluation should be conducted to identify what worked and what did not, and to learn from the experience. These findings should be used to improve protocols and future preparedness.

Effective communication and coordination are essential to ensure a coordinated and safe response in hostage situations. Teaming up with other professionals and law enforcement helps leverage the strengths of each discipline and maximizes the chances of a peaceful and safe resolution.

Preparation for Tactical Intervention: In high-risk situations, negotiators must be prepared for the possibility of tactical intervention by law enforcement. They should be in constant contact with tactical teams and follow established safety procedures.

Coordination with Tactical Teams: Negotiators must establish constant and effective communication with tactical or rapid response teams. This coordination is crucial to ensure that both parties work in sync and minimize the risk of conflict or misunderstandings.

Establishment of Safety Procedures: Negotiators must adhere to rigorous and well-established safety procedures. These procedures include measures to ensure the safety of the hostages, law enforcement, and negotiators.

Assessment of the Need for Tactical Intervention: The decision to resort to tactical intervention must be based on a careful assessment of the situation. Negotiators and tactical teams must consider factors such as the severity of the threat, the feasibility of negotiation, and the safety of the hostages.

Physical and Mental Preparedness: Tactical teams must be physically and mentally prepared for a potential intervention. This includes training in rescue tactics, handling high-stress situations, and readiness to face unforeseen circumstances.

Tactical Intervention Planning: Tactical intervention must be meticulously planned, including determining entry and exit routes, coordinating movements, and assigning specific roles to team members.

Communication During Intervention: Communication during a tactical intervention is crucial. There must be clear and secure communication channels to ensure coordination between tactical teams and negotiators.

Maintaining Calm and Discipline: Both negotiators and tactical teams must maintain calm and discipline during an intervention. This is essential to avoid errors and ensure that safety procedures are followed.

Continuous Situation Assessment: During a tactical intervention, it's important to continuously assess the situation to adapt the strategy as necessary.

Hostage Safety: Hostage safety should be the top concern during a tactical intervention. Tactical teams must be prepared to protect the hostages and minimize the risk of harm.

Debriefing and Post-Intervention Review: After a tactical intervention, a debriefing process should be carried out to review what worked and what didn't. This is essential for learning from the experience and improving preparedness for future situations.

Preparation for Tactical Intervention is a critical part of managing hostage situations and should be carried out by highly trained and coordinated teams. The safety of the hostages and all parties involved is the top priority in this scenario.

Exit Strategy: Negotiators must develop an exit strategy in case the negotiation is unsuccessful. This may include rescue plans, evasion, or subsequent actions to ensure the safety of the hostages.

Development of Rescue Plans: Negotiators and tactical teams must have robust rescue plans in place in case rescuing the hostages is deemed necessary. These plans should be meticulously crafted and consider all possible contingencies.

Assessment of Negotiation Viability: As the situation evolves, negotiators must constantly assess the viability of negotiation. If it appears that negotiation objectives cannot be met or hostage safety is at risk, an exit strategy should be considered.

Communicating Consequences to Kidnappers: Negotiators can communicate the consequences of not reaching an agreement or ensuring the safety of the hostages. This can be part of the exit strategy and may influence the behavior of the kidnappers.

Establishing Clear Limits: Negotiators must set clear limits on what actions or demands are unacceptable. This provides a foundation for the exit strategy and can help prevent excessive or dangerous demands.

Hostage Evacuation Preparation: If the exit strategy involves the evacuation of hostages, detailed plans must be prepared to ensure their safety during the operation.

Coordination with Tactical Teams: Tactical teams must be in full coordination with negotiators in case a rescue action or evacuation is required. Constant communication and synchronization are essential.

Hostage Safety Assessment: Hostage safety should be the primary consideration in any exit strategy. Measures must be taken to ensure they are as safe as possible during any exit operation.

Risk and Short- and Long-Term Consequences Assessment: Any exit action must be assessed in terms of short- and long-term risks and consequences. Negotiators must consider how their actions may affect the situation and the parties involved.

Preservation of Scene Integrity: In the case of an exit operation, the integrity of the scene must be preserved for evidence collection and subsequent investigations.

Review and Continuous Improvement: After any exit operation or evacuation, a thorough review must be conducted to identify lessons learned and improve protocols and future preparedness.

The exit strategy is an essential component of managing hostage situations. It should be developed in advance, practiced, and ready for implementation if necessary. Hostage safety and risk minimization are fundamental priorities in this context.

Continuous Reassessment: Decision-making in hostage situations is a dynamic process. Decisions must be continuously reassessed as the situation evolves.

Changes in the Situation: Hostage situations can change in a matter of seconds. Kidnappers can alter their demands, hostages may be at risk, or new developments may arise. Continuous reassessment allows negotiators to stay informed about these changes and adjust their strategies accordingly.

Hostage Safety: Hostage safety is the top priority. Negotiators must be alert to any signs that hostage safety is in danger and take immediate steps to mitigate that risk.

Assessment of Demands and Concessions: Kidnappers' demands and the concessions offered must be continuously assessed based on their impact on the situation. Negotiators must consider whether proposed concessions are safe and align with the established objectives.

Communication with Kidnappers: Communication with kidnappers is an ever-evolving process. Negotiators must adapt their approach and communication tactics as they gather new information about the kidnappers and their behavior.

Changes in Kidnapper Dynamics: Kidnappers may experience changes in attitude or behavior as the situation unfolds. Continuous reassessment allows negotiators to detect and respond to these changes.

Impact of Communication Strategy: The communication strategy must be reviewed and adapted based on its effectiveness. Negotiators should be vigilant about whether their communication approach is achieving the desired progress toward objectives.

Risk and Long-Term Consequences Assessment: As the situation progresses, risks and the consequences of decisions must be continuously evaluated. This includes considering the long-term impact of concessions made and actions taken.

Communication with Other Professionals and Tactical Teams: Continuous reassessment involves maintaining constant communication with other professionals and tactical teams. This ensures that everyone is aware of developments and can adjust their strategies accordingly.

Informed Decision-Making: Continuous reassessment enables negotiators to make informed decisions and adapt their approach as the situation unfolds.

Flexibility and Adaptability: Continuous reassessment reflects the flexibility and adaptability required in hostage situations. Negotiators must be prepared to change their focus or tactics as needed.

Continuous reassessment is essential to ensure hostage safety and work toward a peaceful resolution in hostage situations. Staying aware of changes and adjusting the strategy accordingly is a fundamental practice in managing these highly dynamic situations.

Emotional Support and Debriefing: After a hostage situation, it's important for negotiators to receive emotional support and participate in a debriefing process to review the decisions made and learn from the experience.

Emotional Support: Acknowledgment of Stress: Negotiators and other professionals should acknowledge that they have experienced a highly stressful situation and that it is normal to feel stress, anxiety, and even symptoms of trauma.

Access to Professional Support: They should have access to emotional support from mental health professionals such as psychologists or counselors to help them process the experience and emotions.

Support from Colleagues: Camaraderie among colleagues can be valuable. Talking to others who have faced similar situations can provide support and understanding.

Space to Express Emotions: It's important to provide a safe and confidential environment where negotiators can express their emotions and experiences without fear of judgment.

Debriefing: Reviewing the Experience: Debriefing involves a structured review of the situation, the decisions made, and the outcomes. This allows participants to share their experiences and learn from the situation.

Identifying Lessons Learned: During debriefing, lessons learned, what worked well, and what could be improved in future situations should be identified.

Improving Protocols and Procedures: The results of the debriefing should be used to improve protocols, procedures, and preparedness for future hostage situations.

Evaluation of Response and Coordination: It's essential to evaluate how tactical teams and negotiators coordinated and if there were challenges in communication and collaboration.

Assessment of Emotional Support: Debriefing should include an assessment of the emotional support provided to participants and how it can be improved in the future.

Preparation for Future Incidents: Debriefing is also an opportunity to review the preparedness and training for hostage situations and adjust them as needed.

Continuous Support: It's important that emotional support and debriefing are available in the long term, as some emotional responses may emerge weeks or months after the incident.

Emotional support and debriefing are essential components of caring for individuals who have faced hostage situations. They help promote mental health and well-being for the professionals involved and contribute to the continuous improvement of practices and response protocols in high-risk situations.

Decision-making in hostage situations is complex and requires a combination of communication, strategy, psychology, and risk assessment skills. Hostage safety should be the top priority at all times, and decisions should be made with a focus on achieving a peaceful resolution of the situation.

13.Psychology of Kidnappers and Hostages

The psychology of both kidnappers and hostages in hostage situations is a complex and multifaceted topic. Understanding the psychological dynamics of both parties is essential for negotiators and tactical teams facing these situations.

Psychology of Kidnappers: Varied Motivations: Kidnappers can have a variety of motivations, ranging from financial gain to seeking media attention, revenge, the release of prisoners, or political objectives. Understanding their motivations is crucial for addressing their demands.

Financial Gain: One of the most common motivators in kidnapping cases is the desire to obtain a ransom or financial benefit. Kidnappers may demand a ransom in exchange for the safe release of hostages. Seeking Media Attention: Some kidnappers seek notoriety and media attention.

They may use the hostage situation to attract media attention and spread their message or cause.

Revenge: In other cases, the motivation behind a hostage-taking can be revenge. Kidnappers may have a personal grievance or a desire to harm specific individuals or entities. Release of

Prisoners: In political or conflict situations, kidnappers may seek the release of prisoners affiliated with their group or cause. They may hold hostages as leverage to achieve this goal.

Political or Ideological Objectives: Some kidnappers may have political or ideological motivations. Their goal may be to effect political change or promote their cause, and they may use hostages as bargaining chips.

Mental Health Issues: In some cases, kidnappers may be dealing with mental health issues that lead them to commit violent and extreme acts, such as hostage-taking. Personal or Family Issues: In less common situations, kidnappers may be motivated by personal or family issues, such as family disputes or personal disagreements.

Understanding kidnappers' motivations is essential for addressing demands strategically and assessing the level of risk and potential resolution strategies. Negotiators and professionals involved must tailor their approaches based on the specific motivation behind the kidnapping and work to achieve negotiation or resolution goals safely and effectively.

Stress and Tension: Kidnappers can also experience stress and tension during the situation, which can influence their behavior. Stress can increase the risk of impulsive or violent actions.

Risk of Impulsive Acts: Stress can increase the likelihood of kidnappers making impulsive or irrational decisions. They may feel extreme pressure to achieve their goals and act impulsively in response to unforeseen or challenging situations.

Threats to Their Safety: If kidnappers feel that their own safety is jeopardized due to police or tactical intervention, they are more likely to react violently or desperately. The fear of being captured or harmed can heighten stress.

Frustration and Anxiety: Lack of progress in negotiations or the perception that their demands are not being met can lead kidnappers to experience higher levels of frustration and anxiety, increasing tension in the situation. Fatigue and Exhaustion: Hostage situations are often prolonged, and fatigue and exhaustion can play a significant role. Kidnappers may become more irrational or impulsive as time passes. Communication Difficulties: Stress can hinder kidnappers' ability to communicate effectively with negotiators. They may become more aggressive, incoherent, or difficult to deal with, complicating negotiations. Possibility of

Escalating Violence: In high-stress situations, kidnappers may resort to violence as a way to express their frustration or as an attempt to pressure authorities or hostages. Distrust and

Paranoia: Stress can lead kidnappers to distrust the intentions of authorities or hostages, making it difficult to build a relationship of trust during negotiations. Response to Changes in the

Situation: Changes in the situation, such as the arrival of tactical teams or increased media pressure, can increase kidnappers' stress and trigger unpredictable responses.

Managing kidnappers' stress is a critical aspect of hostage situation management. Negotiators and tactical teams must carefully consider how to address and mitigate kidnappers' stress to reduce the risk of violence and work toward a peaceful resolution.

Need for Control: Many kidnappers seek to have a sense of control over the situation and the people involved. The loss of control can increase anxiety and aggression. Sense of Power and

Authority: Kidnappers often aim to establish a sense of power and authority over the situation and the people involved. This can be a source of personal gratification and meet their needs for dominance and control.

Reducing Uncertainty: For some kidnappers, having control over the situation allows them to reduce uncertainty and perceived risk. Uncertainty can be uncomfortable and stressful, so they seek to minimize it through control.

Manipulating Authorities and Hostages: By maintaining control, kidnappers may attempt to manipulate authorities and hostages to fulfill their demands. This can include threats and tactics aimed at gaining obedience.

Maintaining the Focus of Attention: By holding hostages and maintaining control, kidnappers can often keep the attention of authorities and the media. This can be part of their strategy to achieve their goals or gain notoriety.

Fear of Losing Control: The loss of control over the situation or the intervention of law enforcement can be a source of anxiety for kidnappers. This fear can increase their aggression or resistance.

Reaction to Loss of Control: If kidnappers feel they are losing control of the situation, they may react violently or desperately to try to regain it.

Impulsive Decision-Making: The need for control can sometimes lead kidnappers to make impulsive or irrational decisions in an effort to assert their authority and dominance over the situation.

Negotiators and professionals involved must take into account kidnappers' need for control when interacting with them and designing negotiation strategies. Recognizing and addressing this need can be essential for establishing effective communication and working toward a safe resolution of the situation. At the same time, it's important to do so without compromising the safety of the hostages and while following established procedures.

Negotiation as a Strategy: Some kidnappers may view negotiation as a strategy to achieve their goals. Negotiators must be aware of this dynamic and use it effectively.

Communication as a Bridge: Negotiators act as a bridge between kidnappers and authorities, and they can use communication as a tool to maintain an ongoing dialogue. This allows kidnappers to feel that they are making progress with their demands, which can increase their cooperation. Managing

Expectations: Negotiators must strategically manage kidnappers' expectations. They can use communication to set clear and realistic boundaries on what is feasible and what is not.

Controlled Concessions: Negotiators can offer controlled and specific concessions as part of the negotiation strategy. This can help maintain kidnappers' cooperation while protecting the safety of hostages and avoiding excessive concessions.

Building Trust: Building trust is essential in negotiation. Negotiators can work to gain the trust of kidnappers through strategic communication and the fulfillment of commitments, as long as they are safe and reasonable.

Continuous Evaluation of Demands and Concessions: Negotiators must constantly assess the demands of the kidnappers and make informed decisions about the concessions they are willing to make. This involves a delicate balance between advancing in negotiations and protecting the safety of the hostages.

Maintaining Calm and Patience: Negotiations can take time and require patience. Negotiators must remain calm and avoid emotional reactions, even when dealing with emotionally charged kidnappers.

Strategic Communication: Strategic communication involves carefully choosing words and adapting the tone and approach of communication to influence the behavior of the kidnappers. This may include persuasion and empathy techniques.

Active Listening Strategy: Actively listening to the kidnappers and showing interest in their concerns can help establish effective communication and enhance mutual understanding.

Assessing Risks and Consequences: Negotiators must consider how their negotiation actions may affect the safety of the hostages and law enforcement and evaluate short- and long-term risks and consequences.

Coordination with Other Professionals: Communication and coordination with other professionals, such as psychologists and tactical teams, are essential to ensure an integrated and synchronized response.

Negotiation as a Strategy is a valuable tool in managing hostage situations. Negotiators must be skilled in the art of strategic communication and expectation management to achieve a peaceful and safe resolution of the situation.

Changes in Attitude: The attitude of the kidnappers can change throughout the situation. They may become more cooperative or hostile depending on various factors, such as the progress of negotiations or tactical intervention.

Progress in Negotiations: If kidnappers perceive that negotiations are progressing positively and some of their demands are being met, they are more likely to become more cooperative and willing to continue dialogue.

Tactical Intervention or Police Pressure: Tactical intervention by law enforcement, such as the deployment of tactical teams, can drastically change the kidnappers' attitude. They may become more hostile, desperate, or violent in response to the perceived threat.

Frustration or Lack of Progress: If negotiations stall or kidnappers feel that they are not achieving their goals, they may become more hostile or anxious. A lack of progress can increase frustration.

Effective Communication: Effective communication by negotiators can positively influence the kidnappers' attitude. If they feel their concerns are heard and considered, they are more likely to cooperate.

Changes in Hostage Dynamics: Changes in the dynamics among the hostages, such as the emergence of leaders or internal conflicts, can influence the kidnappers' attitude. They may adapt their approach based on these dynamics.

Professional Negotiation Strategy: The negotiation strategy used by professionals can influence the kidnappers' attitude. Adapting persuasive approaches and building trust can lead to a more cooperative attitude.

Emotional and Psychological Factors: Kidnappers may experience changes in their emotional and psychological state over time, which can influence their attitude. They may feel more desperate, guilty, or anxious.

Assessment of Risks and Consequences: As the situation progresses, kidnappers may assess the risks and consequences of their actions more accurately. If they perceive that negative consequences are imminent, they may become more cooperative.

Professionals involved in managing hostage situations must be flexible and prepared to adapt their strategies in response to changes in kidnappers' attitudes. Constantly assessing the situation and effective communication are key elements in addressing these changes and working toward a safe resolution.

Psychology of Hostages: Stress and Trauma: Hostages often experience high levels of stress and trauma during a hostage situation. They may suffer symptoms of post-traumatic stress disorder (PTSD) after the incident.

Acute Stress: Hostages typically experience acute stress from the outset of the hostage situation. Fear of violence, uncertainty about their safety, and the restriction of their freedom can generate high levels of anxiety and tension.

PTSD Symptoms: Prolonged stress in hostage situations can lead to the development of post-traumatic stress disorder (PTSD) symptoms. These symptoms may include nightmares, intrusive memories of the traumatic event, avoidance of related situations, and mood changes.

Stockholm Syndrome: Some hostages may develop the so-called "Stockholm Syndrome," characterized by emotional identification with their captors. This may lead them to feel empathy or even affection for the kidnappers, which can be a coping strategy to ensure their survival.

Long-Term Impact: The stress and trauma experienced by hostages can have a lasting impact on their emotional well-being. It's important to provide them with emotional support and resources to address the long-term effects of trauma.

Need for Psychological Support: Hostages who have experienced a hostage situation often require psychological support and treatment to manage stress and trauma. Mental health professionals can help them deal with the emotional consequences of the event.

Debriefing and Follow-Up: After a hostage situation, it is common to conduct a debriefing process with the hostages, where they can discuss their experience and receive support. Long-term follow-up is essential to ensure they receive the necessary care.

Impact on Relationships and Daily Life: Stress and trauma can affect the personal relationships, work capacity, and quality of life of hostages. It is important to consider these aspects when providing support.

Managing the Stress and Trauma of Hostages is a critical part of the response to hostage situations. Mental health professionals and intervention teams must be prepared to address the emotional needs of hostages and provide the necessary support for their recovery.

Stockholm Syndrome: Some hostages may develop an emotional connection with their captors, known as "Stockholm Syndrome." This can make them appear collaborative or defenders of the kidnappers. Stockholm Syndrome is a psychological phenomenon observed in some hostage situations where hostages develop an emotional connection or identification with their captors.

This syndrome is named after an event that took place in Stockholm, Sweden, in 1973, when hostages in a bank taken by robbers began to develop sympathy for their captors. Although the syndrome is relatively uncommon, it has been studied in hostage and kidnapping cases.

Some characteristics of Stockholm Syndrome include:

Identification with Captors: Hostages may begin to see their captors in a more human and understanding way. They may develop feelings of empathy toward them and view them as victims of circumstances.

Collaboration or Defense of Captors: In some cases, hostages may collaborate or even defend their captors. They may assist in criminal activities or justify the actions of the kidnappers.

Denial or Minimization of Danger: Hostages may deny or minimize the threat or danger of the situation. They may believe that their captors will not harm them, despite objective evidence that they are in danger.

Coping Mechanism: Stockholm Syndrome has been described as a psychological coping mechanism. Hostages may develop this emotional connection as a way to reduce stress and increase their chances of survival.

It is important to note that Stockholm Syndrome does not manifest in all hostage cases, and not all hostages will develop this type of emotional connection with their captors. Its occurrence depends on a variety of factors, including the personality traits of the hostages, the duration of the situation, and the specific dynamics of the hostage-taking.

Professionals involved in the management of hostage situations must be aware of Stockholm Syndrome and be prepared to handle it appropriately. This involves maintaining a focus on the safety of the hostages and the resolution of the situation while providing psychological support and addressing the emotional needs of the hostages.

Coping Strategies: Hostages can develop coping strategies to deal with the situation, such as denial, depersonalization, or apathy. These strategies can influence their behavior and their willingness to cooperate with negotiators.

Denial: Some hostages may deny the seriousness of the situation or downplay the risk in an effort to reduce their anxiety. This denial may manifest as a belief that they will not be harmed or that the situation will be resolved smoothly.

Depersonalization: Hostages may depersonalize, which means they emotionally disconnect from the situation. They may try to distance themselves emotionally from the perceived threat and their own emotions to reduce distress.

Apathy: Some hostages may develop an apathetic or resigned attitude. They may stop caring about the consequences and simply follow the instructions of the kidnappers without resistance in an attempt to survive.

Identification with Captors: As mentioned earlier in relation to Stockholm Syndrome, hostages may develop empathy for their captors and view them more favorably. This can lead them to cooperate with the kidnappers.

Establishment of Routines: Hostages may try to establish daily routines or habits to create a sense of normalcy and control in a chaotic situation.

Conversation and Relationship with Other Hostages: Interaction and mutual support among hostages can be a coping strategy. They may talk to each other to stay calm and share information that might be useful for their safety.

Hope of Being Safely Released: Many hostages maintain hope of being safely released, which can be a coping strategy to maintain morale and motivation.

Attachment to Authority: Some hostages may seek security in authorities and negotiators. They may cooperate closely with them to ensure their safety.

These coping strategies can be effective in helping hostages survive extremely stressful situations. However, they can also influence their behavior and their willingness to cooperate with authorities. Negotiators and professionals involved must be aware of these strategies and use effective communication strategies to address the emotional needs of the hostages and ensure their safety.

Emotional and Psychological Support: Providing emotional and psychological support is essential to help hostages recover from the emotional consequences of a hostage situation. By creating a safe and professional environment for them to talk about their experiences and emotions, the long-term impact of trauma can be reduced.

Identification of Leaders and Hostage Conflicts: Hostages may form leaders among themselves or internal conflicts may arise. Negotiators should be aware of these dynamics and consider how they can influence the situation.

Identification of Leaders among Hostages:

Natural Leaders: In stressful situations, some individuals may stand out as natural leaders due to their charisma, decision-making abilities, or communication skills. Other hostages may turn to these leaders for guidance and emotional support.

Coordination and Communication: Leaders among hostages can play a crucial role in coordinating actions and communicating with the kidnappers or authorities. They can help maintain calm among the hostages and ensure that safety instructions are followed.

Relationship with Captors: Leaders among hostages may act as intermediaries between the kidnappers and the hostages, which can facilitate communication and mutual understanding.

Conflicts among Hostages:

Differences of Opinion and Coping Strategies: Hostages may have different opinions on how to approach the situation and develop coping strategies. This can lead to internal conflicts and tensions within the group of hostages.

Competition for the Attention of Kidnappers: Some hostages may seek the attention of the kidnappers, either for their own safety or to obtain certain concessions. This can lead to rivalries and conflicts.

Stress and Agitation: Stress and anxiety can increase agitation among hostages, which, in turn, can lead to conflicts. It is important for negotiators and authorities to work to reduce agitation and fear.

Negotiators and authorities must be prepared to address these dynamics strategically. This may include:

Communication with Leaders among Hostages: Negotiators can establish effective communication with leaders among hostages to understand the group's needs and concerns and collaborate in managing the situation.

Conflict Resolution: Crisis management professionals can help resolve internal conflicts among hostages and reduce tensions. This can contribute to maintaining a safer and more cooperative environment.

Coordination of Actions and Effective Communication: Negotiators must work closely with leaders among hostages to coordinate actions and ensure effective communication with the kidnappers.

Understanding and managing hostage dynamics is essential to ensure the safety of all involved and to achieve a peaceful resolution of the situation. Cooperation and effective leadership among hostages can be important assets in managing hostage situations.

Fear of Retaliation: Hostages often fear retaliation if they cooperate with authorities. This fear can hinder their willingness to assist in negotiations.

Threats and Coercion: Kidnappers may use direct or implied threats to keep hostages in line. This can include threats of physical violence, harm to family members, or legal consequences.

Distrust of Safety Promises: Hostages may distrust safety promises made by authorities or negotiators. They may believe that promises of protection will not be kept and that they will face retaliation if they cooperate.

Continual Psychological Pressure: The ongoing psychological pressure exerted by kidnappers can keep hostages in a constant state of anxiety and fear. This can make it difficult to make decisions that involve cooperating with authorities.

Isolation and Control: Kidnappers often isolate hostages and exert strict control over them, limiting their options and their ability to communicate with the outside world.

Emotional Support and Confidentiality: It is essential for hostages to receive emotional support and be assured of confidentiality when cooperating with authorities. This can help reduce their fear of retaliation.

Effective Negotiation: Negotiators must be sensitive to the concerns of the hostages and work to gain their trust. This involves establishing effective communication and providing credible security guarantees.

Planning for Hostage Safety: Authorities and negotiators must consider the safety of the hostages at all times and take measures to ensure that they do not face retaliation once the situation is resolved.

Fear of retaliation is a complex dynamic in hostage situations and can vary depending on the specific circumstances of each case. Professionals involved in managing these situations must be aware of these concerns and collaborate with the hostages to ensure their safety and a peaceful resolution of the situation.

Understanding the psychology of both kidnappers and hostages is essential for addressing these situations effectively. Negotiators and professionals involved must adapt their approaches and strategies based on the specific dynamics of each case, taking into account the psychological complexities of all parties involved.

14.Persuasion and Reverse Persuasion Techniques

Persuasion and Reverse Persuasion techniques are strategies used in communication and psychology to influence people's behavior, but they operate in opposite ways. Here is a description of both:

Persuasion Techniques: Persuasion is the process of influencing a person's beliefs, attitudes, opinions, or behavior to achieve a specific goal. Some common persuasion techniques include:

Solid Evidence and Arguments: Presenting facts, evidence, and compelling arguments to support your viewpoint.

Reciprocity: Offering something in return before asking for something from the other person, creating a sense of obligation.

Scarcity: Emphasizing the limited time or quantity of what you are offering, which can increase its appeal.

Authority: Using credibility and authority to support your message.

Consistency: Getting the person to commit to small steps that lead to a greater willingness to accept a larger commitment.

Emotional Attachment: Emotionally connecting with the person and appealing to their emotions.

Persuasive Stories and Narratives: Telling stories that exemplify your viewpoint or product persuasively.

Social Proof: Showing examples of other people who have adopted the same attitude or action.

Reverse Persuasion: Reverse persuasion involves using tactics that seemingly go against your goal to achieve it. It is a psychological strategy that involves resisting or challenging someone's position in a way that makes the person more inclined to support the opposite position. Some reverse persuasion techniques include:

Counter-Resistance: Making the person feel as if they are being pressured or manipulated into a decision or action, which can lead them to rebel and do the opposite.

Appearance of Disinterest: Making it seem like you are not interested in persuading someone, which can make the person lower their guard and become more receptive.

Questions Instead of Statements: Instead of directly stating something, asking questions that make the person reflect and arrive at the desired conclusion themselves.

Using Humor: Humor can break down resistance and make someone more willing to listen.

Playing Devil's Advocate: Making arguments against your own position so the person sees you are considering both sides.

It is important to remember that persuasion, whether conventional or reverse, should be used ethically and with respect for the other person. The misuse of these techniques can be manipulative and harmful to interpersonal relationships.

It is important to emphasize that hostage situations are extremely delicate and dangerous, involving human lives at risk, and ethics and safety are of the utmost importance in these cases. Persuasion and reverse persuasion are concepts that have been used in different contexts, but when it comes to a hostage situation, the top priority is the safety of the people involved.

Persuasion Techniques in Hostage Situations:

Peaceful Negotiation: Security forces, such as the police or negotiation teams, often attempt to persuade kidnappers to release hostages through peaceful negotiation. This may involve the use of persuasion tactics, such as showing empathy toward the kidnappers' motives and seeking a peaceful solution that benefits both sides.

Establishing a Communication Channel: Maintaining an open communication channel with kidnappers is crucial to attempting to persuade them to release the hostages safely. Constant communication can help maintain calm and cooperation.

Appearance of Resistance: In some situations, negotiators may use an appearance of resistance or weakness with the purpose of deceiving the kidnappers. This could involve showing less interest in reaching an agreement, which might cause kidnappers to lower their guard and be more likely to yield to their demands.

Using Sympathy or Fear: Negotiators can use emotional strategies to influence kidnappers. For example, expressing concern for the safety of the hostages or making them understand the potential legal consequences of their actions.

However, reverse persuasion in hostage situations is extremely risky and can worsen the situation if not executed correctly. The top priority remains the safety of the hostages and the peaceful resolution of the incident. Professionals handling negotiations in these cases are trained in specific communication and persuasion techniques to manage these situations safely and effectively.

Ultimately, hostage situations require careful attention and coordination by security and negotiation experts to ensure the safety of all individuals involved.

Establishing a Communication Channel: Maintaining an open communication channel with kidnappers is crucial to attempting to persuade them to release the hostages safely. Constant communication can help maintain calm and cooperation.

Establishing and maintaining an open communication channel with kidnappers is one of the key strategies in managing hostage situations. Here are some key reasons why this is crucial:

Keeping Calm: Constant contact with kidnappers can help keep the situation calm. Communication allows security forces or peaceful negotiators to assess the emotional state of both the kidnappers and the hostages, which can be vital for making informed decisions.

Establishing Trust: Through communication, negotiators can work to earn the trust of the kidnappers. This is crucial for persuading them to release the hostages safely and for maintaining constructive dialogue.

Gathering Information: Maintaining constant communication provides the opportunity to gather valuable information. Negotiators can obtain information about the kidnappers' demands, motivations, and the overall situation, which can be useful for making strategic decisions.

Avoiding Mistakes and Misunderstandings: Open communication can help prevent misunderstandings and errors that could worsen the situation. By keeping a clear channel of communication, it is more likely that all parties involved understand each other's intentions and actions.

Negotiation: Constant communication is essential for conducting effective negotiations. Through dialogue, negotiators can explore potential solutions and agreements that allow for the safe release of hostages.

It is important to highlight that managing hostage situations is an extremely delicate and risky task. Security forces and peaceful negotiators must receive specialized training to handle these situations as effectively as possible, always prioritizing the safety of the hostages. Any hostage rescue operation is carried out with the goal of minimizing violence and protecting the lives of all individuals involved.

Appearance of Resistance: In some situations, negotiators may use an appearance of resistance or weakness with the purpose of deceiving the kidnappers. This could involve showing less interest in reaching an agreement, which might cause the kidnappers to lower their guard and be more prone to yielding to their demands.

The strategy of displaying an "appearance of resistance" or "weakness" in negotiations with kidnappers is a risky approach that is sometimes used in extreme hostage situations but must be applied with extreme caution. The idea behind this technique is to deceive kidnappers into lowering their guard and becoming more likely to yield to their demands. However, this strategy can be very dangerous and has its limitations. Here are some key considerations:

Potential Risks: Displaying an appearance of resistance can anger the kidnappers and escalate the tension in the situation. It may lead to retaliation or even a higher level of violence.

Skill and Training: To successfully implement this strategy, negotiators must be highly trained and have a deep understanding of the psychology of kidnappers. Any false sign of weakness must be convincing and credible.

Ongoing Assessment: Negotiators must be prepared to adjust their approach based on the kidnappers' response. If the kidnappers do not respond as desired, negotiators must be flexible in their approach.

Priority on Hostage Safety: Ultimately, the safety of the hostages must be the top priority. Any strategy used, including the appearance of resistance, should not jeopardize the hostages' lives.

Rescue Operation: In hostage situations, the implementation of reverse persuasion strategies occurs while simultaneously planning a possible rescue operation. This operation should be carried out if the hostages' lives are in imminent danger or if negotiations do not progress safely.

Reverse persuasion is an advanced and risky tactic that should only be used by highly trained professionals in extreme situations. Hostage-taking is a highly volatile situation, and decisions made should prioritize the safety of all individuals involved. The reverse persuasion strategy must be carefully considered and used judiciously, if decided to be used at all.

Using Sympathy or Fear: Negotiators can use emotional strategies to influence kidnappers. For example, expressing concern for the safety of the hostages or making them understand the potential legal consequences of their actions.

The use of emotional strategies, such as sympathy or fear, by negotiators in hostage situations is a valid tactic, but it must also be applied with extreme caution and sensitivity. Here are some important considerations:

Sympathy: Showing sympathy can help establish an emotional connection with the kidnappers. By genuinely expressing concern for their well-being and listening to their concerns, negotiators can attempt to gain the kidnappers' trust and foster a more cooperative dialogue.

Fear: Introducing fear must be done with caution. Negotiators can make kidnappers understand the potential legal consequences of their actions, which could dissuade them from continuing with their plan. However, it is important that this strategy does not provoke a violent or impulsive reaction from the kidnappers.

Ethics and Limits: It is essential for negotiators to maintain an ethical focus at all times. The use of fear should not be excessive or unfair, nor should it take advantage of the kidnappers' vulnerability.

Effective Communication: The key lies in effective communication. Negotiators must be experts in crisis management and psychology to apply these strategies appropriately.

Hostage Safety: Safety is the top priority at all times. Any strategy used must be designed to protect the lives of the hostages and minimize the risk of harm.

Ongoing Assessment: Negotiators must continually assess the effectiveness of emotional strategies. If they are not achieving the desired result or if the situation becomes more dangerous, other options, such as a rescue operation, must be considered.

The management of hostage situations is highly complex and delicate. Emotional strategies can be useful for influencing kidnappers' decisions, but their application must be carefully considered and monitored at all times. Professionals involved in these situations must receive specialized training to ensure safety and a peaceful resolution of the incident.

15.Crisis Management in Hostage Situations

Crisis management in hostage situations is a highly specialized process involving a multidisciplinary team of professionals trained to deal with extremely dangerous and delicate situations.

Situation Assessment: The first thing that security forces do is assess the situation. This involves gathering information about the number of kidnappers, the number of hostages, their health status, the location, the kidnappers' demands, and any other relevant information. Situation assessment is the first and most crucial stage in managing a hostage crisis.

Information Gathering: Security forces, including tactical response teams and negotiators, collect detailed information about the situation. This may include the number of kidnappers, the hostages' identity and health status, the exact location of the hostage-taking, and any information about the kidnappers' demands.

Information Verification: It's important to verify the authenticity of the collected information. This may require the cooperation of witnesses or the use of surveillance and communication technology to obtain accurate information.

Risk Analysis: A risk analysis is conducted to determine the level of danger that the hostages face and how the situation might evolve. This is based on the information collected and the experience of the professionals involved.

Establishment of a Response Team: Response teams, which may include the police, SWAT units, negotiators, medical teams, and other experts, are mobilized to address the situation in a coordinated manner.

Perimeter and Command Post: A security perimeter is established around the hostage-taking location to keep unauthorized individuals and the media at a distance. Additionally, a central command post is set up from which all operations are coordinated.

Communication with Kidnappers: An attempt to establish communication with the kidnappers is initiated, whether through a phone or another secure means. Highly trained negotiators handle this communication.

Communication with Families: Security forces also contact the families of the hostages to provide them with information and keep them informed about the situation.

Rescue Operation Planning: While seeking a peaceful solution through negotiation, security forces also plan a potential rescue operation if the situation requires it or if negotiation is unsuccessful.

The situation assessment is fundamental for making informed decisions and ensuring the safety of everyone involved. It is a delicate and highly coordinated process that requires the collaboration of experts in various fields and the ability to adapt as the situation evolves. The top priority is always the lives and safety of the hostages.

Establishment of a Perimeter: A security perimeter is established around the hostage-taking location to keep onlookers and the media at a distance. Additionally, a central command post is set up from which all operations are coordinated.

Establishing a Perimeter and a Central Command Post:

Control of Access: The perimeter is established to control access to the hostage-taking area. This is done to prevent unauthorized individuals from entering the area, which could complicate the situation or endanger the lives of the hostages.

Preventing Onlookers: The presence of onlookers or uninvolved individuals can interfere with security operations and, at times, be dangerous. Establishing a perimeter helps keep people at a safe distance from the scene.

Media Control: Access control to the area also applies to the media. This is done to ensure that information is handled in a controlled and accurate manner. In many hostage situations, the irresponsible release of information could endanger the hostages or compromise security operations.

Central Command Post:

Coordination: The central command post is where all operations are coordinated. It's where all agencies and units involved, such as the police, negotiating teams, tactical units, and other experts, come together and collaborate.

Decision-Making: The central command post is the center for making strategic decisions. Real-time information is analyzed here, available options are assessed, and decisions about crisis management are made.

Communication: The central command post is essential for maintaining effective communication among all parties involved. This ensures that information flows properly and that operations are carried out in a coordinated manner.

The establishment of a perimeter and a central command post is carried out with the aim of maintaining security and efficiency in crisis management. Every detail and action is carefully planned and coordinated to protect the hostages, ensure the safety of everyone involved, and seek a peaceful resolution of the situation, whenever possible.

Communication: A communication channel is established with the kidnappers. Highly trained negotiators are responsible for maintaining contact with the kidnappers and attempting to establish a dialogue that allows for the safe release of the hostages.

Highly Trained Negotiators: To carry out communication with the kidnappers, highly trained and experienced negotiators are employed in crisis situations. These negotiators are experts in managing communication in extremely tense and potentially dangerous circumstances.

Establishment of a Secure Channel: Communication occurs through a secure channel, such as a phone or a dedicated communication line. The security and confidentiality of communication are crucial to protect the lives of the hostages and prevent potential information leaks.

Active Listening: Negotiators strive to maintain active listening and understand the demands and concerns of the kidnappers. This involves showing empathy and patience, which can contribute to gaining the trust of the kidnappers.

Establishing Dialogue: Through communication, negotiators seek to establish a constructive dialogue with the kidnappers. The goal is to persuade the kidnappers to release the hostages safely and to seek a peaceful resolution.

Peaceful Negotiation: Communication is also used to conduct negotiations. Negotiators explore possible solutions that are acceptable to both parties and that allow for the release of the hostages. This may include discussing the kidnappers' demands and seeking compromises that reduce tension.

Maintaining Calm: Communication is conducted with the premise of maintaining calm in the situation. Patience is key to avoiding impulsive or violent responses from the kidnappers.

Ongoing Assessment: The effectiveness of communication is continually evaluated. If progress is not being made toward a safe resolution or if the situation becomes more dangerous, other approaches, such as a rescue operation, may be considered.

Communication in a hostage situation is a delicate and highly specialized process. Negotiators play a crucial role in crisis management as they can influence the kidnappers' decisions and, ultimately, the safe release of the hostages. The safety and well-being of the hostages are always the top priority in these situations.

Peaceful Negotiation: The primary goal of communication is to achieve a peaceful resolution. Negotiators work to persuade the kidnappers to release the hostages while also attempting to understand their demands and motivations.

Persuasion and Empathy: Highly trained negotiators use persuasion and empathy to influence the kidnappers and try to persuade them to release the hostages.

This involves showing understanding and concern for the demands and motivations of the hostage-takers, even if one does not necessarily agree with their actions.

Constructive dialogue: Communication is essential for establishing a constructive dialogue among the involved parties. Negotiators aim to maintain a calm and cooperative atmosphere where demands and concerns can be effectively discussed.

Exploration of solutions: Negotiators work to explore possible solutions that are acceptable to both the hostage-takers and the security forces. This may involve discussing the demands of the hostage-takers and seeking compromises that allow for the safe release of the hostages.

Risk assessment: During negotiations, there is a constant assessment of risks and the safety of the hostages. Decisions are made with the goal of protecting the lives and well-being of the hostages at all times.

Flexibility: Negotiators must be flexible in their approach and be prepared to adapt as the situation evolves. They may need to adjust their strategy based on the response of the hostage-takers or new developments.

Safety and well-being of the hostages: The number one priority is the safety and well-being of the hostages. Decisions made during negotiations are based on this principle.

Maintaining calm: Communication is conducted with the intention of maintaining a sense of calm in the situation. Patience and professionalism are essential to avoid violent or impulsive responses from the hostage-takers.

Peaceful negotiation is a delicate and highly specialized process based on effective communication, empathy, and persuasion. Its goal is to achieve a non-violent resolution of hostage situations whenever possible. However, it's important to note that reaching an agreement is not always possible, and in some cases, other measures such as a rescue operation may be necessary if the lives of the hostages are in imminent danger.

Operational planning: Simultaneously, detailed planning for a possible rescue operation is conducted in case negotiations are unsuccessful or if the lives of the hostages are in imminent danger.

Planning rescue operations in hostage situations is a critical part of crisis management. This planning occurs alongside negotiations and is considered a last-resort measure that is implemented if negotiations are unsuccessful or if the lives of the hostages are in imminent danger.

Risk assessment: Before conducting a rescue operation, security forces conduct a thorough risk assessment. This involves considering the location of the hostage situation, the number of hostage-takers, the hostages' condition, and any additional information that could impact the operation.

Strategic planning: A detailed plan is created that includes the strategy, tactics, logistics, and personnel required to carry out the rescue operation. Planning is meticulous and based on available information and best practices in similar situations.

Coordination: Coordination is essential to ensure the success of the rescue operation. All involved agencies and units work together to ensure that the operation proceeds smoothly and safely.

Technology and specialized equipment: Rescue operations often involve the use of advanced technology and specialized equipment. This can include armored vehicles, night vision devices, communication systems, and other specific resources.

Drills and training: Security forces undergo drills and extensive training to be prepared for a rescue operation. This includes training scenarios that replicate the hostage situation to practice and perfect tactics and procedures.

Real-time decision-making: The decision to carry out a rescue operation is made in real-time and is based on updated information and the assessment of the situation. It's a critical decision, and efforts are made to minimize the risk to the hostages.

Communication: Communication between rescue units and the central command point is crucial during the operation. Accurate information and coordination are essential for success.

Prioritizing hostage safety: The top priority in any rescue operation is the safety of the hostages. All actions are taken with the aim of ensuring their safe release and minimizing any harm.

It's important to emphasize that rescue operations are extremely risky and are carried out only when all other options have been exhausted or when the lives of the hostages are in imminent danger. Planning and executing these operations require a high level of preparation and professionalism on the part of the involved security forces.

Maintaining calm: Security forces and negotiators must maintain their composure at all times. Hostage situations can be extremely tense, and patience is essential to achieve a peaceful resolution.

Maintaining calm is a fundamental principle in the management of hostage situations. Both security forces and negotiators must demonstrate a high level of professionalism and self-control in these extremely tense situations.

Preventing violence: The tension in a hostage situation can be overwhelming, and violent or impulsive reactions can worsen the situation. Maintaining composure and patience helps reduce the risk of the hostage-takers becoming more aggressive.

Effective communication: Calm is essential to maintain effective communication with the hostage-takers. Constructive dialogue is only possible if all involved parties remain calm and professional.

Informed decision-making: Informed decision-making is based on the assessment of the situation. Maintaining composure allows security forces and negotiators to analyze information and consider available options logically and rationally.

Hostage safety: Hostage safety is the top priority in these situations. Composure and patience are essential to ensure that actions taken are designed to protect the hostages and minimize risks.

Error prevention: In high-pressure situations, errors can easily occur. Maintaining composure helps prevent mistakes that could worsen the situation or endanger those involved.

Professionalism: Professional conduct is essential to maintain the trust of the hostage-takers and the involved parties. Calm and professionalism contribute to creating an environment in which constructive work can be done to resolve the crisis.

Managing hostage situations is an extremely complex and dangerous challenge. Both security forces and negotiators receive specialized training to be prepared for these situations and to act calmly and professionally at all times. The safety and well-being of the hostages are always the highest priority.

Hostage safety: Hostage safety is the absolute priority. All actions and decisions taken by security forces, negotiators, and any other personnel involved in crisis management are aimed at minimizing risk to the hostages and ensuring their well-being.

Physical protection: Every possible measure is taken to physically protect the hostages. This includes ensuring that they are not subjected to physical harm and that their basic needs, such as food, water, and medical attention if necessary, are met.

Maintaining calm: Maintaining a sense of calm and composure is essential to create an environment in which the hostages are as safe as possible. Violent or impulsive reactions can endanger their lives.

Continuous evaluation: The safety of the hostages is continually assessed as the situation evolves. If at any point their lives are considered to be in imminent danger, additional measures may be taken, such as a rescue operation.

Effective communication: Communication with the hostage-takers is used to keep the hostages as safe as possible. Negotiators work to persuade the hostage-takers to release the hostages safely.

Rescue operation planning: Rescue operation planning is carried out to be prepared in case negotiations are unsuccessful or if the lives of the hostages are in danger. The rescue operation is conducted with the priority of ensuring the safety of the hostages.

Collaboration with families: Security forces maintain contact with the families of the hostages to provide them with information and emotional support. Communication with the families is an important part of maintaining their well-being.

Specialized training: Both negotiators and security forces receive specialized training in crisis management and hostage situations to ensure they know how to approach these situations in a way that minimizes risks to the hostages.

Managing a hostage situation is a delicate and extremely complex task, where every decision is made considering its impact on the safety of the people involved. The highest priority is always to ensure that the hostages are safely released, and unnecessary harm is avoided.

Communication with families: Security forces also maintain contact with the families of the hostages to provide them with information and emotional support.

Communication with the families of the hostages is a fundamental part of managing a hostage situation. Providing information and emotional support to the families is essential to keep them informed and help them cope with the situation.

Up-to-date information: Security forces make an effort to provide families with up-to-date and accurate information about the situation. This can include details about the progress of the negotiations, relevant events, and any changes in the situation.

Emotional support: Communication with families also involves providing emotional support. Hostage situations can be extremely stressful and distressing for families, so it is essential to provide them with a space to express their concerns and fears.

Confidentiality: At the same time, it's important to respect the confidentiality of sensitive information related to the situation. Details that could compromise the safety of the hostages or ongoing operations are not disclosed.

Coordination with crisis management experts: Security forces often work closely with crisis management experts and psychologists specialized in hostage situations to ensure that communication with the families is as effective as possible.

Providing clear and honest information: The information provided to families should be clear and honest, avoiding false hopes or misleading information. Transparency is essential to establish a trusting relationship.

Coordination with the central command point: Communication with families is part of the overall coordination of the operation. The information shared with families is based on the information available at the central command point, ensuring that it is up-to-date and accurate.

Preparation for various situations: Families must also be prepared for various scenarios, including the possibility that negotiations may not succeed and a rescue operation may be necessary. Communication includes providing families with information about the different possibilities.

Communication with families is a delicate part of managing a hostage situation, as it involves addressing not only the situation of the hostages but also the concerns and needs of those closest to them. Providing adequate information and support to families is essential to maintain calm and cooperation in a crisis situation.

Strategic decision-making: Decisions about whether to continue with negotiations, carry out a rescue operation, or explore other options are made based on up-to-date information and an assessment of the situation.

Strategic decision-making is a critical part of managing hostage situations. These decisions determine the course of the crisis response and have a direct impact on the safety of the hostages and security forces.

Up-to-date information: Decisions are based on up-to-date and accurate information about the situation. This includes details about the number of hostage-takers, the condition of the hostages, the demands of the hostage-takers, and any changes in the situation's dynamics.

Risk assessment: Continuous risk assessment is conducted. This involves considering the danger to the hostages, the chances of negotiation success, the security of the security forces, and any other factors that may affect decision-making.

Clear objectives: Decisions are made with clear objectives of protecting the lives and safety of the hostages. The top priority is to ensure their safe release.

Rescue operation planning: Planning for a rescue operation is carried out in parallel with negotiations. If, at any point, the lives of the hostages are considered to be in imminent danger or if negotiations are unsuccessful, a rescue operation may be executed.

Coordination and communication: Strategic decisions are made collaboratively among the involved agencies and units. Effective communication between the central command point and operational units is essential to coordinate actions.

Evaluation of options: Different options and strategies are explored based on the evolving situation. This can include continuing negotiations, seeking compromises with the hostage-takers, or executing a rescue operation.

Professionalism: The decision-making process is conducted with a high level of professionalism and self-control. Calmness is fundamental to ensure decisions are made rationally and logically.

Expert support: In crisis management, it's common to have the support of crisis management experts, psychologists, and tactical strategists to advise on strategic decision-making.

Strategic decision-making in hostage situations is a highly delicate task, where a careful balance is struck between the need to protect the lives of the hostages and the responsibility to ensure the security of the security forces. These decisions are critical to the outcome of the crisis and must be made with care and consideration.

Resolution: The ultimate goal is to secure the safe release of the hostages. This can involve using persuasion strategies, exchanging demands, or ultimately executing a rescue operation if deemed necessary.

The resolution of a hostage situation primarily aims at the safe release of the hostages. This resolution can take various forms, and the chosen strategy depends on the specific dynamics of the situation and real-time risk assessments.

Peaceful negotiation: As mentioned earlier, peaceful negotiation is a fundamental strategy. Negotiators work to persuade the hostage-takers to release the hostages safely. This involves listening to the hostage-takers, understanding their demands, and seeking mutually acceptable solutions.

Demand exchange: In some situations, it may be possible to reach an agreement through the exchange of demands. This entails involved parties conceding certain points to reach a compromise that allows for the release of the hostages. For example, the hostage-takers may receive certain concessions in exchange for releasing the hostages.

Rescue operation planning: If negotiations are unsuccessful or if the lives of the hostages are in imminent danger, a rescue operation may be carried out. This is a last-resort measure and is executed with the aim of safely freeing the hostages, although it can be highly risky.

Diplomatic intervention: In international situations, diplomatic intervention can be an effective approach. Governments and international organizations can get involved to mediate the situation and seek a peaceful resolution.

Time negotiation: In some situations, buying time can be a useful strategy to reduce tension and allow for a peaceful resolution to be sought. Buying time often involves maintaining a dialogue with the hostage-takers without necessarily reaching an immediate agreement.

Expert support: In crisis management, it's common to have the support of crisis management experts and psychologists specialized in hostage situations. These professionals can advise on strategies to be pursued.

The choice of strategy depends on the specific dynamics of each situation and real-time risk assessments. The top priority is always the safety of the hostages, and decisions are made with this principle in mind. Each step is planned and coordinated carefully to ensure the safe release of the hostages and the most effective resolution of the crisis.

16.Conflict Resolution in Hostage Situations

Conflict resolution in hostage situations is an extremely delicate task that requires careful planning and a coordinated response by authorities such as the police or special forces. These situations are highly dangerous and may involve innocent people at risk.

Communication: Establishing an open and constant line of communication with the hostage-takers is crucial. Negotiation is a key tool in conflict resolution. Negotiators must be trained in communication techniques, active listening, and conflict resolution.

Establishing effective communication with the hostage-takers is essential in hostage conflict resolution.

Negotiation Team: A trained negotiation team must be designated to establish and maintain communication with the hostage-takers. These negotiators should be experts in communication and conflict resolution techniques, as well as stress management.

Establishing Communication Channels: Negotiators must establish secure and confidential communication channels with the hostage-takers. This can include phones, radios, or other agreed-upon means of communication.

Active Listening: Negotiators must actively listen to the hostage-takers to understand their demands, concerns, and emotions. This involves paying attention to what they say, how they say it, and what they might be indirectly conveying.

Empathy: Negotiators must show empathy towards the hostage-takers without justifying their actions. Showing understanding of their concerns can help build a relationship of trust.

Clear and Precise Communication: Negotiators must communicate clearly and precisely. Ambiguity in communication can lead to misunderstandings and increased tensions.

Communication Strategy: Negotiators must develop a communication strategy that takes into account the demands and concerns of the hostage-takers, as well as the authorities' objectives to ensure the safety of the hostages.

Building Trust: Over time, negotiators can work to gain the trust of the hostage-takers, which can be crucial for achieving a peaceful resolution.

Maintaining Calm: It is essential for negotiators to remain calm at all times, even in high-pressure situations. Their behavior can influence the behavior of the hostage-takers.

Conflict Resolution: Negotiators should use conflict resolution techniques to seek mutually acceptable solutions. This may include exploring alternatives and finding common ground.

Flexibility: Negotiators must be flexible and adapt to changing circumstances. Communication strategies may need adjustments as the situation unfolds.

Record of Conversations: A record of all conversations and agreements reached with the hostage-takers should be maintained. This is essential for documentation and future investigations.

Communication and negotiation are critical tools in managing hostage situations, but it's important to remember that each situation is unique, and specific tactics may vary depending on the circumstances. The top priority should always be the safety of the hostages.

Assess the Situation: Authorities must obtain accurate information about the number of hostage-takers, the quantity of hostages, the weapons involved, and any demands or motives behind the kidnapping. This assessment will help determine the most appropriate strategy.

Evaluating the situation in a hostage situation is a critical step in determining the most appropriate and safe strategy for everyone involved.

Information Gathering: Authorities must collect all available information about the situation. This can include witness reports, communication with the hostage-takers (if possible), security camera footage, and any other relevant data sources.

Number of Hostage-Takers: It is crucial to determine how many hostage-takers are involved in the situation. This will affect the strategy to be followed and how negotiations or tactical assaults will be approached.

Quantity of Hostages: Counting and verifying the number of hostages is crucial. It is also important to know if there are additional hostages who may be hidden or not initially identified.

Weapons Involved: Identifying the type of weapons in the possession of the hostage-takers is essential. This will help authorities assess the level of danger and prepare the appropriate response.

Demands and Motives: Understanding the demands and motives behind the kidnapping is key to developing an effective negotiation strategy. Authorities must investigate and verify the legitimacy of the demands.

Psychological Motives: In addition to explicit demands, it is important to consider the psychological factors that may be influencing the hostage-takers. These may include ideological, emotional, or personal motivations.

Contingency Planning: Based on the information gathered, authorities must develop contingency plans for different scenarios. This includes considering what will happen if negotiations fail or if there is an imminent threat to the hostages.

Available Resources: Evaluating available resources, such as special forces units, negotiation teams, medical personnel, and other professionals, to ensure an appropriate response capability.

Risk Analysis: Evaluating the risks associated with any action taken. This includes considering the possibility of collateral damage, the safety of the hostages, and the safety of response personnel.

Continuous Update: The situation assessment should be an ongoing process as the incident unfolds. Circumstances can change rapidly, and authorities must be prepared to adapt accordingly.

The information gathered and the situation assessment should be used to inform decisions made by authorities, whether through negotiation, tactical assault, or other measures. The top priority at all times should be the safety and well-being of the hostages.

Establish Priorities: The lives and safety of the hostages are the highest priority. Decisions should focus on protecting the hostages, even if it means delaying the conflict's resolution.

Hostage Safety: Hostage safety must be the primary and absolute priority in any hostage situation. All decisions and actions should be focused on minimizing any harm or risk to them.

Maintain Calm: It is important for authorities and response teams to stay calm and avoid hasty actions that may endanger the hostages. Patience and prudence are essential.

Continuous Communication: In many cases, negotiation is a key tool to keep the hostages safe. Authorities must maintain an open and constant line of communication with the hostage-takers to attempt a peaceful resolution.

Do Not Yield to Unreasonable Demands: While hostage safety is the priority, it is not always possible or prudent to concede to all of the hostage-takers' demands. Authorities must assess the legitimacy and feasibility of the demands and seek solutions that do not compromise long-term safety.

Contingency Planning: Despite focusing on hostage safety, authorities must develop contingency plans for situations in which negotiation is ineffective, and lethal force is imminent.

Medical Care and Psychological Support: Ensuring that hostages have access to medical care and psychological support is essential. The situation can be extremely stressful and traumatic for them, so providing the necessary support is critical.

Coordination: Authorities must effectively coordinate their efforts, including the police, special forces, negotiation teams, and other professionals, to ensure a comprehensive and cohesive response.

Avoiding Unnecessary Confrontations: Actions that could trigger a violent confrontation should be avoided without a careful assessment of the risks and benefits. This could include premature tactical assaults.

Continuous Evaluation: The situation must be continuously evaluated as it unfolds. Circumstances can change rapidly, and authorities must be prepared to adapt accordingly.

Safety of Response Professionals: In addition to the safety of the hostages, the safety of response professionals, such as negotiators and special forces, is also important. They must take measures to protect themselves while working to resolve the situation.

The management of hostage situations is extremely delicate and requires a careful and strategic approach. The lives and safety of the hostages should guide all decisions and actions taken by the authorities.

Intervention Strategy: Authorities must develop an intervention strategy that may include negotiation, tactical assault, or a combination of both, depending on the situation assessment.

The intervention strategy in hostage situations is a critical component to ensure the safety of the hostages and effectively resolve the crisis. The choice of strategy should be based on a careful assessment of the situation and should be flexible to adapt to changing circumstances.

Negotiation: Peaceful Approach: Negotiation focuses on peacefully resolving the conflict through dialogue with the hostage-takers. Negotiation Team: A highly trained negotiation team is appointed to establish communication with the hostage-takers and work towards a mutually acceptable solution. Limited Concessions: Although the primary goal is the safety of the hostages, authorities must avoid giving in to demands that compromise long-term safety or are clearly unreasonable. Maintaining Calm: Patience and prudence are essential in negotiations. It is important for negotiators to remain calm and avoid provoking the hostage-takers.

Tactical Assault: Focus on Rapid Action: Tactical assault involves an immediate and energetic response to free the hostages. It can be carried out by special forces or trained elite units.

Risk Assessment: Before conducting a tactical assault, a comprehensive risk assessment, including the location and number of hostage-takers, the disposition of the hostages, and the presence of weapons, must be conducted.

Meticulous Planning: Assault planning must be meticulous, including tactics, communication, and coordination. The goal is to minimize the risk of harm to the hostages. Last Resort: Tactical assault is considered a last resort, used when the lives of the hostages are believed to be in imminent danger and negotiations have been unsuccessful.

In many cases, the intervention strategy may combine elements of negotiation and tactical assault, depending on how the situation unfolds. The choice of strategy should be based on the situation assessment and the priority of protecting the hostages. It is important to be prepared to adapt as circumstances change and new information and opportunities arise. The safety of the hostages remains the primary consideration in any intervention approach.

Negotiation: Negotiators must be trained professionals who can establish a dialogue with the hostage-takers. They should seek to gain the trust of the hostage-takers and pursue a peaceful solution.

Negotiation plays a crucial role in resolving hostage situations. Negotiators must be highly trained professionals experienced in communication and conflict resolution techniques to effectively carry out their work.

Trained Professionals: Negotiators should be individuals with experience and training in managing hostage situations. This may include police officers, psychologists, communication experts, or security professionals.

Establishing Communication: The first step is to establish a secure and confidential communication line with the hostage-takers. This is often done through designated phones or radios.

Building Trust: Negotiators must work to gain the trust of the hostage-takers. This may require empathy, active listening, and demonstrating an understanding of the hostage-takers' concerns without justifying their actions.

Establishing a Working Relationship: Over time, negotiators must establish a working relationship with the hostage-takers. This involves developing effective and open communication to peacefully resolve the conflict.

Understanding Demands and Motives: Negotiators must listen and understand the demands and motives behind the kidnapping. This provides valuable information for seeking mutually acceptable solutions.

Maintaining Calm: It is essential for negotiators to remain calm at all times, even in high-pressure situations. Their behavior can influence the behavior of the hostage-takers.

Limited Concessions: While the primary goal is the safety of the hostages, negotiators must avoid conceding to demands that compromise long-term safety or are clearly unreasonable.

Exploring Alternatives: Negotiators should explore alternatives and solutions that do not endanger the lives of the hostages. This may include compromises in areas that do not directly affect the safety of the hostages.

Contingency Planning: Negotiators must be prepared for situations where negotiations are unsuccessful or if the situation worsens. They must collaborate closely with other response teams.

Record of Conversations: A detailed record of all conversations and agreements reached with the hostage-takers must be maintained. This is essential for documentation and future investigations.

Negotiation is a continuous process that can take time and patience. Negotiators must be flexible and adapt as circumstances change. Their primary goal is to achieve a peaceful resolution of the situation, with the safety of the hostages as the top priority.

Time: Often, time is on the side of negotiators, as it can allow tensions to decrease and the hostage-takers to reconsider their actions. However, it is important to balance the need for time with the safety of the hostages.

The factor of time in managing hostage situations is a crucial element, and its proper handling is essential to achieve a safe and effective resolution.

Time Advantage: The passage of time can be an advantage for negotiators and authorities. As time goes on, tensions can decrease, leading to a greater willingness on the part of the hostage-takers to consider peaceful solutions.

Gaining Information: Over time, negotiators can gain valuable information about the hostage-takers, their motivations, and their demands. This can help in formulating more effective negotiation strategies.

Reconsideration of Actions: Hostage-takers may also reconsider their actions as time passes. This is particularly true if their original demands are not met or if they begin to feel the pressure of time and isolation.

Reducing Tensions: Time can help reduce tensions for both hostage-takers and hostages. This can decrease the risk of impulsive decisions that endanger lives.

Balancing with security: Although time can be beneficial, it is important to balance it with the safety of the hostages. Authorities must ensure that everything possible is being done to guarantee their well-being and be prepared to act if the safety of the hostages is in imminent danger.

Contingency planning: Authorities should develop contingency plans that consider the factor of time. This involves setting time limits for negotiations and being prepared to take action if negotiations do not succeed within a reasonable timeframe.

Constant communication: Ongoing communication with the hostage-takers is key to maintaining control of the situation and ensuring that progress is being made, even if it's gradual.

Patience strategy: The strategy of patience, involving waiting for the hostage-takers to reconsider their actions, can be effective when applied appropriately and safely.

In summary, managing time in hostage situations is a matter of balance. Leveraging the advantage of time can be beneficial, but it must always be done in coordination with the priority of keeping the safety of the hostages in mind at all times.

Tactical assault: In extreme situations, when the lives of the hostages are in imminent danger, special forces may carry out a tactical assault. This is dangerous and should be the last resort.

Tactical assault is an extreme and dangerous measure that should only be considered as a last resort in hostage situations. It is used when there is an imminent and serious threat to the lives of the hostages, and other options, such as negotiation, have failed or are not viable.

Risk assessment: Before conducting a tactical assault, authorities must conduct a thorough risk assessment. This includes considering the location and number of hostage-takers, the disposition of the hostages, the presence of weapons, and the special forces' ability to carry out the operation.

Meticulous planning: Tactical assault planning must be meticulous and detailed. It includes strategy, specific tactics, communication, coordination, and role assignments for special forces.

Minimizing collateral damage: The priority is to minimize any collateral damage. Special forces must act with precision to avoid harming or killing innocent hostages.

Effective communication: Communication between special forces and negotiators is crucial to ensure informed decision-making and to avoid conflict when possible.

Last resort: Tactical assault should be considered a last option. It is carried out when there is no other viable alternative to save the hostages' lives.

Physical and mental readiness: Members of special forces must be physically and mentally prepared for the assault. The tension and stress in such an operation are extreme, and intensive training is required to handle these situations.

Medical support: Authorities must ensure that trained medical personnel are available in case of injuries, both for special forces and hostages.

Post-assault evaluation: After the assault, a detailed assessment must be conducted to analyze the results and learn from the experience. This can help improve tactics and preparation for future situations.

It is essential to emphasize that tactical assault must be used with extreme caution, as there is a risk of endangering the hostages and provoking additional violence. The decision to conduct a tactical assault is made after careful analysis of the situation and ultimately aims to preserve the lives of the hostages when there are no other viable options. The safety of the hostages remains the top priority at all times.

Coordination: Effective coordination among all involved agencies, such as the police, the military, negotiation teams, and medical services, is essential for a successful resolution.

Effective coordination among all agencies and teams involved in managing hostage situations is crucial to ensure a safe and effective resolution.

Unified command system: A unified command system that brings together all agencies and teams involved in responding to the hostage situation must be established. This ensures a clear and consistent chain of command.

Constant communication: Ongoing and effective communication is fundamental for coordinating operations. Clear and secure communication channels must be established to allow real-time information transmission.

Information exchange: All agencies must share relevant information, including details about the situation, the hostage-takers' demands, risk assessments, and any significant developments.

Clear roles and responsibilities: Each agency and team must have clearly defined roles and responsibilities. This prevents duplication of efforts and ensures that each entity focuses on its area of expertise.

Joint contingency planning: Coordination includes contingency planning for various scenarios. Agencies must work together to develop action plans that address different possible situations.

Joint preparation: Joint training and exercises are essential to ensure that all agencies are prepared to respond in a coordinated manner to a hostage situation.

Negotiation team and special forces: Coordination between negotiation teams and special forces is particularly important. They must work together to ensure that decisions regarding negotiation and tactical assault are made in an informed manner.

Assessment and feedback: After the situation has been resolved, it is important to conduct a joint assessment to analyze what went well and what could be improved in future operations.

Medical and healthcare teams: Coordination with medical teams is essential to provide immediate medical care to hostages or anyone injured during the operation.

Media and communication management: Coordination with media management teams is important to ensure that information is communicated accurately and controlled, avoiding unwanted publicity of the situation.

Effective coordination among all parties involved is crucial to minimize chaos, reduce the risk of errors, and ensure that the best possible decisions are made based on the evolving situation. The safety of the hostages should be the primary focus of this coordination.

Contingency planning: Contingency plans should be developed for various situations and possible outcomes.

Contingency planning in hostage situations is a critical element to ensure an effective and safe response. Contingency plans help authorities and response teams prepare for various situations and possible outcomes.

Scenario identification: The first step is to identify a range of possible scenarios that could arise during a hostage situation. This includes considering variability in the behavior of the hostage-takers and the evolving situation.

Risk assessment: Each scenario must be evaluated based on its level of risk and threat to the hostages. This helps prioritize and allocate resources effectively.

Strategy development: For each scenario, specific strategies must be developed that describe how to address the situation. This may include negotiation strategies, tactical assault, or a combination of both, depending on risk assessments.

Tactical planning: Contingency planning should include tactical details, such as the locations of special forces, access routes, communication, and escape plans.

Communication planning: Communication is crucial in hostage situations. Plans should address how to maintain effective communication with the hostage-takers and among response teams.

Roles and responsibilities: Every team member should understand their role and responsibility in each scenario. This ensures a coordinated and efficient response.

Resources and logistics: The necessary resources, such as weaponry, medical equipment, vehicles, and personnel, should be considered. Contingency plans should include logistics to ensure that resources are available when needed.

Continuous evaluation: Contingency planning is not static. It must be reviewed and updated periodically to reflect changes in the situation or lessons learned from previous incidents.

Simulations and exercises: Conducting periodic simulations and exercises helps teams practice the implementation of contingency plans and become familiar with the procedures.

Communication with the public and the media: Contingency planning should also address how to manage communication with the public and the media in hostage situations, with the goal of minimizing the spread of uncontrolled information.

Contingency planning is an integral part of preparing for hostage situations, as it helps ensure that authorities are ready to respond effectively and safely in highly volatile circumstances. Continuous review and updating of these plans are crucial to maintaining response capability in constantly changing situations.

Psychological support: Providing psychological support to hostages before, during, and after the crisis is crucial, as they may experience significant trauma.

Psychological support for hostages in hostage situations is of utmost importance, as traumatic experiences can have a significant impact on their mental and emotional well-being.

Before the crisis: In high-risk situations, such as workplaces or conflict zones, it's important to provide people with tools to cope with hostage situations. This may include training in stress management and exposure to security procedures.

During the crisis: Hostages can experience high levels of stress, fear, and anxiety during a hostage situation. Response teams and negotiators should be trained to treat hostages with empathy and care during the crisis.

After the crisis: Once the hostage situation has ended, psychological support is crucial to help hostages recover from traumatic experiences. This may include access to mental health professionals, such as psychologists or counselors.

Trauma assessment: Hostages may have experienced significant trauma. Early trauma assessment and the diagnosis of post-traumatic stress disorder (PTSD) are important for ensuring appropriate treatment.

Supportive therapy: Supportive therapy is a common approach to treating hostages who have experienced trauma. Mental health professionals may use therapies like cognitive-behavioral therapy (CBT) to help individuals process and overcome the trauma.

Peer support groups: Support groups formed by individuals who have experienced similar situations can be helpful for hostages to share their experiences and support each other in their recovery.

Privacy and confidentiality: Ensuring the privacy and confidentiality of conversations and psychological treatment of hostages is important, as they may fear retaliation or stigmatization.

Trauma education: Providing information to hostages about how trauma can affect their well-being and what to expect during the recovery process is important to reduce uncertainty and anxiety.

Social and occupational reintegration: Assisting hostages in reintegrating into society and their work lives is essential. This may include helping them find employment support or education.

Psychological support should be an integral component of the care and support provided to hostages at all stages of the crisis. Recognizing and addressing the psychological impact of hostage situations is essential to help people recover and return to normal life.

After the incident: Once the hostage situation has been resolved, it's important to conduct investigations to determine the causes and prevent future incidents.

After a hostage situation has been resolved, it is essential to conduct thorough investigations to determine the causes of the incident and prevent future similar incidents.

Police investigation: Law enforcement authorities must conduct a comprehensive investigation to determine who the hostage-takers were, how the kidnapping was planned and executed, and whether there were accomplices. Gathering evidence and testimonies is crucial.

Interviews with witnesses and hostages: Interviews with witnesses and hostages should be conducted to gather information about what transpired and obtain specific details that may be useful in the investigation.

Forensic examination: A forensic examination of the crime scene should be conducted to collect evidence, including fingerprints, DNA samples, and other tests that can help identify the hostage-takers.

Assessment of demands: If specific demands were made by the hostage-takers, these should be evaluated in terms of their legitimacy and feasibility. This may include verifying the authenticity of the demands and considering possible measures to address underlying concerns.

Review of security procedures: It is important to review and evaluate security procedures and hostage prevention measures to identify potential weaknesses and areas for improvement.

Lessons learned: Agencies and response teams should conduct an internal review to identify lessons learned during the management of the hostage situation. This includes what worked well and what could be improved in future incidents.

Rehabilitation and support for hostages: Hostages should receive ongoing medical and psychological support to aid in their recovery. This may include trauma treatment and assistance with reintegrating into everyday life.

Communication with the public and the media: Managing communication with the public and the media after a hostage situation is important to provide accurate and controlled information about the incident.

Prevention of future incidents: Based on the information gathered during the investigation and the review of procedures, steps should be taken to prevent future hostage incidents. This may include improvements in security and preparedness.

International coordination: In cases involving foreign citizens or incidents that occur abroad, international coordination is important to ensure an appropriate response and cooperation in investigations.

The resolution of a hostage situation does not mark the end of the response; it is the beginning of a process that includes investigation, victim support, and the prevention of future incidents. Learning from each incident is crucial to enhance preparedness and response in the future.

It is important to emphasize that each hostage situation is unique and may require specific approaches. Authorities must adapt to changing circumstances and make decisions based on the safety and well-being of the hostages. Prevention and preparedness are also critical to reduce the likelihood of hostage situations.

17.The Importance of Empathy in Hostage Negotiation

Empathy plays a fundamental role in hostage negotiation for several important reasons:

Establishing a human connection: Empathy allows the negotiator and the hostage-takers to connect on a deeper human level. This can help reduce initial hostility and distrust, creating a conducive environment for effective communication and negotiation.

Listening actively: Actively listening to both the hostage-takers and the hostages is essential to show that you care about their perspectives and concerns. Pay attention to what they say and validate their emotions and experiences.

Showing empathy: Expressing understanding and empathy toward the emotions and experiences of the hostage-takers and hostages implies showing sympathy for what they are going through without necessarily agreeing with their actions.

Maintaining calm: Staying calm at all times is important to convey confidence and serenity. Agitation or panic can increase tension in the situation.

Finding common ground: Identifying shared interests or common concerns among the parties can help find mutually beneficial solutions.

Avoiding threatening language: Avoid language that can be perceived as threatening. Use a calm and respectful tone in your communications.

Establishing a dialogue: Encourage open and continuous communication. Ask open-ended questions that allow the hostage-takers to express their needs and concerns.

Offering choices: Provide hostage-takers with options and alternatives to achieve their goals without resorting to violence.

Acknowledging difficulties: Recognize the challenges and hardships that hostage-takers and hostages are facing. This can help reduce the feeling of being misunderstood.

Showing respect: Treat all parties with respect, regardless of the situation. Mutual respect can facilitate a peaceful resolution.

Working collaboratively: Promote collaboration among the parties involved in the negotiation. Instead of a confrontational approach, seek solutions that meet everyone's needs.

It is important to remember that empathy does not necessarily mean sympathizing with the actions of the hostage-takers but understanding their motivations and emotions to seek a peaceful and safe resolution. In hostage situations, the priority should be the safety of the hostages and the peaceful resolution of the conflict.

Promotes trust: Showing empathy towards the hostage-takers demonstrates that the negotiator cares about understanding their concerns and feelings. This can contribute to gaining the trust of the hostage-takers and increasing the likelihood of a peaceful outcome.

Showing empathy in a hostage situation is essential to promote trust. When negotiators genuinely show concern for understanding the concerns and feelings of the hostage-takers, they send an important message that they are willing to cooperate and find a solution that takes into account the needs and desires of both parties.

Trust is essential in hostage negotiation, as the parties involved are often in a high-tension situation with initial distrust. Showing empathy can help reduce that distrust by establishing a bridge of understanding and communication between the negotiator and the hostage-takers. When the hostage-takers perceive that their concerns are being heard and considered with empathy, they are more likely to be willing to cooperate and trust the negotiation process.

This mutual trust is critical for achieving a peaceful and safe resolution of the hostage situation, as it facilitates open communication, joint decision-making, and the search for solutions that avoid violence and protect the lives and well-being of the hostages. In this context, empathy acts as an emotional bridge that contributes to building the necessary trust for a successful negotiation.

Promoting trust in a hostage situation is essential for achieving a peaceful and safe resolution. Empathy plays a key role in this process by demonstrating a genuine understanding of the emotions and concerns of the hostage-takers. Here are some ways in which empathy promotes trust in a hostage situation:

Active listening: Actively listening to the hostage-takers demonstrates that you are willing to understand their perspective and concerns. This can help establish a connection and foster trust.

Respectful communication: Use respectful language and tone in your interactions with the hostage-takers. Avoid using provocative or threatening language, as this can undermine trust.

Validation of emotions: Recognize and validate the emotions of the hostage-takers. You can say something like "I understand that you're feeling frustration/anger/fear" to show empathy toward their feelings.

Treating everyone with respect: Treat all those involved in the situation with respect, including both the hostages and the hostage-takers. This contributes to creating an atmosphere of mutual respect.

Offering options and solutions: Show empathy by providing options and solutions that can meet the needs of both parties. This demonstrates your willingness to find common ground and work together to resolve the conflict.

Transparency: Transparent communication can help establish trust. Clearly explain your intentions and the measures being taken to ensure the safety of the hostages.

Keeping promises: If you make promises or agreements, ensure that you follow through on them. This reinforces credibility and trust in the negotiation process.

Patience and perseverance: Building trust can take time, so it's important to show patience and perseverance in the negotiation process.

Trust is essential in the resolution of hostage situations, as it can help prevent violence and ensure the safety of all parties involved. Empathy is a valuable tool for fostering this trust, as it demonstrates a genuine understanding of the emotions and concerns of the hostage-takers, which, in turn, can lead to a safer and more peaceful outcome.

Facilitates communication: Empathy promotes openness in communication. When the hostage-takers feel that they are being heard and understood, they are more likely to share relevant information and be willing to discuss their demands and concerns.

Empathy plays a fundamental role in facilitating communication in hostage situations. When the hostage-takers feel that they are being heard and understood, it creates an environment conducive to more open and effective communication.

Reduction of hostility: Empathy can help reduce the initial hostility and aggression often experienced in hostage situations. When the hostage-takers perceive that someone is trying to understand their motivations and concerns, they are less likely to feel attacked or threatened.

Fostering trust: Empathy contributes to building trust among the parties involved. When the hostage-takers feel that the negotiator cares about understanding their viewpoints, they are more likely to trust the negotiation process.

Facilitating effective communication: Empathy opens the door to more effective communication. Hostage-takers may be more willing to express their demands and concerns clearly and directly when they feel that someone is genuinely listening.

Creating a collaborative environment: Empathy can help shift the tone of the conversation from confrontational to collaborative. When the parties feel that they are working together to find a solution, they are more likely to communicate openly and constructively.

Facilitates the identification of mutually beneficial solutions: Through empathy, the negotiator can identify potential solutions that meet the needs of both parties. This is crucial for finding common ground and reaching an agreement that benefits both sides.

Correct, empathy can facilitate the identification of mutually beneficial solutions in hostage situations. By demonstrating a deep understanding of the needs and concerns of the hostage-takers, the negotiator can work together with them to explore alternatives that meet their demands without jeopardizing the safety of the hostages or resorting to violence.

Understanding demands: Empathy helps the negotiator understand why the hostage-takers are carrying out the hostage situation and what their fundamental demands are. This understanding can guide the search for solutions that effectively address those demands.

Exploring alternatives: By showing empathy, the negotiator can collaborate with the hostage-takers to explore alternatives that meet their goals without endangering the lives or safety of the hostages. This can include concessions or agreements that both parties find acceptable.

Finding common ground: Empathy can help find points of agreement and common ground between the parties. This may include identifying shared interests or concerns that both parties wish to address.

Respect for human dignity: Empathy also involves respecting the dignity and human rights of all people involved. This can be a fundamental principle for seeking fair and respectful solutions.

Prevention of violence escalation: By identifying solutions that satisfy the needs of the hostage-takers through empathy, the likelihood of resorting to violence as a last resort is reduced.

It's important to highlight that empathy in hostage negotiation doesn't mean giving in to all the demands of the hostage-takers but rather seeking solutions that balance the needs of all parties while ensuring the safety of the hostages. Empathy, when combined with a strategic approach and the assistance of security professionals, can help find peaceful and safe solutions in hostage situations.

Reduces the risk of violence: Showing empathy can help deter hostage-takers from resorting to violence as a means to achieve their goals. When they feel they are being heard and treated with respect, they are less likely to become violent.

Showing empathy can contribute to reducing the risk of violence in hostage situations. Here are some reasons why empathy can play an important role in violence prevention:

Emotional de-escalation: Empathy can help calm the emotions of the hostage-takers, thereby reducing the likelihood that they will react impulsively with violence due to frustration, anger, or fear.

Feeling heard: When hostage-takers feel that they are being heard and understood, they are less likely to feel desperate and resort to violence as a way to draw attention to their demands.

Human connection: Empathy establishes a human connection between the negotiator and the hostage-takers. This can make the hostage-takers see the negotiator as someone with whom they can communicate and collaborate, rather than an enemy they must confront with violence.

Exploration of alternative solutions: Empathy can open the door to seeking peaceful and alternative solutions to meet the demands of the hostage-takers. This reduces the need to resort to violence as a means to achieve their goals.

Building trust: Showing empathy can contribute to gaining the trust of the hostage-takers, which, in turn, reduces the likelihood of resorting to violence. Trust can be a key element in violence prevention.

While empathy can be an effective tool in reducing the risk of violence in hostage situations, it's important to remember that it doesn't guarantee a peaceful resolution on its own. Hostage negotiation is a complex process that requires careful planning, the collaboration of security forces, and effective communication strategies. Empathy, when used appropriately and in conjunction with other approaches, can be an integral part of the strategy to prevent violence and ensure the safety of the hostages.

Mitigates stress and anxiety: Both hostages and hostage-takers experience high levels of stress and anxiety in these situations. Empathy can contribute to alleviating some of this tension by showing understanding and emotional support.

Empathy can play an important role in mitigating the stress and anxiety of both hostages and hostage-takers in hostage situations.

Validation of emotions: Showing empathy involves recognizing and validating the emotions of the people involved. This can make them feel heard and understood, which, in turn, can alleviate some of their anxiety.

Reducing the sense of isolation: Both hostages and hostage-takers can feel isolated and trapped in the situation. Empathy can help break that sense of loneliness by demonstrating that there is someone willing to understand their emotions and concerns.

Emotional support: Empathy involves providing emotional support to people in high-stress situations. This can help alleviate anxiety and provide a sense of companionship during a difficult time.

Promoting communication: When people feel understood and supported, they are more likely to communicate more effectively, which can reduce anxiety related to a lack of information or uncertainty.

Improving mental health: Empathy can contribute to the mental health of individuals in hostage situations by reducing the impact of stress and anxiety. This can be especially important for emotional recovery after the situation is resolved.

It is essential to recognize that empathy is only a part of a broader strategy in hostage negotiation. The safety of the hostages and the prevention of violence remain the top priorities. Empathy should be used in conjunction with effective negotiation techniques and a multidisciplinary approach involving security experts and psychologists, among others, to ensure a safe and peaceful resolution of the situation.

Contributes to the safety of the hostages: By establishing a relationship of trust with the hostage-takers, negotiators can work more effectively to ensure the safety of the hostages and seek a peaceful resolution.

Empathy can contribute to the safety of hostages in hostage situations. Here are some ways in which empathy can play a role in hostage safety:

Building trust: Empathy can help establish a relationship of trust between the negotiator and the hostage-takers. When the hostage-takers feel they are being treated with understanding and respect, they are more likely to trust the negotiation process and cooperate with the authorities.

Effective communication: Empathy promotes effective communication among all parties involved. This can allow the transmission of important information about the safety of the hostages and the intentions of the hostage-takers, which, in turn, can help authorities take appropriate measures to protect the hostages.

Identification of peaceful solutions: Empathy can help identify solutions that meet the needs of the hostage-takers without endangering the safety of the hostages. By seeking peaceful alternatives, the risk of violence and harm to the hostages is reduced.

Prevention of violence escalation: Empathy can deter hostage-takers from resorting to violence as a means to achieve their goals. Feeling that their demands are being heard and considered makes it less likely that they will see violence as the only option.

Collaboration in hostage release: Once a level of trust and cooperation has been established with the hostage-takers, a safe release of the hostages is more likely to be achieved without jeopardizing their lives.

Empathy should be used in conjunction with other approaches and strategies and should be part of a multidisciplinary approach involving security and psychological experts. The top priority in any hostage situation is to ensure the safety of the hostages and prevent violence, and empathy can be an effective tool to achieve this goal when used in conjunction with careful planning and execution.

Empathy in hostage negotiation doesn't necessarily mean sympathizing with the hostage-takers or justifying their actions. Instead, it involves trying to understand their motivations and emotions to achieve a peaceful and safe solution for all parties involved. Empathy should be combined with careful planning, effective communication strategies, and the collaboration of security forces to ensure a successful outcome.

18.Media in Hostage Negotiations

Media plays a significant role in hostage negotiations and can have both a positive and negative impact on the resolution of such situations. Here is a description of the influence of the media on hostage negotiations:

Amplification of public attention: The media has the ability to amplify public attention in hostage cases. Intensive media coverage can pressurize the involved parties, such as the kidnappers or authorities, to reach an agreement more quickly as constant media attention can increase pressure on them.

Amplifying public attention is an important aspect of the media's influence on hostage negotiations.

Continuous coverage: The media often dedicates significant attention to hostage incidents, leading to constant coverage in news broadcasts, newspapers, websites, and social media. This continuous coverage ensures that the public is informed and aware of the situation.

Human interest stories: The media tends to focus on human interest stories related to hostages and their families. This can generate empathy and sympathy among the public, which can increase pressure on the parties involved in negotiations to find a quick and safe solution.

Public debate: Media coverage can trigger public debates on how hostage cases should be handled. This can influence public opinion and authorities' decision-making.

Sensationalism: The media can sensationalize hostage cases, which can attract more attention. While this may increase pressure on the kidnappers, it can also create problems, such as the risk of other criminals seeking notoriety.

Calls to action: Media coverage can lead to calls to action from the public, such as raising funds for a rescue or pressuring authorities to act more quickly.

Amplifying public attention through the media can have a significant impact on the dynamics of hostage negotiations. It can be a powerful tool to pressure the involved parties to seek a solution, but it also carries risks, such as glorifying the kidnappers and additional pressure on the hostages. Therefore, it is important for authorities, negotiators, and the media to work together responsibly and strategically to achieve a successful resolution in these cases.

Dissemination of demands and messages: Kidnappers often use the media as a platform to convey their demands and messages. This can be helpful for authorities and negotiators as it provides information about what the kidnappers are seeking, which can facilitate negotiation and decision-making.

Kidnappers often use the media as a platform to convey their demands and messages in hostage situations. This can have several implications:

Communication with authorities: Through the media, kidnappers can directly or indirectly communicate with the authorities responsible for resolving the crisis. They can set specific conditions or demands they want to be met in exchange for the release of hostages.

Visibility of demands: Broadcasting demands through the media can make the public and authorities aware of what the kidnappers' primary concerns are. This can be helpful for authorities in developing negotiation strategies.

Public pressure: By making their demands public, kidnappers may attempt to generate support or sympathy in the public, pressuring authorities to comply with their demands or find a favorable solution.

Establishing a negotiation channel: Communication through the media can establish a negotiation channel, allowing kidnappers and authorities to exchange messages and reach agreements indirectly. This can be useful in situations where direct talks are difficult or dangerous.

Propaganda and notoriety: By using the media to convey their messages, kidnappers can also seek notoriety and publicity for their actions, which can be detrimental in terms of encouraging others to seek similar attention.

To address the risk of glorification, the media often follows ethical and editorial guidelines aimed at balancing the responsibility of reporting an incident with the need to avoid providing unnecessary platforms to kidnappers. This may include limiting the publication of specific details about kidnappers' tactics or minimizing media coverage of their motivations.

Careful management of media coverage is essential to minimize the risk of glorification and its negative consequences. Journalists and media organizations play a critical role in balancing the need to inform the public with the responsibility to avoid incentivizing future hostage-takings or violent acts.

Disinformation and speculation: Media coverage can sometimes be filled with disinformation and speculation, which can complicate negotiations by creating an atmosphere of uncertainty. The lack of accurate information can hinder the work of negotiators.

Risk of Negotiation Errors: Negotiators responsible for resolving hostage situations heavily rely on accurate and up-to-date information. Misinformation can lead to erroneous decision-making, which could have negative consequences, such as endangering the safety of the hostages.

Manipulation of Information: Kidnappers may attempt to manipulate the information disseminated through the media to their advantage. They can provide false or confusing information with the aim of creating chaos and enhancing their bargaining position in negotiations.

False Public Expectations: Speculation and misinformation in media coverage can create false expectations in the public regarding the crisis's development. This can lead to frustration and mistrust in authorities if things do not unfold as expected.

Pressure on Authorities: Media coverage often generates expectations of quick results, which can put additional pressure on authorities to resolve the crisis promptly. This pressure can be detrimental if it leads to hasty decisions.

To mitigate the negative effects of misinformation and speculation in media coverage of hostage situations, it is essential for the media, authorities, and negotiators to collaborate effectively.

Strategic Communication: Authorities and negotiators should work closely with the media to strategically provide accurate and updated information without compromising the safety of the hostages or ongoing operations.

Information Verification: The media should make extra efforts to verify information before reporting, especially in crisis situations. Sourcing verification and data confirmation are crucial.

Official Statements: Authorities can issue official statements to provide verified and up-to-date information to the media and the public. This can help reduce speculation.

Public Education: Public education about the importance of awaiting confirmed information and avoiding the spread of rumors can help reduce speculation in hostage situations.

Misinformation and speculation in media coverage of hostage situations are challenges that must be effectively addressed to ensure proper crisis management and hostage safety. Collaboration between authorities, negotiators, and the media plays a crucial role in this process.

Media Pressure and Hostages: Constant media coverage can be exhausting for the hostages themselves, who are often aware of the attention they receive. This can generate additional stress and impact their psychological well-being.

Constant media pressure can be an extremely stressful and challenging experience for the hostages in hostage situations.

Psychological Stress: Hostages often become aware of the media attention they receive, and, in some cases, they may be exposed to media coverage through electronic devices or statements from the kidnappers. This can increase their stress and anxiety levels, as they may feel observed or judged by the public.

Sense of Vulnerability: Constant media coverage can make hostages feel more vulnerable and exposed to risk. They may fear that their captors are aware of the media attention and may retaliate in response to public pressure.

Loss of Privacy: Hostages often experience a significant loss of privacy when their situation becomes a media topic of interest. Constant exposure can make them feel as though their personal lives are in the public domain, which can be distressing.

Expectations and Desperation: Media attention can raise public expectations of a swift resolution to the crisis. When these expectations are not met, hostages may feel desperate and concerned for their well-being and safety.

Traumatic Experiences: Hostages are already going through a traumatic experience, and constant media pressure can worsen their situation. They may feel that they are at the center of a media storm they cannot control.

To address these challenges, it is important for authorities, negotiators, and mental health professionals to provide proper support and care for the hostages during and after the crisis. This may include restricting the hostages' access to media coverage, regular communication with the hostages to provide accurate and reassuring information, and psychological support to help manage stress and anxiety.

Furthermore, the media also plays a significant role in the responsible treatment of hostage stories, avoiding the publication of information that could jeopardize the safety of the hostages and showing empathy and sensitivity to their situation.

Constant media pressure can have a negative impact on hostages in hostage situations, and it is essential to address their needs and concerns both during and after the crisis to ensure their well-being and recovery.

Communication Strategy: Authorities and negotiators sometimes use the media as part of their communication strategy to influence public perception and the kidnappers. They can choose when and how to disclose information based on their objectives.

The communication strategy plays a crucial role in managing hostage situations. Authorities and negotiators often use the media as part of their strategy to influence public perception and, in some cases, to send messages to the kidnappers.

Controlled Communication: Authorities can use the media to provide accurate and controlled information about the situation. This may include confirming facts, disclosing actions taken to resolve the crisis, and reassuring the public.

Messages to Kidnappers: In some cases, authorities can use media coverage to send direct messages to the kidnappers. These messages may include reminders that the law will be fully enforced or promises that steps are being taken to meet certain reasonable demands.

Influence on Public Perception: Media coverage can influence public perception of the situation. Statements from authorities can help shape public opinion and provide appropriate context for the crisis.

Maintaining Calm: An effective communication strategy can help maintain calm among the public and reduce widespread anxiety. This is particularly important in high-stress situations, as public reaction can affect the crisis's dynamics.

Avoiding Glorification: Authorities can use media coverage to avoid glorifying kidnappers and their cause, focusing on the safety of the hostages and law enforcement.

Discreet Negotiation: In some cases, authorities can use media coverage to conceal the true negotiation strategy or tactics they are using to resolve the crisis. This can help preserve confidentiality and the security of rescue operations.

The communication strategy in hostage situations must be carefully planned and coordinated to ensure that it does not endanger the safety of the hostages or provide information that could be used to the detriment of the rescue operation. Effective collaboration between authorities and the media is essential to ensure that the communication strategy objectives are met while protecting the safety of all involved parties.

Censorship and Information Control: In some cases, authorities may impose restrictions on media coverage to prevent kidnappers from obtaining a platform for their demands. This can be a strategy to limit the media's influence on negotiations.

The imposition of restrictions on media coverage in hostage situations is a strategy that authorities can use to control information and protect the safety of the hostages. This strategy is based on the idea of limiting the platform that kidnappers have through the media, which can have several implications:

Reducing publicity for kidnappers: By limiting media coverage, authorities seek to reduce the publicity kidnappers can gain from their actions. This can decrease their incentive to commit similar acts in the future to seek notoriety.

Minimizing the risk of manipulation: Kidnappers often use media coverage to convey their demands and messages. Limiting this coverage can reduce the risk of kidnappers using media attention as a bargaining or manipulation tool.

Focus on hostage safety: By restricting the information disclosed through the media, authorities can shift the focus to hostage safety and crisis resolution, instead of allowing media attention to shift toward kidnappers and their demands.

The imposition of restrictions on media coverage raises issues related to freedom of the press and the right to information. The media plays a significant role in society by keeping the public informed, and restrictions on media coverage can be perceived as a limitation of these rights.

Therefore, it is essential that any restriction on media coverage is based on legitimate security considerations and applied proportionately. Authorities must balance the need to protect the hostages and ensure public safety with respect for the rights of freedom of the press and information. Restrictions should be temporary and specific and must be adequately justified.

Imposing restrictions on media coverage in hostage situations can be a legitimate strategy to protect the safety of the hostages and minimize the influence of kidnappers in the media. However, precautions must be taken to ensure that these restrictions are applied proportionately and in compliance with fundamental rights.

The media has a significant impact on hostage negotiations by amplifying public attention, providing a platform for kidnappers' demands, and playing a role in the authorities' communication strategy. However, they also pose challenges in terms of misinformation, glorification, and media pressure on hostages. Proper management of media coverage is essential to achieve a successful resolution in hostage situations.

19.Negotiating with Terrorist Groups

Negotiating with terrorist groups is a complex and controversial topic in international politics and security. Strategies for dealing with these groups vary depending on the situation and objectives, and there is no single or universal approach.

Recognition: Before any negotiations, it's important to determine if the group in question is willing to engage in dialogue and if it has a hierarchy or leadership with whom dialogue can be established. Not all terrorist groups are willing to negotiate.

Recognizing the willingness of the terrorist group to negotiate is a crucial first step in any negotiation attempt. Some terrorist groups may be more inclined to negotiate, while others may outright reject it. Here are some additional considerations related to recognition:

Indirect communication: In some cases, it is possible to establish channels of indirect communication or informal contacts to gauge the group's willingness to negotiate before fully committing to a formal negotiation process. This can help evaluate the prospects for success and reduce risks.

Internal group factors: Willingness to negotiate can vary within the group. Some members may be more inclined to seek a peaceful solution, while others may be more radical and resistant to negotiation. This can complicate the determination of whether the group as a whole is willing to engage in dialogue.

Leadership changes: Changes in the leadership of the terrorist group can influence its willingness to negotiate. A new leader or direction may have a different attitude toward negotiation compared to the previous administration.

International pressure: International pressure, through sanctions, diplomatic isolation, or other measures, can influence the group's decision to explore the negotiation route as a way to alleviate pressure.

Contextual factors: The political, social, and economic environment can influence the group's willingness to negotiate. Changes in the context, such as a military weakness, can make a group more prone to seeking a negotiated solution.

Preparation for possible responses: It's important that the involved parties are prepared for the possibility that a terrorist group may reject negotiation. This may require an alternative strategy, which could include the use of military force or other security measures.

The recognition of the terrorist group's willingness to negotiate is a critical step in the negotiation process, and the assessment of this willingness should be based on a careful analysis of multiple factors, including communication, internal group dynamics, and the surrounding context.

Clear Objectives: It is essential to have clear objectives for the negotiation. This involves defining what you aim to achieve through negotiation, such as the demobilization of the group, the release of hostages, or the resolution of underlying conflicts.

Having clear objectives is crucial in any negotiation process with terrorist groups. Here are some additional considerations related to defining clear objectives:

Prioritizing objectives: It's important to prioritize negotiation objectives, as achieving everything at once can be challenging. For example, if the terrorist group is involved in hostage-taking and has political demands, it must be decided which is the priority and focus efforts in that area.

Precise definition: Objectives should be defined precisely and as specific as possible. For example, if the goal is the "resolution of underlying conflicts," it's important to specify the exact issues and matters to be addressed.

Flexibility: While it's important to have clear objectives, it's also essential to be flexible and willing to adapt them as the negotiation progresses. Discussions may reveal new opportunities or challenges that require adjustments to the objectives.

Internal consistency: Objectives should be consistent with the policies and values of the government or entity negotiating. They should also align with the expectations of the local population and the international community.

Communication: It's crucial to communicate objectives clearly and transparently to all involved parties, including the public, to ensure the legitimacy and support of the negotiation process.

Balance between security and concessions: When defining objectives, a balance must be struck between security and concessions. This involves carefully assessing how much one is willing to concede for the sake of peace and stability.

Short and long-term objectives: Objectives can be divided into short-term and long-term goals. Short-term objectives may include the release of hostages or a ceasefire, while long-term objectives may relate to demobilization and the resolution of deeper conflicts.

Consultation with experts: In complex situations, it may be helpful to consult with experts in conflict resolution, diplomacy, or issues related to the terrorist group to effectively define objectives.

Having clear objectives provides a solid foundation for the negotiation process and helps the parties measure progress and success over time. However, it's important to remember that negotiating with terrorist groups is a delicate process that can take significant time and effort to achieve desired objectives.

Pressure Mechanisms: On some occasions, negotiation can be backed by pressure mechanisms such as economic sanctions or limited military actions to compel the group to come to the negotiation table.

The use of pressure mechanisms in negotiations with terrorist groups is a strategy that can be employed as part of a comprehensive approach to promote dialogue and move toward a peaceful resolution. Here are some key considerations regarding the use of pressure mechanisms:

Economic sanctions: Economic sanctions can include trade, financial, and diplomatic restrictions aimed at pressuring the terrorist group through resource deprivation and economic isolation. These sanctions can be used as leverage to compel the group to reconsider its actions and engage in negotiation talks.

Limited military actions: Limited military actions can be used to exert pressure on a terrorist group and persuade it to seek a peaceful solution. This may involve military operations aimed at weakening the group's capacity or demonstrating the government's determination to use force if negotiations fail.

International coordination: In some cases, international coordination is essential to ensure the effectiveness of pressure mechanisms. The international community can impose sanctions or take military action in support of a government's position seeking negotiation.

Risk assessment: It's important to carefully assess the risks and potential consequences of pressure actions. The use of military force, for example, must be carried out with caution to minimize the risks of collateral damage and increase the likelihood of success.

Communication: Clear communication is essential when using pressure mechanisms. The terrorist group must be informed about the consequences of its lack of cooperation and what steps it can take to avoid sanctions or military actions.

Preparation for dialogue: The application of pressure mechanisms should be supported by a well-thought-out negotiation strategy. The ultimate goal remains to reach an agreement through dialogue, so one must be prepared to engage in meaningful conversations once the terrorist group is willing.

Monitoring and adjustments: As pressure mechanisms are applied, it's important to monitor their effectiveness and be prepared to adjust the strategy if needed. If pressure mechanisms fail to achieve their goal or if the terrorist group shows signs of willingness to negotiate, one should be ready to take appropriate actions.

Ultimately, the use of pressure mechanisms in negotiations with terrorist groups is a strategy that must be used judiciously and in the context of a broader approach aimed at a peaceful and sustainable resolution. Combining pressure mechanisms with diplomatic efforts can be an effective approach to conflict resolution.

Third-Party Mediators: In many negotiations with terrorist groups, third-party mediators are employed, such as neutral governments, international organizations, or respected figures. These mediators can help facilitate dialogue and maintain confidentiality.

The involvement of third-party mediators in negotiations with terrorist groups is a common and valuable strategy to facilitate the negotiation process. Third-party mediators play an important role by acting as impartial intermediaries and de-escalating tensions in the discussions.

Neutrality: Third-party mediators must be perceived as neutral and impartial by all parties involved in the negotiation. This is crucial for gaining the trust of both the terrorist groups and the government or entity seeking to negotiate.

Trust: Trust is essential in any negotiation process. Third-party mediators must build and maintain the trust of all parties, which involves maintaining confidentiality, being consistent in their approach, and adhering to agreed-upon commitments.

Diplomatic skills: Third-party mediators must possess strong diplomatic and negotiation skills. They should be able to manage discussions effectively, resolve conflicts, and overcome obstacles on the path to an agreement.

Effective communication: Third-party mediators must be able to communicate effectively with all parties, conveying their concerns and proposals clearly and constructively.

Contextual understanding: It's important that third-party mediators understand the context in which the negotiation takes place, including the conflict's history, regional dynamics, and specific challenges faced by the terrorist group.

Clear mandate: Third-party mediators should have a clear mandate that defines their role and authority in the negotiation process. This helps prevent misunderstandings and conflicts over their function.

Facilitating ceasefire agreements: Third-party mediators often play a key role in facilitating ceasefire agreements or temporary truces, which can lay the groundwork for broader discussions.

Inclusive process: Third-party mediators should work to ensure that negotiations are as inclusive as possible, involving all relevant and representative parties, even if there are multiple factions within the terrorist group.

International coordination: In some cases, third-party mediators may work in coordination with international actors, such as United Nations bodies or interested governments, to ensure a coherent approach and unified pressure on the terrorist group.

Continuous Assessment: As negotiations progress, third-party mediators must continually assess the effectiveness of their intervention and be willing to adjust their approach if necessary.

Third-party mediators can play a crucial role in conflict resolution and facilitating agreements between governments and terrorist groups. However, it is important to remember that there is no guarantee of success in negotiations with terrorist groups, and the process can be lengthy and complex.

Cessation of Hostilities: A common initial step in negotiations is to achieve a ceasefire or cessation of hostilities, which can create a more conducive environment for dialogue.

Cessation of hostilities or a ceasefire is a critical and common step in negotiations with terrorist groups and conflict resolution in general. This step can be essential in creating an environment conducive to dialogue and moving towards a peaceful solution.

Violence Reduction: A ceasefire or cessation of hostilities entails a reduction in violence, which can save lives, prevent damage to infrastructure, and improve the security of the civilian population.

Building Trust: The cessation of hostilities can contribute to building trust among the parties involved. By halting military operations, a message is sent that there is a commitment to a peaceful process.

Facilitation of Negotiation: By stopping violence, a more conducive environment for negotiation is created. Parties can focus on discussing the issues rather than worrying about immediate security.

Ceasefire Agreements: Ceasefire agreements must be clear and specific, defining terms and conditions such as duration, geographic areas covered, and monitoring measures.

Monitoring Mechanisms: It is important to establish monitoring mechanisms to ensure compliance with the ceasefire by all parties. Third-party mediators or the international community often play a role in monitoring.

Dispute Resolution: Ceasefire agreements should also include procedures for resolving disputes and violations of the ceasefire. This helps prevent hostilities from resuming due to misunderstandings or provocations.

Humanitarian Support: The cessation of hostilities can enable safer access for delivering humanitarian aid to populations affected by the conflict.

Transition to Peace: Cessation of hostilities is generally considered an intermediate step in the peace process. It can be followed by negotiation talks to address the underlying causes of the conflict and seek a long-term solution.

Relapse Risks: It's important to note that ceasefire agreements are not always permanent, and there is a risk of hostilities resuming if the parties are not committed to a sustainable peace process.

International Community Involvement: The international community, through organizations such as the United Nations or other entities, often plays a key role in facilitating and monitoring ceasefire agreements.

Cessation of hostilities is an essential step in seeking peace and stability in conflict-affected areas involving terrorist groups. However, its success depends largely on the willingness and commitment of all parties involved to adhere to the terms of the agreement and progress towards a long-term conflict resolution.

Release Conditions: In cases where the release of hostages is negotiated, it is important to agree on the conditions and terms of release. This may include ransom delivery or the release of prisoners.

When negotiating the release of hostages in situations involving terrorist groups, it is essential to establish clear conditions and terms to ensure the safety of hostages and the integrity of the negotiation process.

Hostage Safety: Hostage safety should be the top priority. Release conditions should guarantee that hostages are freed in a safe location and in good health.

Communication: Parties should establish a reliable and secure line of communication to coordinate the release of hostages and ensure their well-being.

Identity Verification: Procedures should be in place to verify the identity of hostages and ensure that there are no errors or confusion during the release process.

Delivery Conditions: Delivery conditions may include the location, date, and time of the release. These details should be agreed upon and secure for all parties.

Monitoring: The presence of third-party mediators or international organizations can be helpful in monitoring the release and ensuring that the agreed-upon conditions are met.

Prisoner Exchange: In some cases, the release of hostages may be linked to the exchange of prisoners or other commitments by the negotiating government or entity.

Written Agreement: It is advisable to document the release conditions in a formal agreement signed by all parties involved. This provides a clear record of commitments.

Confidentiality: Negotiating release conditions and the release process itself are often conducted confidentially to avoid complications and ensure the safety of hostages.

Commitment to Compliance: All parties involved must commit to complying with the agreed conditions. Any violation of the terms could jeopardize the safety of hostages and undermine trust in the negotiation process.

Post-Release Follow-Up: After the release of hostages, it is important to follow up to ensure their continued well-being and provide psychological and medical support if needed.

Release conditions are a fundamental aspect of negotiations with terrorist groups when it comes to hostages. The goal is to ensure that hostages are released safely and that the negotiation process is conducted transparently and effectively. However, it is also important to consider the ethical and legal implications of any release agreement, especially if it involves compliance with demands from the terrorist group.

Compliance Guarantees: For negotiations to succeed, both parties must trust that the other will fulfill the agreements. Verification mechanisms and guarantees can be implemented to ensure compliance with commitments.

Trust and compliance guarantees are essential in any negotiation process, including negotiations with terrorist groups. The involved parties must be convinced that the agreed commitments will be carried out honestly and effectively.

Monitoring Mechanisms: It is important to establish monitoring mechanisms to verify compliance with agreements. These mechanisms can include impartial observers, third-party mediators, or monitoring teams.

Transparency: Transparency in the negotiation process and in the implementation of agreements is key. Parties should provide verifiable information about their compliance.

Consequences for Non-Compliance: Agreements should specify consequences in case of non-compliance. This may include sanctions, the suspension of agreements, or the resumption of hostilities.

Open Communication: Parties should maintain open and continuous communication to address any concerns or issues that may arise during the implementation of agreements.

Verifiability: The agreed commitments must be verifiable and measurable. They should be clear and specific so that it is possible to determine whether they are being fulfilled.

International Coordination: The international community, including international organizations such as the United Nations, often plays a role in monitoring and ensuring compliance with agreements. Their presence can enhance trust in the process.

Confidentiality: In some cases, confidentiality may be necessary to protect the safety of the parties and the success of the negotiation. However, it must be balanced with the need for transparency and accountability.

Mutual Trust: Mutual trust is essential in negotiations. Parties must work on building this trust throughout the negotiation process.

Public Communication: Effectively communicating progress in the negotiations and the implementation of agreements to both the local population and the international community is important. This helps generate support and understanding.

Continuous Assessment: As agreements are implemented, continuous assessments are important to ensure they are being upheld and to address challenges as they arise.

Compliance guarantees are a critical component in building a successful negotiation process and consolidating peace in contexts involving terrorist groups. Without a high level of trust and effective monitoring, it is difficult to make significant progress in conflict resolution and seeking peaceful solutions.

Legitimacy: The legitimacy of the terrorist group and its representativeness are also crucial issues. International recognition or recognition by the local population can sometimes play an important role in negotiations.

International Recognition: International recognition of a terrorist group as a legitimate entity can be an important factor in their willingness to participate in negotiations. Recognition can come from foreign governments, international organizations, or regional actors.

Legitimacy from the Local Population: Acceptance and support from the local population are essential for the legitimacy of a terrorist group. If a group is perceived as representative of the interests and aspirations of the population in a conflict region, it is more likely to be considered a legitimate actor in the negotiation process.

Validation by Mediators and Impartial Observers: The legitimacy of a group can be validated by third-party mediators, international organizations, or respected figures in the field of diplomacy and conflict resolution.

Representation of Internal Factions: Some terrorist groups may have internal factions with varying levels of influence and control. It is important to determine who has the real authority to make decisions and negotiate on behalf of the group.

Leadership Changes: Leadership changes within a group can influence its legitimacy and representativeness. New leadership may be perceived differently compared to the previous administration.

Consultation with Affected Populations: Successful negotiations often involve consulting the local population and the affected parties to understand their needs and demands. This can help determine if the terrorist group is viewed as a legitimate actor in the process.

Legitimacy Challenges: Some terrorist groups may struggle to gain legitimacy due to the nature of their violent methods and extremist goals. In such cases, significant effort may be required for the group to become an acceptable interlocutor in negotiations.

Validation through Elections or Democratic Processes: In some contexts, terrorist groups may seek legitimacy through elections or democratic processes. This can be a controversial approach and requires careful analysis of the situation.

The issue of legitimacy and representativeness in negotiations with terrorist groups is complex and often subject to debate. Striking a balance between international recognition, local acceptance, and the negotiation process is crucial to move toward a peaceful solution in conflict situations.

Risks: Negotiations with terrorist groups carry risks, such as the possibility of the group exploiting the process to gain time or resources. It is essential to assess these risks and exercise caution.

Gaining Time and Resources: There is a risk that a terrorist group may exploit the negotiation process to gain time and resources to reorganize, recruit new members, or plan future attacks. This is especially true if the group does not have sincere intentions of seeking a peaceful solution.

Propaganda and Legitimization: Negotiations can provide a platform for a terrorist group to legitimize itself and promote its narrative. They can use the talks to present themselves as legitimate political actors, which can be detrimental to stability and security.

Radicalization: The negotiation process can lead to divisions within the terrorist group, with some members becoming further radicalized in response to concessions made in the process.

Lack of Commitment: The terrorist group may fail to fulfill its commitments or may withdraw from the process at any time, undermining the credibility of the talks and the trust of the parties involved.

Security Challenges: The negotiations themselves can be targets of terrorist attacks, presenting significant security challenges for the parties involved in the talks.

Pressure on Governments: Negotiations can generate criticism and public pressure on the government or entity seeking negotiation, especially if it is perceived that too many concessions are being made or the process is ineffective.

Collateral Damage: Attempts at negotiation can cause collateral damage, especially if limited military actions are taken to support the process.

Return to Violence: If negotiations fail or do not result in a sustainable agreement, the terrorist group may resume hostilities with renewed determination.

Distrust of Third-Party Mediators: There may be distrust toward third-party mediators by one or both parties, which can hinder the process.

Given the complexity and risks involved in negotiations with terrorist groups, a thorough assessment and adequate security measures are crucial. Moreover, parties should be prepared for various contingencies and have a plan of action in case negotiations do not succeed. The approach should be pragmatic, realistic, and based on clear objectives to minimize risks and move toward a peaceful solution if possible.

Alternatives: In some cases, negotiating with terrorist groups may not be possible or advisable, and military force may be the only option. Decision-making should be based on a detailed analysis of the situation.

In some cases, negotiating with terrorist groups may be unfeasible or inadvisable, and military force may be the only option to address the threat they pose. Decision-making in these situations should be based on a careful and comprehensive analysis of the situation, taking into account various factors such as the terrorist group's capabilities, willingness to negotiate, the severity of the threat, local population support, and long-term objectives.

Threat Assessment: Accurately assessing the threat posed by the terrorist group is crucial. Is it an imminent threat to public security and stability? Are there viable alternatives to military action?

Clear Objectives: Before resorting to military force, clear and well-defined objectives are necessary. What are the desired outcomes of the military action? How will success be measured?

Military Strategy: Military action must be supported by a strong military strategy that takes into account the group's capabilities, regional implications, and the consequences of the operation.

Minimizing Collateral Damage: Measures should be taken to minimize collateral damage and protect the civilian population to the greatest extent possible. This may include careful operation planning and coordination with humanitarian organizations.

International Coordination: In some cases, military action may require cooperation and coordination with other countries or international actors, especially if the terrorist group operates in multiple jurisdictions.

Local Population Support: Gaining the support of the local population in the fight against terrorism is important. This may involve implementing security measures that minimize inconveniences and suffering for the civilian population.

Follow-Up Measures: Military action can be the initial phase of a broader approach to address terrorism. After military action, it is important to consider follow-up measures, such as stabilization, reconstruction, and prevention of radicalization.

Diplomacy and Reconciliation: Although military action may be necessary in certain cases, diplomacy and the pursuit of long-term political solutions remain important to address the underlying causes of terrorism and prevent its resurgence.

The decision to resort to military force instead of negotiation should be made carefully and as a last resort, as it can have significant consequences. Comprehensive planning and consideration of alternatives are essential to ensure that military action is effective and proportionate to the threat posed by the terrorist group.

Negotiating with terrorist groups is a delicate process that requires a strategic approach and a deep understanding of the situation. Specific policies and strategies will vary depending on the context and the goals of the government or entity seeking negotiations. Additionally, it is important to consider the ethical and legal implications of dealing with groups that have committed acts of violence and terrorism.

20.Famous Hostage Negotiation Cases

There have been several famous hostage negotiations throughout history involving governments, terrorist groups, and international organizations. Here are some notable examples:

Iran Hostage Crisis (1979-1981): In 1979, a group of Iranian students seized the United States Embassy in Tehran and held 52 American hostages for 444 days. The negotiations for their release were complex, ultimately resulting in an agreement known as the "Algiers Accords." The hostages were released on January 20, 1981, shortly after President Ronald Reagan's inauguration.

The Iran Hostage Crisis, which took place between 1979 and 1981, was a highly significant episode in the history of U.S.-Iran relations. Here are more details about this crisis:

Context: The Iran Hostage Crisis originated when, on November 4, 1979, a group of Iranian students seized the U.S. Embassy in Tehran, demanding the extradition of exiled Shah Mohammad Reza Pahlavi, who had been overthrown in 1979 and sought asylum in the United States. The students took 52 American diplomats and citizens hostage who were present at the embassy at the time. The images of the hostage-taking were broadcast worldwide and became a symbol of the growing hostility between the United States and Iran.

Development: The hostages were held captive for 444 days, from November 1979 to January 1981. During that time, negotiations for their release were complex and often unsuccessful. Tensions between the United States and Iran escalated during this period, and there were several attempts at negotiation and mediation by third-party countries and organizations. U.S. President Jimmy Carter attempted to resolve the crisis diplomatically, but the talks did not lead to a resolution. The situation became even more complicated when a U.S. military rescue attempt, known as "Operation Eagle Claw," in April 1980, resulted in failure and loss of life.

Resolution: The Iran Hostage Crisis finally came to an end on January 20, 1981, the same day Ronald Reagan assumed the U.S. presidency. Negotiations for the release of the hostages were conducted secretly through Algerian intermediaries. As part of the agreement, the United States agreed to release frozen Iranian financial assets held in U.S. banks, and both sides agreed not to take legal actions against each other regarding the incident.

The hostages were ultimately released and returned to the United States, while Iran regained access to its financial assets. The release of the hostages marked the official end of the crisis.

The Iran Hostage Crisis had a lasting impact on U.S.-Iran relations and left a profound mark on international politics at the time. Despite being resolved through diplomacy, the episode continues to be a point of contention and distrust in bilateral relations between the two countries.

Achille Lauro Cruise Ship Hijacking (1985): In 1985, a Palestinian group hijacked the Italian passenger ship Achille Lauro and held hostages on board. The release of the hostages was achieved after a series of negotiations between the Italian government and the hijacking group.

The hijacking of the Italian passenger ship Achille Lauro in 1985 was an internationally known incident that involved a Palestinian group and made a significant impact on public opinion. Here are the key details of this incident:

Context: On October 7, 1985, the Italian passenger ship Achille Lauro, with 440 passengers on board, was hijacked in the Mediterranean Sea by a Palestinian group called the "Palestine Liberation Organization - Palestine Liberation Front" (PLO-PLF). The group demanded the release of Palestinian prisoners held in Israel.

Development: The hijackers took approximately 450 people, including passengers and crew, as hostages. The ship was diverted to several ports in the Mediterranean. During the hijacking, the hijackers murdered American citizen Leon Klinghoffer, a wheelchair-bound passenger, and threw his body into the sea. Klinghoffer's murder generated international condemnation and strong media attention. As the crisis escalated, the Reagan administration in the United States and other governments became involved in negotiations for the release of the hostages.

Resolution: After intense negotiations and diplomatic pressure, the hijackers finally abandoned the Achille Lauro off the coast of Egypt on October 10, 1985. The hostages were released. Later, some of the hijackers were arrested and brought to trial in Italy and other countries for their involvement in the hijacking and the murder of Leon Klinghoffer. The Achille Lauro hijacking and the murder of Leon Klinghoffer sparked widespread international condemnation and a renewed focus on the fight against terrorism. It also raised questions about how to address international terrorism and hostage negotiations, especially in cases where violence is committed against hostages. This incident is remembered as a significant event in the history of hijackings and the fight against terrorism.

Ingrid Betancourt Kidnapping (2002): Colombian politician Ingrid Betancourt was kidnapped by the Revolutionary Armed Forces of Colombia (FARC) in 2002. She spent over six years in captivity before being rescued in a military operation in 2008.

The 2002 kidnapping of Ingrid Betancourt was a highly publicized event that involved Colombian politician Ingrid Betancourt, who was kidnapped by the Revolutionary Armed Forces of Colombia (FARC), a Colombian guerrilla group. Here are the key details of this event:

Context: Ingrid Betancourt was a Colombian politician and former senator who ran for the Colombian presidency in the 2002 elections. As part of her election campaign, she decided to travel to remote areas of Colombia, despite warnings about the dangers of FARC-controlled regions. On February 23, 2002, Ingrid Betancourt was kidnapped by the FARC while traveling in a jungle area of southern Colombia. She was one of many victims of FARC kidnappings during decades of armed conflict in Colombia.

Development: During her captivity, Ingrid Betancourt became an international symbol of kidnappings in Colombia. Her situation, as well as that of other hostages held by the FARC, raised widespread concern and calls for their release. The Colombian government, with the support of the international community, made efforts to negotiate the release of Betancourt and other FARC hostages. However, negotiations were complex and marked by disagreements and obstacles.

Resolution: Ingrid Betancourt spent more than six years in captivity in extremely harsh conditions in the Colombian jungle. Finally, on July 2, 2008, she was rescued in a military operation called "Operation Jaque" carried out by the Colombian Army. The rescue operation was successful and led to the liberation of Ingrid Betancourt and other hostages held by the FARC. The news of her release was met with celebration in both Colombia and the international community.

The kidnapping of Ingrid Betancourt and her subsequent release are events that captured the world's attention and underscored the severity of the kidnapping problem in Colombia during the armed conflict. Her story served as a reminder of the risks and suffering faced by kidnapping victims and their families in Colombia and elsewhere. The successful rescue operation marked an important moment in this history and brought an end to a long period of captivity for Ingrid Betancourt and other hostages.

The "Operation Jaque" is the name of the successful Colombian military operation carried out on July 2, 2008, to rescue a group of hostages, including Ingrid Betancourt, who had been held by the Revolutionary Armed Forces of Colombia (FARC) for several years. Here are more details about this operation:

Context: The "Operation Jaque" took place in the midst of the armed conflict in Colombia, during which the FARC had kidnapped numerous hostages, including politicians, military personnel, and civilians, some of whom had been in captivity for over six years. Ingrid Betancourt, a Colombian politician and former senator who ran for the Colombian presidency in 2002, was one of the individuals kidnapped by the FARC. Her kidnapping drew international attention and calls for her release.

Development of the Operation: The "Operation Jaque" was the result of careful intelligence and planning by the Colombian Army. It was conducted with great secrecy and precision. Colombian military forces managed to infiltrate the ranks of the FARC and posed as members of the guerrilla group who were transporting the hostages. During the operation, Colombian forces deceived the FARC kidnappers, making them believe they were being moved to another location. As the operation progressed, the kidnappers and hostages were surprised by disguised Colombian military forces, and the releases took place. The operation resulted in the liberation of 15 hostages, including Ingrid Betancourt and three American contractors who had been in captivity for five years. The news of the operation and the release of the hostages was met with great joy and celebration.

The "Operation Jaque" was a success for the Colombian Army and marked a significant moment in the fight against the FARC and the kidnapping problem in Colombia. It was also a significant event in the lives of Ingrid Betancourt and the other hostages who regained their freedom after years of captivity in extremely harsh conditions in the Colombian jungle. The operation highlighted the importance of intelligence, careful planning, and surprise in hostage rescue operations.

The release of hostages in Colombia in 2010 was a process involving the Revolutionary Armed Forces of Colombia (FARC), a Colombian guerrilla group, and the Colombian government. During this process, negotiations were conducted for the release of various hostages, including military personnel, politicians, and other citizens who had been held by the FARC for extended periods. These releases were the result of talks mediated by neighboring countries and the Red Cross. Here are more details about this process:

Context: Colombia had experienced decades of armed conflict between the Colombian government, guerrilla groups like the FARC, and other armed actors. The FARC had kidnapped numerous hostages over the years as part of their strategy. Among the hostages were military personnel, politicians, and other citizens, some of whom had been in captivity for many years.

Development: In 2010, peace talks were initiated between the Colombian government and the FARC under a process known as "Operation Emmanuel." The goal of these talks was to agree on the release of some of the hostages held by the FARC. The International Red Cross played a crucial role as a neutral intermediary in the negotiations and as the entity responsible for coordinating the release operations. One of the most notable cases during this process was the release of former presidential candidate Íngrid Betancourt, who had been held by the FARC for over six years. The operation to release Betancourt and other hostages was successfully carried out on July 2, 2008. Subsequent releases continued during the peace process, and several hostages were handed over to the Red Cross and representatives of the Colombian government.

Resolution: The hostage release process in Colombia in 2010 represented a significant step toward a peaceful resolution of the conflict. It helped alleviate the suffering of the hostages and their families and marked a milestone in efforts to seek a political solution to the armed conflict in Colombia. Peace talks between the Colombian government and the FARC continued in the years that followed and culminated in a historic peace agreement in 2016. The release of hostages in Colombia in 2010 was a major achievement in the Colombian peace process and contributed to reducing tension in a conflict that had affected the country for decades. It was a milestone in efforts to achieve a peaceful agreement and a signal that the parties were willing to seek negotiated solutions instead of violence.

Al Jazeera Journalists Kidnapping (2005): In 2005, journalists from the Al Jazeera network, including British journalist Alan Johnston, were kidnapped in the Gaza Strip. They were released after an extensive campaign of negotiation and international pressure.

The kidnapping of Al Jazeera journalists, including British journalist Alan Johnston, in 2005 was an event that drew international attention and highlighted the risks faced by journalists working in conflict zones. Here are more details about this incident:

Context: Alan Johnston was a British journalist working as a correspondent for the Al Jazeera news network in the Gaza Strip, which was under the control of the Palestinian faction Hamas. On March 12, 2007, Alan Johnston was kidnapped by an armed group in Gaza while traveling in his car. The kidnapping occurred amid escalating violence and instability in the region.

Development: During his captivity, Alan Johnston was held in extremely challenging conditions and cut off from the outside world. There was international concern for his safety and widespread calls for his release. Throughout his kidnapping, there were negotiation and mediation efforts by Palestinian leaders and the international community to secure Alan Johnston's release.

Resolution: Alan Johnston was released on July 4, 2007, after spending 114 days in captivity. His release was met with relief and celebration both in the UK and the international community. The release of Alan Johnston was achieved through negotiations and diplomatic efforts. At the time of his release, Johnston appeared to be in good health. The kidnapping and subsequent release of Alan Johnston underscored the significant risks faced by journalists covering conflicts and dangerous areas. It also highlighted the importance of diplomatic and mediation efforts to secure the release of hostages in similar situations. The safety of journalists working in conflict areas has remained a significant concern in the journalistic community and the international community.

Chibok Schoolgirls Kidnapping (2014): The terrorist group Boko Haram kidnapped over 200 schoolgirls from the Chibok secondary school in Nigeria. While some hostages were released through negotiations, many of them remain missing.

Context:

On the night of April 14-15, 2014, the terrorist group Boko Haram attacked the girls' secondary school in Chibok, a town in northeastern Nigeria. Boko Haram is an extremist Islamic group that has carried out a series of deadly attacks in Nigeria with the aim of establishing an Islamic state in the region.

Development: In the attack, Boko Haram kidnapped more than 200 students, the majority of them teenagers. The young girls were taken to an unknown location and became hostages of the terrorist group. The kidnapping of the Chibok schoolgirls sparked outrage and protests both in Nigeria and the international community. The "Bring Back Our Girls" campaign became a symbol of solidarity and a call to action. Nigerian President Goodluck Jonathan declared a state of emergency in northeastern Nigeria and pledged to free the kidnapped students.

Resolution: Despite efforts by the Nigerian government and international pressure, many of the kidnapped students remained in captivity for years. Some managed to escape on their own, while others were released or rescued in military operations. The release of some of the Chibok students occurred at various times over the years. However, a significant number of them remained in Boko Haram's captivity in 2021. The 2014 kidnapping of the Chibok students highlighted the brutality of Boko Haram and the vulnerability of populations in northeastern Nigeria.

Despite international attention and efforts by the Nigerian government to secure the release of the kidnapped students, the incident also underscored the complexity and challenges of addressing the threat posed by Boko Haram in the region. The kidnapped girls and their families faced deep trauma and a long wait for their release, emphasizing the urgency of addressing terrorism and insecurity in the region.

MSF Volunteers Kidnapping (2014): In 2014, members of Médecins Sans Frontières (MSF), also known as Doctors Without Borders, were kidnapped by armed groups in Syria. Negotiations and diplomatic efforts contributed to their release.

The kidnapping of Médecins Sans Frontières (MSF) members in Syria in 2014 was an event that underscored the dangers faced by humanitarian workers in conflict zones and the importance of diplomatic efforts to ensure their release. Here are more details about this incident:

Context: In 2014, Syria was engulfed in a brutal and complex conflict in which multiple armed groups were fighting against the Syrian government and each other. The situation in the country had become increasingly perilous for humanitarian workers and journalists.

Development: In January 2014, several MSF members were kidnapped in the city of Homs in western Syria. The humanitarian workers were in the area to provide medical and humanitarian assistance to the conflict-affected population. MSF publicly condemned the kidnapping and called for the safe release of its workers. The organization also worked closely with governments and international organizations to advocate for their release.

Resolution: After several months in captivity, the kidnapped MSF members were released under safe conditions in October 2014. Negotiations and diplomatic efforts played a significant role in the release of the humanitarian workers from MSF. The humanitarian organization, in collaboration with governments and mediators, worked to ensure the safety and integrity of its employees.

The kidnapping of MSF members in Syria served as a reminder of the risks faced by humanitarian workers providing assistance in conflict zones. Despite the dangers, these organizations continue to provide vital assistance to populations affected by conflicts and disasters worldwide. The safe release of humanitarian workers in this case highlighted the importance of diplomatic and mediation efforts in such situations.

These are just some examples of famous hostage negotiation cases. Each situation is unique and presents specific challenges. Hostage negotiation is a delicate process that requires the involvement of multiple parties, including governments, international organizations, and often impartial mediators, with the goal of ensuring the safe release of hostages.

21.Hostage Release and Post-Negotiation

Hostage release and post-negotiation are two key aspects in hostage-taking situations. Here is a brief explanation of both concepts:

Hostage Release: Hostage release is the process of freeing individuals who have been taken as hostages by kidnappers or captured in hostage situations, with the aim of returning them safely to their loved ones. Hostage release can occur for various reasons, including complying with the demands of the kidnappers, intervention by security forces, or negotiation of an agreement between the involved parties.

Hostage release is the act of freeing individuals who have been taken as hostages, with the primary goal of ensuring their safe return to their loved ones. This process may involve several steps and considerations, such as negotiating with the kidnappers, coordinating with security forces, and ensuring that the released individuals receive necessary medical attention and support after their release. The safety of the released individuals and all involved parties is a priority during this process.

Hostage release typically involves a series of carefully coordinated steps to ensure the safety of the released individuals and minimize the risk of harm to all parties involved.

Post-Negotiation: Post-negotiation is the period following the release of hostages during which a series of actions and measures are taken to ensure long-term stability and security after a hostage crisis. During this phase, various aspects can be addressed:

Assessment of Circumstances: Authorities and involved parties analyze what happened during the hostage-taking, the actions taken, and the outcomes achieved. This may include a thorough review of the response by security forces, negotiation strategies, and the demands of the kidnappers.

Circumstances assessment is an essential part of the hostage-taking or kidnapping situation management process. In this phase, authorities and involved parties, such as security forces and negotiators, conduct a comprehensive review of what occurred during the incident. Some of the aspects considered in this assessment include:

Hostage-Taking Analysis: The circumstances that led to the hostage-taking are examined, including who the kidnappers are, their motivations, and how the situation unfolded.

Response Strategy: The response by authorities and the actions taken to handle the situation are analyzed. This may include coordinating security forces, negotiation strategy, and any other approaches used to resolve the incident.

Outcomes Achieved: The results of the hostage release operation are reviewed, including whether the hostages were safely released and whether the kidnappers' demands (if any) were met.

Lessons Learned: Lessons learned from the situation are identified, involving the strengths and weaknesses of the response and how procedures can be improved for future similar situations.

This assessment is critical for improving response capabilities in future cases and for preventing the repetition of hostage-taking incidents. It can also contribute to the development of more effective policies and strategies in crisis management and security situations.

Victim Support: Psychological and physical support is provided to individuals who were hostages, as well as to their families, as they may have experienced significant trauma.

Indeed, victim support is a fundamental part of managing hostage-taking or kidnapping situations. Individuals who have been hostages often face significant traumas and may require both psychological and physical support to recover from their experiences. Key aspects of victim support include:

Psychological Support: Individuals released from hostage situations may have experienced high levels of stress, anxiety, and trauma during their captivity. It is essential to provide them with access to mental health services and psychological support to help them process their experiences and recover emotionally.

Medical Assessment and Care: Conducting comprehensive medical assessments of individuals released is important to identify any physical injuries or health issues resulting from their captivity. They should receive appropriate medical care and treatment for any injuries or conditions.

Family Reunification: In many hostage-taking situations, the released individuals have been separated from their loved ones for an extended period. Facilitating their safe reunification with their families and supporting the reintegration process can be essential for their recovery.

Ongoing Support: Victim support extends beyond the immediate period after release. Long-term support may be necessary to help individuals overcome the long-term effects of trauma, such as post-traumatic stress disorder (PTSD).

Victim support is essential to help individuals recover from the aftermath of a traumatic situation and rebuild their lives. Crisis care organizations, mental health professionals, and government agencies often play a key role in providing this support.

Long-Term Security: Measures are implemented to ensure the ongoing safety of the released individuals and to prevent future hostage-takings. This may include protecting the released individuals and pursuing those responsible.

Long-term security is a critical concern after the release of hostages in hostage-taking or kidnapping situations. A series of measures are implemented to ensure the continued safety of the released individuals and to prevent future hostage-takings. These measures can include:

Witness Protection: In cases where released individuals may be key witnesses in legal proceedings against the kidnappers, protective measures such as identity concealment or relocation may be offered to ensure their safety and that of their families.

Physical Security: Physical security measures, such as escorts, security systems, and surveillance, may be provided to protect released individuals from potential retaliation or future kidnapping attempts.

Reintegration Programs: To help released individuals safely reintegrate into society, reintegration programs may be implemented, providing support for employment, housing, and assistance in overcoming challenges that may arise after their release.

International Collaboration: In transnational kidnapping situations, international cooperation is crucial to ensuring long-term security. This may involve collaboration with other countries, international organizations, and security agencies to track down and apprehend kidnappers and prevent future incidents.

Security Strengthening: Enhancing security measures in areas where the hostage-taking occurred may be necessary to prevent similar situations in the future. This could involve deploying additional security forces or implementing more rigorous security policies.

Long-term security is a critical component of hostage situation management, ensuring that released individuals are not at risk once they return to their normal lives. Additionally, it deters kidnappers and prevents future hostage-takings by showing that authorities take the protection of victims and the prevention of these crimes seriously.

Post-Conflict Negotiations: In some cases, post-negotiation may include discussions on broader issues that contributed to the hostage-taking, such as political or ideological conflicts.

In some cases, post-conflict negotiations may be part of the post-negotiation phase after a hostage situation. These negotiations can be broader than simply releasing hostages and may address underlying issues that contributed to the hostage-taking, such as political, ideological, or social conflicts. Here are some key points related to these negotiations:

Resolving Underlying Conflicts: In situations where hostage-taking is a symptom of larger conflicts, post-conflict negotiations may address fundamental issues at stake. This could include discussing solutions to the underlying conflict and working towards an agreement that resolves political, ethnic, religious, or other tensions that may have contributed to the kidnapping.

Dialogue and Reconciliation: Post-conflict negotiations often involve a process of dialogue and reconciliation among different parties in conflict. It may be necessary for the involved parties to come to the negotiation table to discuss peaceful solutions and address the root causes of the conflict.

International Engagement: In situations of international or regional conflict-related kidnappings, the engagement of international actors, such as mediators or neutral negotiators, may be essential in facilitating post-conflict discussions.

Peace Process: In some cases, post-conflict negotiations may be part of a broader peace process in which long-term solutions to enduring conflicts are sought. This may include ceasefire agreements, reconciliation processes, and the implementation of political and social reforms.

It's important to note that post-conflict negotiations are often complex and may take a long time. However, they are crucial for addressing the underlying causes of hostage situations and working towards a sustainable resolution of conflicts. These negotiations can help prevent future episodes of kidnapping and contribute to peace and stability in the affected areas.

Post-negotiation is a critical stage in resolving hostage situations, as it can help prevent the recurrence of similar incidents and promote reconciliation and stability in the affected region.

22.Explosive Device Deactivation Techniques

Deactivation of explosive devices is a highly specialized task carried out by explosives and bomb disposal professionals. It is dangerous and requires a high level of training and expertise. Here are some techniques and general considerations used in deactivating explosive devices:

Device Assessment: Before taking any action, bomb disposal experts thoroughly assess the explosive device to determine its type, components, and operation. This helps in understanding the danger and the required deactivation strategy.

Device assessment is one of the fundamental stages in bomb disposal. Bomb disposal experts perform this assessment to gain an in-depth understanding of the device and make informed decisions on how to safely deactivate it. Here are some key aspects of device assessment:

Device Type Identification: Specialists determine the type of explosive device they are dealing with, as deactivation approaches can vary depending on whether it's a homemade bomb, a military artifact, a chemical or biological device, etc.

Components and Main Parts: The components of the device, such as explosives, timers, detonators, wires, and other relevant elements, are identified and analyzed.

Design and Operation: Experts study the device's design to understand how it's constructed and intended to function. This includes identifying any activation mechanisms, such as a timer, a switch, a photocell, etc.

Explosive Capacity: The device's power and potential damage are assessed. This is essential to determine the risk it poses and plan for deactivation appropriately.

Device Condition: The device's condition is checked, as it may be damaged or deteriorated in some way. A deteriorated device can be more unpredictable and dangerous.

Hazardous Materials: If the device contains additional hazardous materials, such as toxic chemicals or biological agents, this threat must be identified and addressed properly.

Device assessment provides a solid foundation for the development of a safe deactivation strategy. It's important to emphasize that this phase is critical and should not be underestimated, as any misunderstanding of the device could lead to catastrophic consequences. Thorough and accurate assessments are essential to ensure the safety of both bomb disposal specialists and the general public.

Area Isolation: A safety perimeter is established around the device to protect bomb disposal teams and the general public. Evacuations may be necessary depending on the threat.

Area isolation is a fundamental safety measure when dealing with the deactivation of explosive devices. This action involves establishing a safety perimeter around the device to protect bomb disposal teams and the general public. Here are some important considerations related to area isolation:

Evacuation: In bomb deactivation situations, it may be necessary to evacuate people in the vicinity of the device. This can include evacuating nearby buildings, streets, and public areas. Evacuation is essential to ensure the safety of people and minimize the risk of injuries in case of an accidental explosion.

Establishment of a Safety Perimeter: An appropriate safety perimeter must be established around the explosive device. The distance of the perimeter depends on various factors, such as the type of device, the quantity and type of explosives, and the potential for an explosion.

Access Control: Access to the isolated area must be strictly controlled. Only authorized personnel, such as bomb disposal specialists, should be present within the safety perimeter.

Communication with the Public: Authorities should clearly communicate the reasons for area isolation and provide instructions to affected individuals on how to stay safe during the deactivation process.

Respect for Isolation Signs: The general public must respect isolation signs and avoid approaching the restricted area. This is essential for their own safety and to allow specialists to perform their work effectively.

Area isolation is a critical preventive measure to minimize risks and protect people from harm in bomb deactivation situations. It should be carried out in an organized and coordinated manner by authorities and emergency response teams, ensuring that established safety protocols are followed.

Remote Handling: If possible, attempts are made to deactivate the device remotely using remotely controlled robots. This reduces the risk to human operators.

Remote handling is a common and safe technique used in the deactivation of explosive devices when possible. It involves the use of remotely controlled robots to approach the device and perform deactivation operations without the need for a human operator to be physically close to the device. Here are some important considerations related to remote handling:

Use of Specialized Robots: Bomb disposal teams often use robots specially designed for this task. These robots are typically equipped with cameras and sensors that allow operators to see and control the environment in real-time.

Safe Distance: Remote handling allows operators to work at a safe distance from the explosive device, significantly reducing the risk of injury in the event of an accidental explosion.

Highly Trained Operators: Operators controlling the robots remotely must be highly trained and experienced in using this technology. They need to be capable of performing precise and delicate maneuvers to deactivate the device without triggering it.

Specialized Sensors and Tools: Robots are often equipped with specialized tools and sensors that enable them to cut wires, remove components, or perform other necessary operations for deactivation.

Constant Communication: Continuous communication between operators and the on-site team is essential to ensure effective coordination and real-time decision-making.

Limitations: While remote handling is a valuable technique, it may have limitations. In some cases, the device may be designed in a way that makes remote handling impossible, or other deactivation strategies may be required.

Remote handling is a safe and effective strategy when feasible. However, it's important to note that not all explosive devices can be deactivated in this manner, and in some cases, manual intervention by bomb disposal experts may be necessary. Safety and expertise are always a priority in these procedures.

Controlled Deactivation: If manual handling is required, specialized tools and techniques are used to neutralize or disarm explosive components in a controlled manner. This may involve the removal of timers, switches, or activation cables.

Controlled deactivation is a technique used when manual handling is necessary to neutralize or disarm the explosive components of a device. This is one of the most delicate and dangerous phases of bomb disposal and requires the expertise of highly trained experts. Here are some important considerations related to controlled deactivation:

Experience and Training: Bomb disposal experts performing controlled deactivation must have a high level of experience and training. This includes a deep understanding of the mechanics and electronics of explosive devices.

Specialized Tools: Specialized tools and equipment, such as precision pliers, cable cutters, mirrors, and other handling devices, are used to address the device's components safely.

Caution: Controlled deactivation is carried out with extreme care and caution, as a small error can result in an explosion. Technicians work slowly and follow specific procedures.

Disarming Components: Technicians disarm explosive components one by one, often starting with the safest ones. This may include removing timers, activation cables, switches, or other activation devices.

Use of Containment Containers: In some cases, a sturdy containment container may be used to isolate the device and contain any potential explosion in case of a failure during deactivation.

Testing and Verification: After each step of deactivation, technicians conduct tests and verifications to ensure that the component has been effectively neutralized.

Personal Protective Equipment: Bomb disposal technicians use personal protective equipment, such as face shields and bulletproof vests, to minimize the risk of injury in case of an explosion.

Controlled deactivation is a highly risky process and should only be carried out by highly qualified bomb disposal experts. Safety and precision are crucial to the success of this task and to ensure the protection of people and property in the vicinity.

Use of Specialized Tools: Bomb disposal specialists use specialized tools and equipment designed specifically to accurately and safely carry out the task of deactivating explosive devices. These tools are essential to ensure that the handling of explosive components is done in a controlled and safe manner. Some of the specialized tools and equipment commonly used in bomb disposal include:

Precision Pliers: Precision pliers are used to manipulate cables, wires, and other delicate components of the device.

Cable Cutters: Cable cutters allow specialists to cut activation cables and other cables accurately without causing undue damage.

Telescopic Mirrors: Telescopic mirrors enable technicians to see hard-to-reach areas of the device without having to physically approach it.

Meters and Detectors: Metal detectors and other meters are used to identify and verify the presence of metallic components in the device.

These specialized tools and equipment are crucial for the safe and effective deactivation of explosive devices.

Cameras and Vision Systems: Cameras and vision systems allow specialists to closely observe the device and monitor their actions with precision.

Measurement and Analysis Instruments: This includes equipment such as oscilloscopes and spectrum analyzers used to analyze electrical signals and electronic components.

X-ray and Gamma-ray Equipment: In some cases, X-ray and gamma-ray devices can be used to examine the interior of the device without physically opening it.

Manipulation and Fastening Tools: Tools designed to manipulate and secure components, such as fasteners and screws, may be necessary during deactivation.

Containment Containers: These sturdy containers are used to isolate the device and contain a potential explosion in case of a failure during deactivation.

The use of specialized tools is essential to ensure that deactivation is carried out safely and accurately. These tools allow bomb disposal specialists to work in a controlled manner and minimize the risk of an accidental explosion. The choice of specific tools and equipment will depend on the nature of the device and its components.

Containment Containers: In some cases, a sturdy containment container is used to isolate the explosive device during deactivation. This helps contain a potential explosion in case of a failure during the deactivation process.

Containment containers are specialized devices used in bomb disposal or situations where it is necessary to safely isolate an explosive device. These containers are designed to withstand the pressure and force generated by an explosion. Here are some important considerations related to the use of containment containers:

Purpose: The primary purpose of a containment container is to protect operators and the surrounding public from the effects of a potential explosion during the deactivation of an explosive device. These containers are designed to withstand the pressure and force generated by the explosion.

Robust Design: Containment containers are often made from strong materials, such as steel or composite materials, that can withstand an explosion without breaking.

Controlled Ventilation: Containers often have controlled ventilation systems that allow the gradual release of pressure generated by the explosion to prevent damage to the surrounding structure.

Observation Windows: Some containers are equipped with observation windows that allow operators to see the device and deactivation operations without the need to open the container.

Remote Manipulation: In some cases, remotely controlled robotic arms can be used to manipulate the device inside the container without a human operator having to be physically close.

Careful Procedures: While containment containers provide a high level of safety, deactivation procedures inside the container must be carried out with extreme caution and precision.

Containment containers are used in situations where it is not possible or safe to deactivate an explosive device in any other way. These containers are a critical safety measure and an important part of the equipment used by bomb disposal specialists to minimize the risks associated with deactivating explosive devices.

Specialists' Consultation: If the method of deactivation cannot be determined with certainty, experts may turn to specialists in explosives and bomb disposal with experience in similar situations.

When bomb disposal specialists cannot determine with certainty how to deactivate an explosive device or if there are significant doubts about the best deactivation strategy, they may opt for the consultation of other experts in explosives and bomb disposal. This involves seeking the knowledge and experience of other experts to more effectively address the device in question. Here are some key considerations related to specialists' consultation:

Consultation and Collaboration: Bomb disposal specialists may consult with colleagues, government agencies, or specialized organizations in explosives for advice and guidance.

Information Exchange: During specialists' consultation, details about the device and the circumstances surrounding the situation are shared. This may include photographs, blueprints, and any relevant information.

Assessment and Recommendations: Consulted specialists may conduct an independent assessment of the device and provide recommendations on how to safely and effectively address deactivation.

Experience in Similar Situations: Bomb disposal specialists with experience in similar situations can provide valuable information about successful strategies and potential risks.

Specialists' consultation is a prudent approach when dealing with complex or unusual explosive devices. It allows for the collective experience of experts in the field and increases the chances of addressing the situation safely and effectively. Collaboration and communication among experts are crucial for successfully resolving bomb deactivation situations.

Personal Protective Equipment: Bomb disposal technicians use specialized suits and equipment to minimize the risk of injuries in case of an accidental explosion.

Personal protective equipment is essential to ensure the safety of bomb disposal technicians while they perform their highly dangerous work. Specialized suits and protective equipment are designed to minimize the risk of injuries in case of an accidental explosion during the deactivation of an explosive device. Here are some common elements of the personal protective equipment used by bomb disposal technicians:

Protective Suits: Protective suits, often made of resistant materials such as Kevlar or other ballistic materials, cover the technician's entire body to protect them from fragments and debris in the event of an explosion.

Helmets: Helmets provide protection for the technician's head and face in case of an explosion. They may include visors and face shields to safeguard the eyes and face.

Protective Eyewear: Protective eyewear is used to shield the technician's eyes from debris and fragments that may be ejected during an explosion.

Gloves: Resistant gloves protect the technician's hands and allow for precise handling of tools and components during deactivation.

Sturdy Boots: Sturdy boots provide protection for the technician's feet and legs and are capable of withstanding various risks, including nails or fragments.

Bulletproof Vests: In situations where there may be an additional risk of gunfire or bullet impacts, bulletproof vests provide additional protection to the torso and upper body.

Communication Equipment: Technicians typically carry radios or communication devices to stay in contact with other team members and coordinate their actions during deactivation.

Respirators: In situations where there may be chemical or biological risks, respirators are used to protect the technician from hazardous inhalations.

Personal protective equipment is critical for the safety of bomb disposal technicians, allowing them to perform their work safely and minimize the risk of injuries. In addition to wearing this equipment, technicians must follow rigorous safety procedures and work with extreme caution to ensure that deactivation is carried out effectively and safely.

Ongoing Training: Bomb disposal professionals receive continuous training and stay up-to-date with the latest techniques and technologies for addressing advanced explosive devices.

Technological Advancements: Technology related to explosive devices, explosives, and deactivation techniques is constantly evolving. Specialists must stay updated on the latest advancements to effectively address new threats.

Changes in Threat: Tactics and techniques used by groups or individuals employing explosive devices can change over time. Ongoing training allows specialists to adapt to evolving threats.

Skill Improvement: Constant practice and training help refine the skills necessary for bomb deactivation, such as handling delicate components, analyzing devices, and making decisions under pressure.

Safety: Ongoing training is essential to maintain high safety standards in the profession. Specialists learn to use personal protective equipment and follow updated safety protocols.

Knowledge Sharing: Continuous training also provides the opportunity to share knowledge and experiences with colleagues and experts in the field, contributing to a better understanding and improvement of deactivation techniques.

Skills Testing: Periodic training may include practical tests to ensure that specialists maintain their skills and knowledge at the highest level.

Ongoing training is a continuous commitment that ensures bomb disposal specialists are prepared to face potentially lethal and complex situations. Furthermore, this training helps ensure public safety by equipping specialists to effectively address threats and minimize the risks associated with bomb and explosive deactivation.

23.Negotiation in Virtual Kidnapping Situations

Negotiating in virtual kidnapping situations, also known as "express kidnapping" or "phone kidnapping," is an extremely dangerous and delicate situation. These situations often involve criminals making false threats that they have a loved one of the victim and demanding a ransom or compliance with their demands in exchange for the safe release of the alleged victim.

Keep Calm: In a virtual kidnapping situation, it is essential to remain calm. Criminals often attempt to create panic and stress in the victims to make them make impulsive decisions. Take deep breaths and try to stay calm.

Keeping calm is one of the most important pieces of advice in a virtual kidnapping situation, as criminals often use intimidation tactics to force victims to act quickly and make mistakes. Some reasons why maintaining composure is crucial include:

Rational Decision-Making: When you are calm, you can make more rational decisions and think clearly. This is essential for evaluating the situation and determining if the threats are legitimate or false.

Effective Communication: If you are calm, you can communicate more effectively with the authorities and those close to you. This facilitates the coordination of efforts to resolve the situation safely.

Avoiding Impulsive Errors: If you are in a state of panic or stress, you are more likely to give in to the kidnappers' demands without verifying the authenticity of the situation. Keeping calm allows you to resist the pressure and act more informatively.

Gathering Information: When you are calm, you can record important details, such as the kidnappers' voices or accents, which can be valuable for later investigations.

Protecting Your Personal Safety: Remaining calm also allows you to take measures to protect your safety and that of your loved ones.

Remember that in a virtual kidnapping situation, fear and anxiety can be tools used by criminals to manipulate you. Staying calm will help you resist these tactics and make safer and more effective decisions.

Verify the Safety of Your Loved Ones: Try to communicate with the alleged hostages or loved ones who are supposedly in danger. Call their phone number or send text messages to ensure they are okay. Do not share personal information with the kidnappers without verifying the situation.

Verifying the safety of your loved ones is a critical part of a virtual kidnapping situation.

Maintain Calm: Before attempting to communicate with your loved ones, make sure to stay as calm as possible. This will help you make more informed decisions and communicate effectively.

Use a Secure Channel: Instead of responding directly to the kidnapper's call or message, use a different channel to contact your loved ones. For example, call a phone number you know is safe or use a messaging app to send a message.

Avoid Mentioning the Situation: When speaking with your loved ones, avoid directly mentioning the supposed threat or virtual kidnapping. You can use subtle phrases or codes that only your family or friends would understand so that you do not reveal sensitive information to the kidnappers.

Request Proof of Life: Ask your loved ones to independently confirm their safety. It could be a specific question or action that only they could answer or perform.

Do Not Share Sensitive Information: Do not disclose personal details, such as your location or intentions, to the kidnappers while trying to verify the safety of your loved ones.

Keep Communication Open: Let your loved ones know that you are in contact with the authorities and follow their recommendations. This can be reassuring for them and aid in resolving the situation.

In a virtual kidnapping situation, it is essential to prioritize the safety of your loved ones, but you must also be cautious and avoid putting anyone at risk. Secure and discreet communication is crucial to protect all those involved.

Contacting the authorities is one of the most important actions you should take in a virtual kidnapping situation.

Call the Emergency Number: In most countries, the emergency number is 911. Call this number as soon as possible to report the situation. Local police can respond quickly and provide assistance.

Be Clear and Concise: When speaking with the police, be clear and concise when providing information. Describe the situation accurately, including the threat, the demand, and any relevant details about the kidnappers.

Follow Their Instructions: Listen carefully to the authorities' instructions and follow them to the letter. They can give you advice on how to proceed and gather additional information.

Provide Details: Provide all the information you have about the kidnappers, such as phone numbers, names they may have mentioned, accents, voices, and any other details you can remember.

Cooperate with the Specialized Unit: In cases of virtual kidnapping, units specializing in kidnapping or cybercrime investigations may have specific expertise. Collaborate closely with them and provide all the information they require for the investigation.

Record the Case Number: Make sure to obtain a case number or police report. This will allow you to follow up on the investigation and keep a record of the actions taken.

Do Not Take Hasty Actions: The police may advise you not to comply with the kidnappers' demands without verifying the authenticity of the situation. Follow their recommendations and avoid taking hasty actions.

Remember that the authorities are trained to deal with virtual kidnapping situations and are there to help you. The more information you provide and the faster you communicate with them, the greater the chances of resolving the situation safely.

Do Not Give in to Demands: Do not comply with the kidnappers' demands without verifying the authenticity of the situation. It may be tempting to pay a ransom or meet their demands, but this does not guarantee the safety of the allegedly kidnapped person and can encourage criminals to continue this type of activity.

Not giving in to the demands of the kidnappers without verifying the authenticity of the situation is fundamental advice in a virtual kidnapping situation.

Safety of Loved Ones: Complying with the kidnappers' demands does not ensure the safety of the allegedly kidnapped person. It is essential to first verify that the threat is real before taking any action.

Encouragement of Further Extortion: By paying a ransom or complying with the kidnappers' demands, you can encourage them to continue with this type of criminal activity. They may attempt to extort you or others in the future.

Financial Risk: Complying with the demands can result in the loss of a significant amount of money. Furthermore, there is no guarantee that the kidnappers will hold up their end of the deal.

Legal Risk: In some countries, paying a ransom or complying with certain demands can be illegal. You could face legal consequences if the authorities discover your involvement in illegal activities.

Lack of Verification: If you do not verify the authenticity of the threat, you could be a victim of fraud or deception. It is essential to confirm that the situation is real before taking action.

Instead of immediately complying with the demands, follow the above advice to remain calm, communicate with the authorities, and verify the safety of your loved ones. The authorities will be in a better position to assess the authenticity of the threat and take appropriate measures to resolve the situation safely and legally.

Record Details: Keep a record of all communications, including phone numbers, voices, accents, and any information you can obtain from the kidnappers. This can be valuable for police investigations.

Recording details is a crucial part of a virtual kidnapping situation.

Maintain a Written Record: Use paper and pencil or a mobile app to record all details related to the situation. It is important to have a written record for future reference.

Date and Time: Note the date and time of all calls, text messages, or interactions with the kidnappers. This can be valuable for police investigations.

Phone Numbers: Record all phone numbers used by the kidnappers. This includes both the numbers from which they contacted you and the numbers they asked you to call.

Voice Characteristics: Describe the voices of the kidnappers. You can include details such as gender, apparent age, accent, and any distinctive features you have noticed.

Accents: If the kidnappers spoke with particular accents, try to identify from which region or country that accent might be.

Lexicon and Language Used: Note any words or phrases that the kidnappers frequently use. This could help identify patterns or clues about their origin.

Threat Details: Record the specific threats made by the kidnappers. This may include the demands they have made or the actions they say they will take.

Any Other Relevant Information: If there is any additional detail you consider relevant, such as background sounds or any information you have obtained from the kidnappers, be sure to note it.

Keep a Backup: Back up your record in several secure places, such as in the cloud, in case your device is lost or confiscated by the kidnappers.

This record of details can be valuable for police investigations and can help authorities track down the criminals. Additionally, having a comprehensive record can be useful for your own safety and peace of mind.

Limit Personal Information: Do not disclose additional personal information to the kidnappers. Do not give them details about your family, address, schedules, or routines.

Limiting personal information is essential to protect yourself in a virtual kidnapping situation.

Do Not Disclose Family Details: Avoid providing information about your loved ones, such as their names, locations, or daily activities. Kidnappers can use this information to threaten or extort others.

Current Location: Do not share details about your current location. If the kidnappers ask where you are, avoid providing accurate information.

Schedules and Routines: Do not disclose your daily schedules or usual routines. This includes information about your movements, workplaces, schools, or recreational activities.

Social Media: Be cautious about the information you share on social media. Kidnappers can use social media to gather information about you and your loved ones. Make sure to set the privacy of your accounts appropriately.

Distrust Personal Questions: If the kidnappers ask you personal questions, be cautious and avoid providing information. They may be trying to obtain information to make their threat seem more credible.

Be Aware of Social Engineering: Kidnappers can use social engineering techniques to obtain personal information. Be cautious of calls or messages asking you to verify or confirm personal information.

Use Strong Passwords: Ensure you use strong passwords on your online accounts, especially those related to sensitive personal information. This will help protect your information from potential cyberattacks.

Family Education: Talk to your family and loved ones about the importance of online safety and protecting personal information. The more aware they are, the better they can protect themselves.

Personal information is valuable and can be used against you by kidnappers. Maintain discretion and privacy as priorities at all times to safeguard your safety and that of your loved ones.

Inform Trusted Individuals: Communicate the virtual kidnapping situation to trusted friends, family members, or colleagues so they are aware of what is happening and can provide emotional support.

Informing trusted individuals about the virtual kidnapping situation is important for several reasons. Here are some additional recommendations on how to do it effectively:

Communicate Discreetly: Ensure you communicate the situation to trusted individuals discreetly and securely. Do not share sensitive information or details that could jeopardize your safety or that of your loved ones.

Provide Relevant Information: Inform your loved ones about the threat and the measures you have taken up to that point. This will help them understand the situation and provide better support.

Provide Alternative Contact Numbers: Ensure that your loved ones have access to alternative contact numbers to reach you if necessary. This can be helpful if the kidnappers are monitoring your communications.

Keep Communication Open: Keep your loved ones informed about any developments in the situation. Open communication can be valuable for coordinating efforts and making informed decisions.

Avoid Panic: It's natural for your loved ones to worry, but it's important to reassure them and focus on resolving the situation calmly and effectively.

Cooperate with Authorities: Communicate to your loved ones that you are working in collaboration with the authorities. This can give them confidence that the right steps are being taken to resolve the situation.

Consider Professional Counseling: In virtual kidnapping situations, both victims and their loved ones can experience high levels of stress and anxiety. Consider seeking support from a mental health professional to help you cope with the emotional and psychological impact of the situation.

Having emotional support from trusted individuals can be comforting and helpful during such a stressful situation as a virtual kidnapping. Keep your loved ones informed and work together to resolve the situation safely and effectively.

Additional Security Measures: If you have reason to believe that your safety is at risk, consider changing your locks, implementing additional security measures at your home, and being cautious on social media to avoid disclosing personal information.

Taking additional security measures is a reasonable precaution in a virtual kidnapping situation or in any circumstance where you feel your personal safety is at risk. Here are some recommendations to enhance your security:

Change Locks: If you have reason to believe your security may be compromised, changing the locks at your home and/or workplace is an effective measure. Make sure that only trusted individuals have access to the new keys.

Install Security Systems: Consider installing security systems at your home, such as surveillance cameras, alarm systems, and electronic locks. These devices can help deter intruders and provide evidence in case of incidents.

Establish a Safety Code: Create a safety code with your loved ones, close friends, and trusted colleagues. This code can be used to verify your identity in emergency situations.

Inform Your Neighbors: Talk to your neighbors about the situation and ask for their support. They can be vigilant for any suspicious activity and notify you or the authorities if they observe anything unusual.

Avoid Predictable Patterns: Vary your daily routines and schedules to prevent kidnappers from predicting your movements. This can make it more challenging for them to follow or locate you.

Limit Online Information: Review and limit the amount of personal information you share online, including on social media and public profiles. Kidnappers can use this information to track you.

Keep an Emergency Phone: Consider carrying an additional mobile phone with a charged battery in case you need it in emergency situations.

Secure Communication: Use secure or encrypted messaging apps to communicate with trusted individuals. Avoid discussing sensitive details over insecure phone calls or messages.

Protect Your Financial Information: Regularly monitor your bank accounts and credit cards for unusual activity. If you suspect your financial data is at risk, notify your financial institution.

Maintain Contact with Authorities: Continue collaborating with the authorities and follow their recommendations at all times.

Remember that, in virtual kidnapping situations, personal safety is paramount. It's always preferable to prevent and be prepared in case problems arise. Consult with local authorities and security professionals for specific guidance on security measures to take in your particular situation.

Collaborate with Authorities: Work closely with law enforcement throughout the investigation. Provide all requested information to the authorities and follow their recommendations.

Close collaboration with law enforcement is crucial for resolving a virtual kidnapping situation safely and effectively. Here are some additional guidelines on working together with the authorities:

Provide Comprehensive and Accurate Information: Be transparent and provide the authorities with all the information you have about the situation, the kidnappers, their demands, and any relevant details. The more information they have, the better they can assist you.

Keep a Record of Interactions: Continue documenting all communications with the kidnappers and any other suspicious activity. Provide this evidence to the authorities, as it can be valuable for the investigation.

Follow Authorities' Instructions: Listen to and follow the recommendations of the authorities. They have experience in dealing with such situations and know how to proceed in the safest and most effective manner.

Respond Promptly: Communicate any developments or new information to the authorities as soon as possible. Quick response can be crucial in these situations.

Cooperate in the Investigation: If the police require your cooperation for further investigations, provide the necessary support. This may include testifying, identifying voices, or providing any other details that may be useful in the case.

Request Protection Measures: If you feel that your personal safety or that of your loved ones is at risk, consult with the authorities about possible protection measures, such as escorts or additional surveillance.

Stay Calm: Despite the stress and anxiety you may experience, try to stay calm and trust the investigative process. Effective collaboration with the authorities increases the chances of a safe resolution.

Follow Legal Procedures: Comply with any legal requirements that the authorities instruct you to follow. This may include filing reports or cooperating in judicial investigations.

Seek Emotional Support: In virtual kidnapping situations, emotional stress can be overwhelming. Consider seeking emotional support from mental health professionals, friends, and family to help you cope with the situation.

Remember that the authorities are there to protect you and resolve the situation as safely as possible. Effective collaboration with them is essential to achieving that goal.

It's important to remember that virtual kidnapping situations are illegal and dangerous. Cooperation with the authorities and staying calm are the keys to managing this situation safely.

24. Hostage Negotiation in the Corporate Setting

Hostage negotiation in the business environment is an extremely delicate and dangerous scenario. Although rare, it can happen that employees of a company are kidnapped for the purpose of obtaining a ransom or other demands. Here are some key steps to follow in case of facing a hostage negotiation situation in the business environment:

Immediate Communication: As soon as you become aware of the kidnapping situation involving employees, you should inform local authorities, such as the police or security forces, to initiate an investigation. It's also important to communicate the situation to the company's security contacts and ensure they are informed.

Immediate communication with local authorities, such as the police or security forces, is a crucial step in any employee kidnapping situation in the business environment.

Call the Emergency Number: In most countries, the emergency number is 911. Call this number as soon as you become aware of the kidnapping situation to notify the authorities and request their intervention.

Be Clear and Concise: When speaking with the police or security forces, be clear and concise when providing information about the situation. Provide details about the location of the kidnapping, the number of employees involved, and any information you have about the kidnappers.

Provide Relevant Details: The more relevant information you can provide, the better the response from the authorities. This may include descriptions of the kidnappers, details about how the kidnapping occurred, and any demands that have been made.

Cooperate with Authorities: Follow the instructions of the authorities and cooperate closely with them throughout the investigation. Provide all the information you are asked for and follow their recommendations.

Avoid Hasty Actions: Avoid taking hasty actions on your own, such as attempting to negotiate with the kidnappers or taking risky actions. Let the authorities handle the situation.

Maintain Confidentiality: Ensure that the situation is kept as confidential as possible. Public disclosure could endanger the safety of the hostages and hinder negotiations.

Inform Superiors and Crisis Management Team: Make sure that the company's senior management and the crisis management team are informed about the situation. They can coordinate the company's response more effectively.

Immediate communication with authorities is essential to ensure that an appropriate response is initiated, maximizing the chances of resolving the situation safely. Collaborating with local authorities and following their recommendations is crucial in an employee kidnapping situation.

Establish a Crisis Management Team: The company should form a crisis management team, which typically includes security experts, lawyers, human resources representatives, and communicators. This team will coordinate the response and actions to be taken.

Forming a crisis management team is essential in an employee kidnapping situation in the business environment. This team is responsible for coordinating and executing an effective and safe response.

Identify Team Leaders: Appoint an experienced crisis management or security leader to coordinate all team activities and decisions.

Recruit Key Experts: The crisis management team should include individuals with specific expertise and knowledge. This can include security experts, lawyers, human resources representatives, communicators, and public relations professionals.

Establish Communication Protocols: Define clear communication protocols and contact lines within the team and with local authorities. Ensure that all team members know how to communicate critical information and maintain confidentiality.

Set Up a Crisis Room: Configure a crisis room that serves as the operations center for the team. This is where decisions will be made and actions coordinated.

Define Roles and Responsibilities: Each team member should know their specific roles and responsibilities. This includes who will handle negotiations, who will manage communication with the hostages and their families, and who will be in charge of coordination with the authorities.

Maintain Accurate Records: Keep detailed records of all actions, decisions, and communications made by the team. These records can be important for future investigations or post-crisis reviews.

Implement Crisis Training: Ensure that team members are trained in crisis management and understand the established procedures.

Prepare a Communication Strategy: Collaborate with communication experts to prepare an effective communication strategy, both internally and externally. Information should be managed carefully and controlled.

Evaluate and Adjust: As the situation evolves, the team should continually evaluate and adjust its strategy and actions as needed. This includes considering new developments and potential changes in the kidnappers' demands.

Support Employees and Their Families: Provide support to the involved employees and their families, including counseling, medical care, and legal assistance.

The formation of a strong and well-trained crisis management team is crucial for handling an employee kidnapping situation safely and effectively. Effective coordination and collaboration of this team can make a difference in the successful resolution of the crisis.

Maintain Confidentiality: The situation should be kept confidential as much as possible. Premature public disclosure could jeopardize the safety of the hostages.

Maintaining confidentiality in an employee kidnapping situation is essential.

Hostage Safety: Public disclosure of the situation could seriously endanger the safety of the hostages. Kidnappers could retaliate or increase their demands if they learn that the company is taking steps to resolve the situation.

Preservation of Negotiation: Confidentiality is critical for successful negotiations. If kidnappers realize that the company is cooperating with the authorities or taking actions, they may become more reluctant to negotiate or increase their demands.

Protection of Company Reputation: Premature public disclosure of a kidnapping can damage the company's reputation and negatively impact its employees, customers, and shareholders. Maintaining confidentiality allows the company to manage the situation in a more controlled manner.

Compliance with Safety Recommendations: Authorities and security experts often advise maintaining confidentiality to protect the hostages. Following these recommendations is essential.

Information Control: The company can better manage information by keeping it secret. This avoids rumors, the spread of misinformation, and ensures that only necessary individuals are aware of the situation.

Respect for Laws and Regulations: In many places, disclosing a kidnapping situation is subject to legal regulations and may require approval from the authorities. Compliance with these laws is crucial.

More Effective Negotiation: By maintaining confidentiality, the company and negotiators have more control over the information shared and can use it strategically in negotiations with the kidnappers.

Ultimately, confidentiality is one of the best practices in kidnapping situations and helps maximize the chances of a safe resolution. The company and the crisis management team must work closely to ensure confidentiality is maintained at all times.

Professional Negotiators: Hiring professional negotiators in hostage situations is a common practice. These experts can speak on behalf of the company and negotiate with the kidnappers, minimizing the risk to the hostages.

Hiring professional negotiators in hostage situations is a common and effective strategy for addressing these cases safely and effectively. These experts are trained to communicate with kidnappers, manage demands, and seek the release of hostages. Here are some additional considerations regarding the hiring of professional negotiators:

Experience and Training: Professional negotiators often have experience in hostage situations and have received specialized training in negotiation techniques and crisis management. Their previous experience allows them to deal with extremely delicate situations.

Effective Communication: These experts know how to communicate effectively with kidnappers, maintaining calm and avoiding emotional responses that could endanger the hostages.

Risk Mitigation: Professional negotiators are trained to minimize risks in hostage situations. They can help avoid impulsive decisions that could worsen the situation.

Setting Boundaries and Strategies: Negotiators establish clear boundaries and develop strategies for negotiation. This may include determining how much the company is willing to concede or what demands are unacceptable.

Coordination with Authorities: Professional negotiators work closely with the authorities and the company's crisis management team. This collaboration ensures a coordinated and effective response.

Maintaining Confidentiality: Negotiators are skilled at maintaining confidentiality, which is essential in kidnapping situations to prevent kidnappers from knowing too much about rescue efforts.

Emotional Support for Hostages: In addition to negotiation, professional negotiators can provide emotional support to the hostages to help them cope with the situation.

Monitoring and Review: Once the situation is resolved, professional negotiators can participate in the review of the response and help identify lessons learned for future cases.

Hiring professional negotiators is an investment in the safety and successful resolution of a hostage situation in the business environment. These experts play a crucial role in negotiations and in protecting the lives and safety of the hostages.

Establish Clear Boundaries: Negotiators must set clear boundaries regarding what the company is willing to do and offer in exchange for the release of the hostages. This may include a maximum limit on ransom or acceptable demands.

Establishing clear boundaries in a business hostage negotiation is a fundamental strategy to protect the company's interests and ensure the safety of the hostages. Here are some additional considerations on how to establish boundaries effectively:

Define Boundaries in Advance: Before negotiations begin, the crisis management team and professional negotiators must clearly define what the boundaries are and how far the company is willing to go in terms of demands or concessions.

Evaluate Demands: It's important to analyze the kidnappers' demands and determine which of them are reasonable and which are unacceptable or dangerous to the hostages' safety.

Determine Maximum to Offer: Set a maximum limit in terms of ransom or any other concession the company is willing to offer. This limit should be carefully considered and effectively communicated to negotiators and kidnappers.

Do Not Compromise Safety: Boundaries should focus on not compromising the safety of the hostages. This means that even in negotiation, the safety of the hostages must always be the top priority.

Internal Communication: Ensure that all team members of the crisis management team and the negotiators are aware of the boundaries and are committed to respecting them.

Strategic Negotiation: During negotiations, boundaries can be used strategically. Negotiators may be willing to compromise in certain areas but not in others, with the goal of achieving a safe and effective resolution.

Real-Time Assessment: As the situation evolves, it's important to continuously evaluate whether boundaries should be adjusted based on new developments or additional information.

Support from Authorities: Work closely with the authorities and follow their recommendations regarding boundaries and actions to take.

Transparency in Communication: If necessary, communicate boundaries and the reasons behind them to the kidnappers in a clear and firm manner. This can help set realistic expectations and avoid misunderstandings.

Establishing clear boundaries is a fundamental part of a successful hostage negotiation in the business environment. This helps protect the hostages and ensures that the company can manage the situation effectively without compromising their safety or interests.

Communication with Kidnappers: Communication with kidnappers must be conducted carefully and planned. Negotiators should act as intermediaries and follow the guidelines of the crisis management team.

Communication with kidnappers in a hostage situation must be extremely careful and well-planned to maximize the safety of the hostages and the effectiveness of negotiations. Here are some additional guidelines on how to conduct this communication safely:

Establish a single point of contact: Designate a professional negotiator or a member of the crisis management team as the sole point of contact with the kidnappers. This avoids confusion and centralizes communication.

Define communication protocols: Set clear communication protocols, such as specific call schedules or communication channels. These protocols should be followed strictly.

Maintain calm and empathy: Negotiators should remain calm at all times and show empathy towards the kidnappers without justifying their actions. Empathy can help establish a trusting relationship.

Active listening: Negotiators should attentively listen to the demands and concerns of the kidnappers. This can provide valuable information for negotiations.

Controlled information sharing: Only provide information that is necessary and safe for negotiation. Communication should be managed in a controlled manner to avoid disclosing unnecessary details.

Avoid promising what cannot be delivered: Negotiators should refrain from making promises that cannot be kept. This can erode the kidnappers' trust and hinder negotiations.

Follow the crisis management team's guidance: Negotiators should adhere to the crisis management team's guidance regarding what can be offered or negotiated. This ensures a consistent and strategic response.

Respect pre-established limits: Pre-established negotiation limits must be respected at all times. Negotiators should effectively communicate these limits.

Avoid revealing personal information: Negotiators should not disclose personal information about themselves, the company, or the hostages. Information security is critical.

Transparency and honesty: While it's important to be careful with information, it's also crucial to be transparent and honest to the extent that it is safe. Lack of honesty can undermine the kidnappers' trust.

Communication with kidnappers is a critical part of hostage negotiation and must be handled professionally and strategically. Negotiators and the crisis management team must work together to ensure that all guidelines are followed and the safety of the hostages is maximized.

Risk assessment: The company should work closely with the authorities to assess the risk and decide when and how any actions for the hostages' release will be carried out.

Risk assessment in a hostage situation is an essential process for making informed decisions and ensuring the safety of the hostages. Working closely with authorities and security experts is crucial in this regard. Here are some additional considerations on how to conduct an effective risk assessment:

Collaboration with authorities: The company should fully cooperate with local authorities and any hostage response units, such as the police, security forces, or the corresponding jurisdiction's crisis response team. These agencies often have experience in managing hostage situations.

Gathering information: Collect all relevant information about the situation, including the nature and demands of the kidnappers, the location of the hostages, the kidnappers' capability and willingness to inflict harm, and any information that can help determine the risks.

Analysis of demands: Evaluate the kidnappers' demands and determine which are reasonable and which are unacceptable or dangerous. This will help define clear boundaries for negotiations.

Assessment of potential threats: Consider potential threats that may arise if certain actions are taken or if certain demands are conceded. This includes assessing the security implications for the hostages and other involved parties.

Determining the viability of negotiations: Assess whether negotiations are a viable option and whether there is a possibility of reaching an agreement with the kidnappers that ensures the safety of the hostages.

Planning rescue actions: If necessary, work with authorities and security experts to plan and coordinate rescue actions. This must be done with extreme caution and consideration of all potential risks.

Communication with kidnappers: Communication with kidnappers should be viewed as a strategic tool and a potential means of ensuring the release of hostages. Evaluate when and how communications will take place.

Ongoing evaluation: Risk assessment should be ongoing as the situation evolves. Changes in the kidnappers' demands, the kidnappers' behavior, or any other developments should be assessed and addressed accordingly.

Risk assessment is a dynamic and ongoing process that should guide decision-making in a hostage situation. Working in collaboration with authorities and security experts is essential to ensure that all actions are carried out safely and effectively. The safety of the hostages should always be the number one priority.

Support for hostages: Providing support for hostages and their families is essential. This may include counseling, medical care, and legal assistance.

Providing support for hostages and their families is of utmost importance in a kidnapping situation. The stress and emotional distress can be overwhelming for those affected, and it is the responsibility of the company and the crisis management team to ensure they receive the necessary support. Here are some additional considerations on how to provide support for hostages and their families:

Counseling and emotional support: Provide access to counseling and emotional support services for hostages and their families. This can help them cope with the trauma and stress associated with the experience.

Medical care: Ensure that hostages receive proper medical care for any injuries or health issues they may have suffered during the kidnapping. This may include medical examinations and psychological care.

Legal assistance: Offer legal guidance to hostages and their families to ensure they are aware of their rights and legal options. This is especially important if testimony is required or if legal issues related to the kidnapping arise.

Ongoing communication: Maintain regular communication with hostages and their families to keep them informed about the progress of negotiations and actions taken. Transparency can help reduce uncertainty.

Privacy and security: Protect the privacy and security of hostages and their families. This includes avoiding the disclosure of information that may jeopardize their safety or is unnecessary for their well-being.

Coordination with support professionals: Collaborate with mental health professionals, lawyers, and victim support experts to ensure that hostages and their families receive the appropriate support.

Reintegration assistance: After the hostages are released, provide support for their reintegration into normal life. This may include therapy services or assistance with job searches.

Continued safety: Work in collaboration with the authorities to ensure the ongoing safety of the hostages and their families after their release.

Kidnap and ransom insurance: In some companies, kidnap and ransom insurance may be in place to provide funds for ransom and support for hostages. Ensure that these insurance policies are active and used as needed.

Supporting hostages and their families is an essential part of the response to a kidnapping situation. Ensuring their emotional, physical, and legal well-being is a priority and contributes to their successful recovery and reintegration.

Limited media information: If the decision is made to communicate the situation to the media, it should be done in a controlled manner and under the guidance of crisis communication experts.

Communicating a kidnapping situation to the media, when necessary, must be done extremely carefully and controlled. Here are some additional guidelines on how to handle media communication in a kidnapping situation:

Coordination with authorities: Before communicating the situation to the media, coordinate with the authorities and follow their recommendations.

This ensures that the communication is consistent with rescue efforts and the safety of the hostages.

Designate a single spokesperson: Appoint an official spokesperson from the company or the crisis management team to be the sole source of information to the media. This avoids contradictory or inaccurate information.

Clear and controlled messaging: Develop a clear and controlled message that will be shared with the media. This message should be reviewed and approved by crisis communication experts and the authorities.

Limited disclosure of details: Avoid disclosing specific details that could endanger the safety of the hostages, such as their exact location or the movements of the authorities. The safety of the hostages should always be the priority.

Limit sensitive information: Do not disclose additional personal information about the hostages or their families. This includes avoiding the disclosure of personal details that could be used by the kidnappers.

Control rumors and speculations: If rumors or inaccurate information are spread, the spokesperson should be prepared to address them professionally and accurately.

Scheduled press conferences: Organize scheduled and controlled press conferences instead of providing information ad hoc. This allows the company to have more control over the communication.

Regular updates: Provide regular updates to the media as needed, maintaining control over the information shared. The frequency of updates should be determined in consultation with the authorities and communication experts.

Monitoring and Tracking: Continuously monitor and track media coverage to ensure that information is being managed in accordance with established guidelines.

Coordination with Hostage Families: If appropriate and safe, coordinate communication with the families of the hostages and ensure they are informed before any media statements.

Media communication in kidnapping situations is a critical part of crisis management. The focus on coordination, safety, and information control is fundamental to safeguarding the hostages' security and maintaining the integrity of the company's response.

Follow-up and Review: Once the hostages are released or the situation is resolved, a thorough review of the company's response should be conducted to learn from the experience and improve safety procedures.

Following up and reviewing the company's response after a kidnapping situation is crucial for learning from the experience and enhancing safety procedures. Here are some additional considerations on how to conduct this review effectively:

Post-event Review: Immediately after the hostages are released or the situation is resolved safely, the crisis management team should conduct a comprehensive review of the event. This may include an assessment of the actions taken, key decisions, and the effectiveness of the response.

Identification of Lessons Learned: During the review, lessons learned should be identified. This includes recognizing what worked well and what did not, as well as areas where improvements can be made.

Documentation of the Review: It's important to document the review in detail, including findings, recommendations, and specific actions to be taken based on the lessons learned.

Implementation of Improvements: Once areas requiring improvement are identified, the crisis management team should implement necessary corrective measures. This may involve changes in procedures, staff training, or the adoption of additional security technologies.

Training and Drills: As a result of the review, crisis management training can be developed or adjusted, and drills can be conducted to ensure that employees are prepared to respond to similar situations in the future.

Coordination with Authorities: Share lessons learned and recommendations with local authorities who were involved in the response, which can help improve coordination in future incidents.

Communication Planning: Develop a communication plan that includes how to handle post-crisis media coverage and how to keep stakeholders, such as employees and shareholders, informed about the actions taken to enhance security.

Policy and Procedure Updates: If necessary, update the company's security policies and procedures based on lessons learned and implemented improvements.

Ongoing Review: Crisis response review should be an ongoing process. As threats and risks change, the company should continue to assess and enhance its ability to handle kidnapping situations and other crises.

Monitoring and review are essential to ensure that the company is better prepared to handle future kidnapping situations more effectively and safely. Learning from experience is fundamental to continuous improvement in safety and crisis management.

The top priority in an employee kidnapping situation is the safety of the hostages. Collaboration with authorities and the use of security and negotiation experts are essential to maximize the likelihood of a safe outcome.

25.Legal and Ethical Aspects of Hostage Negotiation

Hostage negotiation involves a range of legal and ethical considerations that are critical to understand and respect. These aspects may vary by country and specific laws, but here are some general considerations regarding the legal and ethical aspects involved in hostage negotiation:

Legal Aspects: Compliance with the Law: It is essential that all actions taken during a hostage negotiation comply with local, national, and international laws and regulations. This includes cooperation with authorities and adherence to laws related to crisis management and security.

Applicable Jurisdiction: Hostage negotiation may involve multiple legal jurisdictions, especially if hostages are in a foreign country. It is important to understand and respect the laws of each relevant jurisdiction.

Coordination with Authorities: Companies must fully cooperate with local authorities, such as the police, security forces, and crisis response agencies, and follow their guidance. Coordination with authorities is essential to ensure legal compliance.

Compliance with Extortion and Ransom Laws: In many countries, paying ransoms may be illegal and subject to legal sanctions. Companies should be aware of laws related to extortion and ransom payments in their jurisdiction and act in accordance with them.

Confidentiality and Information Security: Legal compliance also involves protecting the confidentiality of information that could jeopardize the safety of hostages or security operations. Irresponsible disclosure of information can have legal consequences.

Compliance with International Regulations: In addition to national laws, companies should consider international regulations related to hostage negotiation, as established by the United Nations and other international organizations.

Legal Responsibility: Companies and their legal representatives must assume legal responsibility for their actions and decisions during a hostage negotiation. This includes any agreements or commitments made.

Legal Counsel: Having specialized legal counsel during a hostage negotiation can be crucial to ensure that all actions comply with the law.

Attorneys with experience in crisis management and security can provide important legal guidance.

Compliance with the law is a fundamental principle in any hostage negotiation. Ensuring that all actions are in accordance with applicable laws and regulations is essential to avoid legal consequences and ensure a legally sound and ethical response.

Hostage Safety: The legal priority is the safety of the hostages. All actions must be evaluated based on their impact on the safety of the hostages, and decisions made must not jeopardize their lives.

Hostage safety is the top priority in any kidnapping or hostage negotiation situation. Every action, decision, or strategy must be assessed in terms of its impact on the safety of the hostages, and measures should be taken to minimize any risks they may face.

Ongoing Risk Assessment: Hostage safety must be continuously assessed as the situation evolves. Actions and decisions must be adjusted as needed to protect the hostages.

Secure Communication: Communication with the kidnappers must be conducted securely to protect the identity and location of the hostages. Local authorities and security experts can provide guidance on how to maintain communication security.

Concede Only When Safe: If the decision to concede to the kidnappers' demands is made, it should be done only if it is deemed safe for the hostages. This should be carefully evaluated to minimize any additional risk.

Safe Ransom or Release: In situations where a ransom or release is planned, it is crucial to ensure that these actions are carried out safely and that any risk to the hostages is minimized.

Professional Negotiation: Negotiating with kidnappers should be conducted by crisis management and hostage negotiation professionals who are trained to ensure the safety of the hostages.

Cooperation with Authorities: Work closely with local authorities and crisis response agencies when using professional negotiators. Coordination is essential to ensure that all actions are in compliance with the law and effective.

No Concession to Violence: Hostage safety involves not conceding to violence as a tactic by the kidnappers. Negotiation should focus on the peaceful resolution of the situation.

Assistance in Medical and Psychological Care: After their release, hostages should receive medical and psychological support to help them overcome trauma and any injuries.

Hostage safety is a shared responsibility among the company, authorities, and professional negotiators. All actions and decisions should consider this fundamental principle to minimize any risks to the lives of the hostages.

Use of Professional Negotiators: Hiring professional negotiators in hostage situations is common and may be subject to legal regulations. It is important to ensure that negotiators comply with applicable standards and regulations.

The use of professional negotiators in hostage situations is common and often essential to ensure effective and safe negotiation. However, the use of professional negotiators may be subject to legal regulations in some jurisdictions. It is important to be aware of these regulations and ensure that negotiators comply with applicable standards and regulations.

Local and National Regulations: Regulations governing the hiring of professional negotiators may vary by jurisdiction. Be sure to be familiar with the specific laws and regulations in your country or region.

Registration and Accreditation: In some jurisdictions, professional negotiators may be required to register or be accredited in some way. Ensure that the negotiators you hire meet these requirements if applicable.

Experience and Training: Evaluate the experience and training of professional negotiators before hiring them. They should have experience in hostage situations and a solid understanding of negotiation tactics and crisis management.

Ethics and Professional Conduct: Ensure that professional negotiators are ethical and adhere to high standards of professional conduct. This is essential to maintain the integrity of negotiations and the safety of the hostages.

Coordination with Authorities: Work closely with local authorities and crisis response agencies when using professional negotiators. Coordination is essential to ensure that all actions are in compliance with the law and are effective.

Ongoing Assessment: Continuously assess the performance of negotiators during the negotiation. Make sure they are following agreed-upon guidelines and strategies and adjust the approach as needed.

Transparency and Communication: Professional negotiators should communicate transparently with the crisis management team and authorities. Effective communication is key to negotiation success.

Confidentiality and Security: Professional negotiators must be committed to confidentiality and the security of information related to the negotiation and the hostages. Hiring professional negotiators in hostage situations is a specialized and highly regulated practice in many jurisdictions. Compliance with applicable regulations and standards is essential to ensure a legal and ethical response to the hostage situation and to protect the safety of all parties involved.

Extortion and Ransom Payments: In many countries, paying ransoms may be illegal and subject to legal sanctions. Companies should be aware of laws related to extortion and ransom payments in their jurisdiction and act in accordance with them. It is true that in many countries, the payment of ransoms is subject to legal regulations and can be illegal in certain circumstances.

Extortion and ransom payments are complex issues that vary based on local and national laws and regulations. Local Laws and Regulations: It is important to be familiar with the specific laws and regulations in your country or jurisdiction regarding extortion and ransom payments. Laws can vary significantly from one place to another.

Company Policy: Some companies have clear policies regarding ransom payments that may align with local laws and regulations. Ensure that your company has a policy in this regard and that it is adhered to.

Collaboration with Authorities: If the hostage situation involves extortion or a possible ransom payment, it is important to collaborate closely with local authorities and follow their guidance. They can provide guidance on how to handle these situations within the legal framework.

Evaluation of Demands: If faced with ransom demands, it is important to carefully assess them in terms of their authenticity and the safety of the hostages. No payment should be made without verifying the situation and its compliance with the law. Kidnap and Ransom Insurance: Some companies have kidnap and ransom insurance that can provide funds for ransoms. This insurance is often subject to specific regulations and should be used in accordance with applicable laws and regulations.

Legal and Ethical Consequences: Ransom payments often have significant ethical and legal implications. They can encourage future kidnappings and fund criminal activities. It is important to carefully weigh the ethical and legal consequences when considering a ransom payment.

Coordination with International Authorities: If the kidnapping involves foreign nationals or crosses international borders, it is essential to coordinate with international authorities and agencies that may be involved in crisis management. In summary, extortion and ransom payments are complex issues that must be handled carefully within a legal and ethical framework.

Collaboration with authorities and compliance with local and national regulations are fundamental to making informed decisions and ensuring the safety of the hostages. Information

Confidentiality: The disclosure of information that could jeopardize the safety of the hostages or security operations may be subject to legal restrictions. It is important to protect confidentiality at all times. Information confidentiality is a critical aspect of managing kidnapping situations and hostage negotiations. Irresponsible disclosure of information can jeopardize the safety of hostages and the effectiveness of security operations.

Secure Communication: Communication between negotiators and kidnappers must be conducted securely to prevent interception or exposure of sensitive information.

Information Control: Designate a team responsible for controlling information and ensuring that it is managed securely and confidentially. This may include document management, communication records, and other data related to the negotiation.

Selective Disclosure: Only relevant and necessary information for security operations and negotiations should be disclosed. Unnecessary disclosure of details can be detrimental.

Legal Restrictions and Regulations: It is important to be aware of the legal restrictions and regulations governing information confidentiality in your jurisdiction. This may include privacy and security laws.

Staff Training: Ensure that staff involved in crisis management are trained in the importance of confidentiality and adhere to specific information handling policies and procedures.

Internal and External Communication: Coordinate internal and external communication to ensure that sensitive information is shared only with necessary and authorized parties. This includes communication with authorities, negotiators, and stakeholders.

Media Coverage Management: If the situation is to be communicated to the media, it is important to do so in a controlled manner and under the guidance of crisis communication experts to avoid the disclosure of sensitive information.

Cybersecurity: Protect cybersecurity to prevent information exposure through cyber threats, such as hacking.

Risk Assessment: Continuously assess the risks associated with information disclosure and adjust communication strategies as necessary. Information confidentiality is essential to ensure the safety of hostages and the effectiveness of security operations. Proper coordination and management of information may be critical to the success of a response to a kidnapping situation.

Ethical Considerations:

Protection of Human Life: The ethics of hostage negotiation are based on the protection of human life. All efforts should be focused on ensuring the safety and well-being of the hostages.

The protection of human life is the fundamental ethical principle in hostage negotiation. The ethics of this process focus on ensuring the safety and well-being of the people involved, both the hostages and the kidnappers.

Non-Concession to Violence: Ethics involve not giving in to violence as a tactic. Negotiation should seek a peaceful resolution of the situation and avoid any actions that jeopardize the lives of the hostages.

Respect for Human Rights: Ethics demand respect for the human rights of all individuals involved in the situation. This includes avoiding the use of torture or inhumane and degrading treatment.

Corporate Responsibility: Companies have an ethical responsibility to do everything possible to ensure the safety of their employees and to comply with applicable laws and regulations in the management of hostage situations.

Transparency and Honesty: Ethics require transparency and honesty in communication, both with authorities and with kidnappers. Lack of honesty can undermine trust in negotiations.

Priority of Safety: Ethics dictate that the top priority is the safety of the hostages. All actions and decisions should be directed toward ensuring their safety and well-being.

Support for Hostages and Their Families: Ethics also involve providing support to hostages and their families, both during and after the crisis. This is essential for their emotional and physical well-being.

Consideration of Long-Term Consequences: Ethics also require consideration of the long-term consequences of actions taken during a hostage negotiation. This includes the possibility that a ransom may finance future criminal activities.

Cooperation with Authorities: Working closely with authorities and following their guidance is essential to ensure the protection of human life and compliance with applicable laws and regulations. The ethics of protecting human life are a fundamental part of managing hostage situations. Focusing on the safety and well-being of all individuals involved is essential for making ethical and effective decisions during such a crisis.

Not yielding to violence: The ethics of negotiation entails not yielding to violence or using it as a tactic. Negotiations should be focused on the peaceful resolution of the situation. The ethics of hostage negotiation clearly emphasizes that one must not yield to violence or use it as a tactic during negotiations. Instead, the aim is a peaceful resolution of the situation.

Protection of human life: Violence can endanger the lives of hostages, kidnappers, and anyone else involved. The ethics of negotiation is based on the protection of human life at all times.

Respect for human rights: Using violence as a negotiation tactic often constitutes a violation of human rights and can lead to severe legal and ethical consequences.

De-escalation of the situation: Violence tends to increase tension and worsen the situation. The ethics of negotiation seeks de-escalation and a reduction in tension to achieve a safer and more peaceful resolution.

Building trust: Violence undermines trust among the parties involved in the negotiation. Trust-building is essential for reaching an agreement that ensures the safety of the hostages.

Prevention of future kidnappings: Yielding to violence can encourage future kidnappings, as criminals may perceive this tactic as effective. The ethics of negotiation aims to avoid creating incentives for future criminal acts.

Effective cooperation: Effective negotiations require cooperation among all parties involved. Violence can hinder cooperation and impede the resolution of the situation.

Sustainable resolution: Peaceful resolution of the situation tends to be more sustainable in the long term and can lay the groundwork for more constructive relationships in the future. In summary, the ethics of hostage negotiation is based on humanitarian principles and the peaceful resolution of conflicts. Not yielding to violence is fundamental to protecting the lives and security of all individuals involved and achieving an ethical and safe resolution.

Respect for human rights: Hostage negotiation must be conducted with respect for the human rights of both hostages and kidnappers. This includes avoiding the use of torture or inhumane and degrading treatment. Respect for human rights is a fundamental principle in hostage negotiation. The ethics of this process is based on respecting the human rights of all individuals involved, including hostages and kidnappers.

Right to life and physical integrity: The right to life and physical integrity of all individuals involved, including hostages and kidnappers, must be respected at all times. This entails avoiding any actions that could endanger their lives or cause physical harm.

Prohibition of torture: Torture and cruel, inhuman, or degrading treatment are prohibited by international law and ethical principles. In hostage negotiation, resorting to torture or similar coercive methods should not occur. Right to a fair trial: Kidnappers have legal rights, including the right to a fair trial if they are captured. If the release of kidnappers is achieved, they should be handed over to the authorities to face a legal process.

Medical and psychological assistance: Hostages and kidnappers who may have experienced trauma or injuries should receive appropriate medical and psychological support. This is essential for their recovery and well-being.

Right to legal defense: If a legal process is conducted against kidnappers, their right to legal defense and a fair trial in accordance with applicable laws and regulations must be ensured.

Right to privacy: Communication and information related to hostage negotiation should be handled in a manner that respects the right to privacy of the individuals involved.

Access to humanitarian representatives: In some situations, representatives from humanitarian organizations may be involved to ensure the well-being of hostages and monitor the compliance with human rights.

Responsible information dissemination: Information related to the hostage situation that is shared with the media or the public should be done in a manner that respects the rights and safety of the individuals involved. Respect for human rights is a fundamental principle guiding the ethics of hostage negotiation. Ensuring that all individuals involved are treated with dignity and respect is essential for an ethical and humanitarian response to these situations.

Corporate Social Responsibility: Companies have an ethical responsibility to do everything possible to ensure the safety of their employees and to comply with laws and regulations in their response to hostage situations. Corporate Social Responsibility (CSR) implies that companies have an ethical obligation to consider the impact of their actions on society and to act in a way that benefits the community at large, in addition to their business interests. In the context of hostage situations, this means that companies have a responsibility to do everything possible to ensure the safety of their employees and to comply with relevant laws and regulations.

Employee protection: CSR implies that a company must take all necessary measures to protect its employees and ensure their safety in hostage situations. This may include security training, the implementation of safety policies, and effective crisis response.

Legal and ethical compliance: The company must comply with local, national, and international laws and regulations in its response to hostage situations. CSR involves acting ethically and legally at all stages of crisis management.

Collaboration with authorities: Cooperation with local authorities and crisis response agencies is crucial to ensuring an effective and ethical response. The company should follow the guidance of authorities and collaborate in crisis management.

Transparency and communication: CSR also involves transparent communication with employees, stakeholders, and the general public during a crisis. Effective communication can provide important information and build trust.

Evaluation and continuous improvement: The company should conduct ongoing evaluations of its response to hostage situations and seek ways to improve its procedures and safety policies.

Support for employees and their families: CSR also involves providing support to employees affected by hostage situations and to their families. This may include counseling, medical care, and legal assistance.

Prevention and risk mitigation: The company has a responsibility to take proactive measures to prevent and mitigate risks related to hostage situations, including employee safety training and the implementation of appropriate safety measures.

Long-term impact: CSR also involves considering the long-term impact of actions taken in response to a hostage situation, both for the company and the community at large. Corporate Social Responsibility is essential in the management of hostage situations, as it guides companies to make ethical and effective decisions that prioritize the safety of their employees and compliance with applicable laws and regulations.

Transparency and honesty: Ethics require transparency and honesty in communication, both with authorities and with kidnappers. Lack of honesty can undermine trust in negotiations. Transparency and honesty in communication are fundamental ethical principles in hostage negotiation. These principles are essential for establishing and maintaining trust among all parties involved and for seeking a peaceful and safe resolution.

Building trust: Transparency and honesty are key to building and maintaining trust in negotiations. When all parties feel that information is communicated openly and honestly, they are more willing to cooperate.

Prevention of misunderstandings: Lack of transparency or dishonesty in communication can lead to misunderstandings and increase tension in the situation. Clarity and honesty prevent misunderstandings and unnecessary conflicts.

Credibility and effective negotiation: Parties in a negotiation must be seen as credible and trustworthy. Lack of honesty can undermine credibility and hinder effective negotiation.

Hostage safety: Lack of honesty in communication can jeopardize the safety of hostages if kidnappers perceive that promises or agreements are not being upheld. Ethics and legality: Ethics and legality in hostage negotiation require open and honest communication. Lack of honesty can have serious legal and ethical consequences.

Cooperation with authorities: Communication with authorities and crisis response agencies should be based on transparency and honesty. This is essential for effective coordination in managing the situation.

Strategic planning: Transparency in communication allows all parties to understand the negotiation strategy and objectives, facilitating strategic planning and informed decision-making.

Respect for human rights: Honest and open communication is also fundamental to respecting the human rights of all individuals involved in the hostage situation. Transparency and honesty are ethical cornerstones in hostage negotiation and in crisis management in general. These principles are essential for establishing a trust-based environment where all parties can collaborate effectively to achieve a safe and ethical resolution.

Support for hostages and their families: Ethics also includes providing support to hostages and their families, both during and after the crisis. This is essential for their emotional and physical well-being. Supporting hostages and their families is a fundamental ethical consideration in the management of hostage situations. This ethic recognizes the importance of caring for the emotional and physical well-being of those involved in a crisis of this nature. Here are some additional considerations regarding support for hostages and their families:

Psychological and Emotional Care: Hostages may experience trauma, fear, and emotional distress during their captivity. It is essential to provide them with access to psychological and emotional support to help them cope with their experiences.

Medical Care: Hostages may have suffered injuries or health issues during their captivity. Providing them with prompt medical care is not only ethical but also necessary for their recovery.

Reintegration Assistance: After their release, hostages may face challenges in reintegrating into society. They may need assistance with medical care, legal matters, and psychological counseling to help them transition back to a normal life.

Support for Families: The families of hostages also go through significant emotional stress and uncertainty. They should receive support, information, and assistance in dealing with the situation.

Privacy and Confidentiality: Respecting the privacy and confidentiality of hostages and their families is crucial. Their personal information and experiences should be handled with the utmost care and discretion.

Long-Term Well-Being: Ethical considerations extend beyond the immediate crisis. Ensuring the long-term well-being of hostages and their families is an ongoing responsibility, which may involve continued support and monitoring.

Legal Rights: Hostages have legal rights that must be respected, including the right to compensation for any harm or suffering endured during their captivity.

Communication and Reassurance: Providing clear and regular communication with hostages and their families is essential for keeping them informed and reassured throughout the crisis.

Cultural Sensitivity: Consider cultural and religious sensitivities when providing support to hostages and their families. Respect their values and beliefs in the assistance you offer.

Supporting hostages and their families is a fundamental ethical duty, and it should be approached with empathy, compassion, and a commitment to their well-being. This support extends not only during the crisis but also throughout the recovery and reintegration process.

Medical and Psychological Care: Hostages who have undergone a traumatic situation may require medical care and psychological support. Ethics entails providing access to trained healthcare professionals to assess and treat any physical or emotional trauma.

Confidentiality and Privacy: Ethics also require respecting the confidentiality and privacy of the hostages and their families in the process of medical and psychological care. This is essential for creating a trusting environment.

Legal Counseling: Hostages and their families may need legal counseling to understand their rights and options. Ethics implies providing access to competent legal advisors.

Communication with Families: Keeping families informed about the situation of the hostages and providing them with emotional support is essential. Ethical communication involves being sensitive and transparent with the families.

Financial Support: Hostages and their families may face financial difficulties due to the situation. Ethics may involve providing financial support to address these needs.

Long-Term Follow-Up: Ethics also entails providing long-term follow-up to the hostages and their families, as emotional and psychological consequences may persist after their release.

Respect for Dignity: The ethics of caring for hostages and their families is based on respecting their dignity and their right to as normal a life as possible after the crisis.

Coordination with Experts: The company or authorities must coordinate with experts in victim assistance and medical and psychological care to ensure that appropriate support is provided.

Support for hostages and their families is essential for their recovery and well-being. Ethics in hostage management requires attention to these considerations and the provision of necessary support to help those affected overcome the aftermath of the crisis in a healthy and constructive manner.

Hostage negotiation is a complex matter that involves a range of legal and ethical considerations. Companies must work closely with security experts, legal advisors, and authorities to ensure that their actions are both legal and ethical. The priority should always be the safety of the hostages and the peaceful resolution of the situation.

26. The Role of Intelligence in Hostage Negotiation.

Intelligence plays a crucial role in hostage negotiation, as it is a highly delicate operation aimed at ensuring the safety of the victims and achieving a peaceful resolution. Here are several reasons why intelligence is fundamental in this context:

Information Gathering: Before embarking on any negotiation, it is essential to gather accurate information about the situation. This includes data about the captors, their demands, the health status of the hostages, and the dynamics of the location. Intelligence helps obtain reliable and up-to-date information.

Identifying the Parties Involved: It is important to determine who the captors are, how many there are, and their relationship with the hostages. This may include information about their identity, criminal backgrounds, and potential links to terrorist groups or criminal organizations.

Assessing Demands: Understanding the captors' demands is crucial. What are they requesting in exchange for the hostages' release? Demands can vary from financial issues to the release of prisoners, to political or other types of demands.

Hostage Health and Safety: Obtaining information about the hostages' health is critical. This includes any necessary medical care and their emotional well-being. It is also important to know their precise location and the conditions they are in.

Location Dynamics: Knowing the location of the hostages and captors, as well as the layout of the place where they are, is crucial for planning the operation and ensuring the safety of everyone involved.

Previous Communication: If there has been any prior communication between the captors and authorities, it is important to review all conversations and records to identify possible clues or useful information.

Threat Assessment: It is important to assess potential threats to the safety of the hostages and response teams. This may include identifying weapons, explosive devices, or any other imminent dangers.

Captors' Motivations: Understanding the motivations behind the kidnapping can help negotiators design effective strategies. This could include political, economic, or personal objectives.

Cultural and Political Conditions: Having knowledge about the cultural and political conditions in the region where the kidnapping takes place can also be useful, as it may influence negotiation dynamics.

Accurate and up-to-date information gathering is essential for making informed decisions during a hostage negotiation. Intelligence plays a crucial role in this phase, providing the basis for developing effective negotiation strategies and ensuring the victims' safety.

Situation Analysis: Intelligence allows for a more accurate assessment of the situation. Negotiators need to understand the captors' motivations and goals, identify potential threats, and predict future behavior. This informed analysis is essential for making strategic decisions.

Understanding Captors' Motivations and Goals: Previously gathered intelligence can provide information about the possible motivations and objectives of the captors. This may include political, economic, religious, or personal matters. Understanding these motivations is essential for designing negotiation strategies that can effectively address captors' demands.

Identifying Potential Threats: Intelligence can help identify potential threats to the safety of hostages and response teams. This could include information about weapons, explosives, or other dangers that may be present at the kidnapping site.

Assessing Future Behavior: Based on the information gathered, negotiators can attempt to predict the captors' future behavior. This includes anticipating how they might react to different scenarios and actions by authorities or hostages.

Developing Psychological Profiles: Intelligence can also help build psychological profiles of the captors, providing valuable insights into their personality, level of motivation, and ability to remain calm in crisis situations. This can guide negotiators in how they communicate with captors.

Identifying Pressure Points: Intelligence can help identify weaknesses or areas in which captors may be willing to compromise. For example, if the group has political demands, intelligence might reveal internal divisions or shifts in public opinion that could influence their decision-making.

Intelligence plays an essential role in situational analysis during a hostage negotiation. It helps negotiators understand captors, anticipate threats, predict future behavior, and design effective strategies for achieving a peaceful and safe resolution. Informed situation analysis is key to making strategic decisions that prioritize the safety of the hostages.

Effective Communication: Intelligence also plays a fundamental role in communication with captors. Negotiators must be able to establish a secure and effective communication channel. Intelligence can help identify captors' communication preferences and ensure that conversations are productive.

Identifying Communication Preferences: Intelligence can provide information about captors' communication preferences, such as the means they favor (phone, email, written messages) or the times when they are most receptive. Knowing these preferences facilitates the establishment of an effective communication channel.

Communication Security: Intelligence is essential to ensuring the security of communications. Negotiators must ensure that conversations are not intercepted by third parties, which could jeopardize the safety of hostages. Intelligence can provide information about security measures that need to be taken.

Building Trust: Intelligence can help negotiators build trust with captors. This might include the ability to mention accurate information about the captors' demands or the conditions of the hostages, demonstrating a willingness to fulfill certain requests as long as they are safe and reasonable.

Negotiating Agreements: Intelligence enables negotiators to develop strong negotiation strategies. With a precise understanding of captors' demands and motivations, negotiators can formulate proposals that are acceptable and, at the same time, ensure the safety of the hostages.

Emotion Management: Intelligence can also provide information about the psychology of captors, allowing negotiators to effectively address emotions and attitudes. This is essential for maintaining a negotiation environment as calm and cooperative as possible.

Adaptation to Changing Situations: Intelligence is crucial for adapting to changing situations during negotiation. If an unexpected twist occurs in the situation, such as a change in demands or the captors' disposition, intelligence can help negotiators reevaluate and adjust their approach.

Intelligence is essential for establishing a secure and effective communication channel with captors during a hostage negotiation. This allows negotiators to build trust, manage communication security, adapt to changing demands and emotions, and work toward an agreement that ensures the safety of the hostages.

Psychological Profiling: Intelligence can help build psychological profiles of captors, allowing negotiators to adapt their strategies based on captors' personalities, motivations, and crisis behavior.

Understanding the captors' personalities and motivations is crucial as it can be instrumental in gaining their trust and reaching an agreement. Psychological profiling is a valuable tool in hostage negotiation, and intelligence plays an essential role in this process.

Analysis of Motivations and Objectives: Previously gathered intelligence provides key information about the possible motivations and objectives of the captors. This may encompass political, economic, ideological, or personal aspects. Understanding these motivations is essential for building accurate psychological profiles.

Personality Assessment: Intelligence can assist negotiators in evaluating the personality of the captors. Are they impulsive or rational? Are they highly ideological or more pragmatic? Do they have known psychological backgrounds? These are some of the factors that can influence how negotiations are approached.

Identification of Pressure Points: Intelligence can also help identify potential psychological pressure points. Psychological profiles can aid in determining areas where captors may be more vulnerable or prone to concessions in their demands. For example, if dealing with a group with strong political beliefs, intelligence could reveal internal divisions or disputes that might influence their decision-making.

Adopting Communication Approaches: Building psychological profiles can guide negotiators in choosing communication approaches. By understanding the personality and motivations of the captors, negotiators can tailor their language, tone, and strategies for more effective communication.

Risk of Violence Assessment: Psychological profiles can also help assess the risk of violence from the captors. Understanding the captors' psychology allows negotiators to anticipate how they might react in stressful situations and take steps to minimize the possibility of the situation turning violent.

Constructing psychological profiles of captors is an important part of hostage negotiation, enabling negotiators to adapt their communication and negotiation strategies effectively. Intelligence plays a central role in providing data to understand captors' psychology, thus making informed decisions to ensure the safety of hostages and achieve a peaceful resolution.

Negotiation Strategies: Intelligence offers valuable information for designing effective negotiation strategies. Negotiators can use the collected data to propose solutions that meet captors' demands within reason while protecting the safety of the hostages.

Intelligence plays a fundamental role in designing effective negotiation strategies in hostage situations.

Understanding Demands and Objectives: Intelligence provides crucial information about the captors' demands and objectives. With this information, negotiators can design strategies that consider the needs and motivations of the captors while safeguarding the hostages' safety. This may involve identifying demands that could be acceptable or concessions that can be made.

Setting Clear Goals: With intelligence as a foundation, negotiators can establish clear and realistic goals for negotiation. This includes determining what is a priority, such as the safety of the hostages, and the limits regarding concessions.

Communication Planning: Intelligence helps plan how conversations with captors will be conducted. This can involve selecting communication channels, the frequency of conversations, and the tone and content of messages. Careful communication planning is essential for maintaining effective dialogue.

Maintaining Calm and Patience: Psychological profiles and information about captors' motivations provided by intelligence can help negotiators remain calm and patient. Knowing how to approach captors strategically and empathetically can be crucial in avoiding crisis situations.

Risk Assessment: Intelligence is also essential for assessing and managing risks at every stage of negotiation. Negotiators must be aware of potential threats to the safety of hostages and how to mitigate them, as well as potential obstacles that may arise.

Flexibility: Intelligence provides the basis for informed decision-making, but it's also essential to be flexible and capable of adapting to changing situations. Intelligence allows negotiators to anticipate possible scenarios and be prepared to adjust their strategies as needed.

Continual Information Gathering: Intelligence is not static; it's an ongoing process. Negotiators must continue gathering information as the situation evolves to stay informed about changes in captors' demands or dispositions.

Intelligence is essential for designing effective negotiation strategies in hostage situations. It provides valuable information that allows negotiators to make informed decisions, plan communication, set clear goals, and assess risks, contributing to a safer and more peaceful resolution of the situation.

Crisis Management: Intelligence is also essential for crisis management. It enables response teams to anticipate potential challenges, make rapid decisions, and adapt their strategies as the situation unfolds.

Crisis management is a critical aspect of hostage negotiation, and intelligence plays a fundamental role in this process.

Anticipating Potential Challenges: Intelligence enables response teams to anticipate potential challenges that may arise during negotiations. This includes identifying possible captor reactions, the evolving situation, changing demands, and any other factors that may pose obstacles to a safe resolution.

Informed Decision-Making: Intelligence provides response teams with up-to-date and accurate information about the situation. This is essential for making informed real-time decisions. Teams can assess intelligence information to decide on the best course of action and how to adapt their strategies.

Adaptation of Strategies: Intelligence allows response teams to adapt their strategies as the situation evolves. If captors change their demands or behavior, teams can adjust their negotiation approaches or response tactics based on the collected information.

Real-Time Risk Assessment: Intelligence is crucial for assessing ongoing risks and taking steps to reduce them. This includes evaluating the safety of hostages, the potential threat of violence from captors, and any other risk situation.

Continuous Communication: Crisis management involves maintaining continuous and effective communication with captors. Intelligence helps response teams stay informed about changes in captor disposition and demands, facilitating the adaptation of communication strategy.

Interagency Coordination: In hostage situations, multiple agencies and teams often work together, including law enforcement, negotiation teams, and intelligence experts. Intelligence plays a crucial role in the effective coordination between these parties to ensure a cohesive response.

Contingency Planning: Intelligence also aids in contingency planning. Response teams can use intelligence information to anticipate possible scenarios and develop alternative action plans in case the situation deteriorates or becomes dangerous.

In summary, intelligence is essential for crisis management in hostage situations. It provides response teams with the necessary information to anticipate challenges, make informed decisions, adapt their strategies, and evaluate real-time risks, all with the goal of ensuring the safety of hostages and achieving a peaceful resolution.

Risk Reduction: Intelligence helps reduce risks for hostages and response teams. By gaining a better understanding of the situation and captors, negotiators can minimize the likelihood of the situation deteriorating or turning violent.

Risk reduction is a primary objective in managing hostage situations, and intelligence plays a crucial role in this aspect.

Identification and Assessment of Threats: Intelligence provides information that allows for the identification and assessment of threats present in the situation. This includes identifying weapons, explosives, dangerous devices, or any other elements that may pose a risk to hostages or response teams.

Understanding Captors: Intelligence offers a deeper understanding of captors, their motivations, and psychology. This knowledge can help anticipate their behavior and assess the likelihood of resorting to violence. By understanding captors' motivations and weaknesses, response teams can adopt strategies to reduce the risk of violence.

Security Planning: Intelligence contributes to security planning to protect hostages and response teams. This may include identifying secure zones, positioning security teams, creating emergency action protocols, and coordinating safe evacuations if necessary.

Real-Time Risk Assessment: Intelligence is not static; it is continually updated as the situation evolves. Response teams use real-time intelligence information to assess ongoing risks and make immediate decisions to reduce them.

Secure Communication: Intelligence also helps ensure secure communication between response teams and captors. This can involve selecting secure communication channels and implementing security protocols to prevent third-party interception of conversations.

Strategic Negotiation: Intelligence is fundamental to strategic negotiation. It allows response teams to formulate proposals that, within reason, can meet captors' demands without jeopardizing the safety of hostages. Strategic negotiation is an important means to reduce the risk of violence.

Coordination of Actions: Intelligence facilitates effective coordination among the various agencies and teams involved in crisis management. Coordination is essential to avoid misunderstandings and ensure a consistent and safe response.

Intelligence is essential for risk reduction in hostage situations. It provides information that enables threat identification, security measures planning, real-time risk assessment, and strategic negotiations, all with the goal of ensuring the safety of hostages and response teams.

Intelligence plays a fundamental role in hostage negotiation by providing accurate information and analysis that enable negotiators to make informed and strategic decisions. This contributes to a safer and more peaceful resolution of the situation, prioritizing the lives and safety of the hostages.

27.International Hostage Negotiation Context

Hostage negotiation in the international context involves additional challenges and special considerations due to the transnational nature of these incidents.

International Diplomacy: Hostage situations often involve foreign citizens or foreign actors, which may require intense international diplomacy. Governments and embassies play a significant role in coordinating efforts and seeking diplomatic solutions.

International diplomacy plays a crucial role in hostage situations involving foreign citizens or foreign actors.

Protection of Foreign Citizens: When citizens of one country are taken hostage abroad, it is the responsibility of their government to protect their interests and ensure their safety. The embassies and consulates of the hostages' home country play a fundamental role in coordinating efforts to secure their release.

Coordination with Foreign Governments: International diplomacy involves coordination and communication with the government of the country where the hostage-taking has occurred. This may require establishing effective communication channels and seeking joint solutions.

Collaboration Between Agencies: Response teams for hostage situations may consist of various government agencies and departments, such as security forces, intelligence services, and diplomatic representatives. Coordination among these entities is essential for an effective response.

Exchange of Information: Governments involved in hostage negotiations often share intelligence information and relevant data to better understand the situation and coordinate efforts. This is important to ensure that all stakeholders have a common understanding of the situation.

Management of International Relations: International diplomacy may require the management of complex relationships between the countries involved. This includes considerations related to bilateral relations, international agreements, and other political issues that may influence negotiations.

Use of International Intermediaries and Mediators: In some cases, international intermediaries or mediators, such as representatives from the United Nations or the Red Cross, may be employed to facilitate communication and negotiation with the captors. These mediators can help bridge the gap between governments and captors.

Maintaining Diplomatic Pressure: Governments often use diplomacy to maintain pressure on captors and seek a peaceful resolution. This may include seeking international support, sanctions, or cooperation with other governments to pressure the captors.

Coordination with International Organizations: Organizations like the United Nations and the European Union can play a significant role in facilitating peaceful solutions in hostage situations. Governments can collaborate with these organizations to seek mediation and support.

International diplomacy is essential in addressing hostage situations involving foreign citizens or foreign actors. Coordination, communication, and the management of international relationships are crucial in seeking a peaceful and secure resolution in these delicate and complex circumstances.

International Cooperation: International cooperation is fundamental in addressing hostage-taking in the international arena. This may include coordination between security forces and intelligence services from multiple countries, as well as collaboration in information gathering.

International cooperation is essential in the management of international hostage situations.

Information Exchange: Governments and security agencies from different countries often share intelligence information to gain a better understanding of the situation and captors. This information is crucial for making informed decisions and designing effective negotiation strategies.

Effort Coordination: International cooperation involves the coordination of efforts among the countries involved to ensure a unified and effective response. This includes collaboration in planning negotiation strategies, rescue operations, and security measures.

Utilization of Joint Capabilities and Resources: Countries can combine their capabilities and resources to address hostage situations more effectively. This may include deploying joint response teams or sharing specialized technology and equipment.

Coordination of Cross-Border Operations: In hostage situations that cross borders, international cooperation is crucial for coordinating cross-border operations. This can involve collaboration in locating and rescuing hostages in different countries.

Diplomacy and International Pressure: Cooperation between countries can help exert diplomatic pressure on captors. International diplomacy may involve seeking support from other governments, coordinating actions within the United Nations framework, or implementing international sanctions.

Support for Mediation and Facilitation: Countries can work together to facilitate mediation and peaceful solutions in hostage situations. This may involve collaboration with international organizations, such as the Red Cross or the UN, to seek neutral mediators.

Management of International Relationships: International cooperation also involves managing complex international relationships. Governments must consider bilateral relations with other countries and international agreements that may influence negotiations and crisis management.

Unified Communication: International cooperation is also crucial to ensure that communications and public statements from different countries are consistent and do not compromise the safety of hostages or response operations.

International cooperation is essential in addressing international hostage situations. Coordination among different countries allows for a more effective and cohesive response, increasing the likelihood of achieving a peaceful and secure resolution in these complex and sensitive circumstances.

Cultural Diversity: In international situations, it is crucial to understand and respect cultural differences and behavioral norms. What may be considered an appropriate approach in one culture may not be in another. Cultural training and cultural intelligence are fundamental.

Cultural diversity is a critical aspect of international hostage situations, and understanding and respecting cultural differences are essential for successful negotiation.

Cultural Sensitivity: Negotiators and response teams must be culturally sensitive and willing to learn and respect the norms and customs of the cultures involved. What might be considered a respectful action in one culture may not be in another.

Intercultural Communication: Effective communication is essential in hostage negotiation, and intercultural communication presents additional challenges. Training in intercultural communication can help response teams understand how to communicate effectively and respectfully with people from different cultural backgrounds.

Translation and Interpretation: Language barriers can be a significant challenge in international hostage situations. Accurate translation and interpretation are essential to ensure that conversations and written communications are accurately understood by all parties involved.

Respect for Religion and Spirituality: Religion plays a significant role in many cultures, and understanding and respecting the religious beliefs of captors or hostages are essential to avoid conflicts and build trust.

Behavioral Norms and Cultural Protocols: Every culture has its own behavioral norms and protocols that must be respected. This may include matters of etiquette, gestures, attire, and social rituals. Ignorance or lack of respect for these cultural norms can have a negative impact on negotiations.

Awareness of Gender Differences: Gender differences should also be considered in intercultural negotiations. People's perceptions and attitudes toward gender can vary significantly between cultures, and it is important to be sensitive to these differences.

Flexibility and Adaptability: Response teams must be flexible and willing to adapt to the needs and expectations of the cultures involved. The ability to adjust negotiation and communication strategies based on cultural differences is crucial.

Consultation with Cultural Experts: In international situations, it can be beneficial to seek the advice of cultural experts and anthropologists to better understand cultural complexities and avoid misunderstandings.

Cultural diversity is a critical factor in international hostage situations. Cultural intelligence training and sensitivity to cultural differences are essential for building trust and facilitating effective communication in an intercultural environment, contributing to successful negotiation and the well-being of hostages.

Intercultural Communication: Effective communication can be a challenge in international situations. Negotiation teams must be aware of the language, cultural, and religious barriers that can complicate communication.

Intercultural communication is a significant challenge in international hostage situations. Negotiation teams must be aware of the language, cultural, and religious barriers that can complicate communication and work to overcome these barriers effectively.

Language Barriers: Language differences can be a significant barrier to communication. Response teams must have trained interpreters and translators who can ensure that conversations are accurately understood. Additionally, it is important to consider dialect and accent differences that can influence communication.

Nonverbal Communication: Nonverbal communication, such as gestures, facial expressions, and posture, can vary significantly between cultures. Response teams must be aware of these differences and avoid misinterpreting nonverbal signals from captors or hostages.

Courtesy and Etiquette Norms: Courtesy and etiquette norms vary between cultures and can influence communication. What is considered polite in one culture may not be in another. Response teams should be informed about the courtesy and etiquette norms of the cultures involved.

Understanding Religious Beliefs: Religion can be a significant factor in international situations. It is essential to understand and respect the religious beliefs of those involved to ensure that communication is sensitive and does not cause offense.

Behavioral Norms and Cultural Protocols: Each culture has its own behavioral norms and protocols that must be respected. This can include matters of etiquette, gestures, dress, and social rituals. Ignorance or disrespect of these cultural norms can impact negotiations.

Gender Awareness: Gender differences should also be taken into account in intercultural negotiations. People's perceptions and attitudes towards gender can vary significantly between cultures, and it is important to be sensitive to these differences.

Flexibility and Adaptability: Response teams must be flexible and willing to adapt to the needs and expectations of the cultures involved. The ability to adjust negotiation and communication strategies based on cultural differences is crucial.

Consultation with Cultural Experts: In international situations, seeking advice from cultural experts and anthropologists can help response teams better understand cultural complexities and avoid misunderstandings.

Intercultural communication is a significant challenge in international hostage situations. Response teams must be aware of language, cultural, and religious barriers and work to overcome them effectively to ensure successful negotiation and the safety of hostages.

Linguistic Barriers: Language differences can be a significant barrier to communication. Response teams must have skilled interpreters and translators to ensure that conversations are accurately understood. Additionally, it's important to consider dialect and accent differences that can influence communication.

Non-Verbal Communication: Non-verbal communication, such as gestures, facial expressions, and posture, can vary significantly between cultures. Response teams must be aware of these differences and avoid misinterpreting non-verbal signals from captors or hostages.

Etiquette and Courtesy Norms: Etiquette and courtesy norms vary among cultures and can influence communication. What is considered polite in one culture may not be in another. Response teams should be informed about the etiquette and courtesy norms of the cultures involved.

Understanding Religious Beliefs: Religion can be an important factor in international situations. It's essential to understand and respect the religious beliefs of the parties involved and avoid any speech or action that may be considered offensive from a religious perspective.

Cultural Sensitivity: Cultural sensitivity is crucial. Response teams must be willing to learn about cultural differences and adapt their communication accordingly. Empathy and an understanding of cultural perspectives are essential.

Avoiding Stereotypes and Prejudices: Cultural stereotypes and prejudices can hinder effective communication. Response teams should avoid falling into the trap of stereotypes and treat people as individuals, taking into account their specific circumstances.

Consulting Cultural Experts: In international situations, it can be beneficial to seek the advice of cultural experts and anthropologists who can provide information and guidance on cultural differences and how to address them in communication.

Active Listening and Patience: Intercultural communication often requires active listening and patience. Response teams must be willing to listen attentively and ask questions to clarify any misunderstandings. Patience is key to building trust.

Intercultural communication is a challenge in international hostage situations, but it's essential for effective negotiation. Response teams must overcome linguistic, cultural, and religious barriers through training, cultural sensitivity, and respect to ensure communication that promotes understanding and a peaceful resolution of the situation.

Political and Diplomatic Considerations: In many cases, hostage situations have a political dimension, which means that decision-making and negotiation strategies may be influenced by political agendas and international relations. Negotiation teams must be aware of these considerations and act prudently.

Political Foreign Policy and International Relations: In international hostage situations, government decisions are influenced by their foreign policy agendas and relationships with other countries. Governments must consider how their actions in negotiations can impact their international relations.

Balancing National Interests and Hostage Safety: Governments must strike a balance between protecting their citizens and promoting their national interests while ensuring the safety of the hostages. This can be challenging, as captors' demands often relate to political or ideological objectives.

International Pressure: International diplomacy can exert pressure on captors. Governments can seek the support of other countries and international organizations to back the release of hostages and pressure captors to seek a peaceful resolution.

Coordination with Other Governments: In international hostage situations, governments often coordinate their efforts and strategies to address the situation effectively. This can include forming international coalitions or working groups.

Role of International Organizations: Organizations such as the United Nations, the Red Cross, and the European Union can play a significant role in mediating and facilitating peaceful solutions. Governments can collaborate with these organizations to seek neutral mediators.

Crisis Management and Decision-Making: Government and diplomatic leaders must make critical decisions in real-time. Political crisis management involves making tough decisions and assessing the risks and consequences of proposed actions.

Strategic Communication: Communication with captors and the international public must be carefully managed. Governments must consider how their communication can influence the perception of the situation and the safety of the hostages.

Resolution of Underlying Political Conflicts: In some cases, hostage-taking may be related to underlying political conflicts or territorial disputes. Resolving these conflicts can be crucial for the release of hostages.

Political and diplomatic considerations are an integral part of hostage situations with a political dimension. Governments must balance their national interests with hostage safety and strategically use international diplomacy and political pressure to seek a peaceful resolution. Decision-making in this context is complex and requires a careful and coordinated approach.

Management of International Media: International media coverage can be intense in hostage situations with international implications. Response teams must coordinate their communication and handle information effectively to prevent the spread of false news or media sensationalism.

International media management is a critical aspect of hostage situations with international implications. Media coverage can be intense and can have a significant impact on the development of the situation and the safety of the hostages.

Controlled Communication: Media management involves controlling and overseeing the information disseminated through the media. This is important to prevent the spread of erroneous information, interference with negotiations, and the protection of hostage safety.

Appointment of an Official Spokesperson: In hostage situations, an official spokesperson is designated to communicate with the media in a carefully planned manner. This spokesperson is the sole authorized source of information and works closely with response teams.

Consistent and Clear Messaging: Media management involves providing consistent and clear messages to the press and the public. The information disclosed must be carefully reviewed and approved to ensure accuracy and not compromise hostage safety.

Avoiding Unwanted Publicity: Media management aims to avoid unwanted publicity that can raise the profile of captors or their demands. This can include limiting media coverage or denying publicity to captors.

Coordination with Other Countries: In international situations, governments of multiple countries may be involved in media management. Coordination between these governments is essential to avoid conflicts and ensure that messages are consistent.

Journalist Safety: Ensuring the safety of journalists covering the situation is also important. Response teams and security agencies can provide guidance and protection to journalists reporting on the hostage situation.

Management of False Information: Media management also involves addressing false information or unconfirmed news that may arise in media coverage. This can help prevent confusion and misinformation.

Social Media Monitoring: Media management should include monitoring social media, as social platforms can be a significant source of information and interaction in hostage situations. Identifying and tracking relevant online information is critical.

International media management in hostage situations is crucial for controlling the information disseminated, avoiding unwanted publicity, and ensuring the safety of hostages and the effectiveness of negotiations. Controlled communication, coordination with other countries, and attention to journalist safety are essential elements of this management.

International Law: The negotiation of hostages in the international arena is often subject to international law and specific treaties and agreements. Response teams must be familiar with these laws and regulations to ensure that their actions align with international standards.

International law plays a significant role in international hostage negotiations.

International Conventions and Treaties: There are international conventions and treaties that regulate issues related to hostage-taking and kidnappings. One of the most important treaties is the 1961 Vienna Convention on Diplomatic Relations and the 1963 Vienna Convention on Consular Relations, which establish the obligations and rights of states and their diplomatic and consular missions. Additionally, there are treaties that specifically focus on kidnapping and international terrorism.

Rights and Responsibilities of States: International law establishes the rights and responsibilities of states in hostage situations. States have the responsibility to protect their citizens abroad and ensure their safety. This can influence how governments respond to hostage situations.

Diplomatic and Consular Immunity: The Vienna Conventions also establish diplomatic and consular immunity, meaning that the buildings and personnel of foreign diplomatic and consular missions are protected by international law. This can be relevant in situations where diplomatic missions become places of refuge for hostages.

Detention and Prosecution of Kidnappers: International law also regulates the pursuit and prosecution of kidnappers in cases of international hostage-taking. States have the responsibility to cooperate in the identification and prosecution of captors.

Consular Access: International law establishes the right of foreign citizens to access consular assistance from their home country when detained or taken hostage abroad. This implies that governments must allow consular representatives to visit their detained citizens and provide legal and consular support.

Prohibition of Concessions to Kidnappers: Some treaties and conventions prohibit the granting of political or economic concessions to kidnappers, as this can incentivize future hostage-taking acts. This can influence government decisions regarding captors' demands.

Arbitration and Dispute Resolution: International law also establishes procedures for resolving disputes between states in connection with hostage situations. This may include the possibility of resorting to international arbitration or international courts.

Protection of Hostages: International law recognizes the obligation to protect hostages and ensure their safety. States must take measures to prevent violence and ensure that hostages receive humane treatment.

International law provides a legal framework for international hostage negotiation and sets rights and responsibilities for both states and individuals involved in these situations. Understanding and respecting international law are essential to ensure that negotiations are conducted in accordance with international legal standards and principles.

Hostage-Taking for Political or Ideological Reasons: In many international cases, kidnappings are carried out for political or ideological reasons, further complicating negotiations. Response teams must be able to address these motivations strategically.

Roles of International Organizations: Organizations such as the United Nations and the Red Cross can play a significant role in mediating and facilitating international negotiations. Response teams can collaborate with these organizations to seek peaceful solutions.

In summary, hostage negotiation in the international context is a complex challenge involving intense international diplomacy and cooperation. Response teams must be prepared to face unique situations and understand the cultural, political, and legal complexities that may arise in this context. Intelligence and crisis management are essential for achieving a safe and peaceful resolution in international hostage situations.

28.Long-Term Psychological Impact on Hostages and Their Families

The long-term psychological impact on hostages and their families is profound and can be enduring. The experience of being a hostage and the distress endured during a kidnapping can leave significant psychological scars on those affected. Here are some of the most common long-term effects:

Impact on Hostages: Post-Traumatic Stress Disorder (PTSD): PTSD is a common response to traumatic situations like kidnapping. Hostages may experience flashbacks, nightmares, anxiety, depression, and physical symptoms related to post-traumatic stress. Post-Traumatic Stress Disorder (PTSD) is a common response to traumatic situations such as kidnapping. Hostages who have experienced traumatic events, such as a kidnapping, may develop PTSD as a result of the distress and extreme danger they have faced.

Flashbacks: Hostages may experience flashbacks, intense and disturbing episodes in which they relive the kidnapping, feeling an overwhelming sense of fear, danger, and distress.

Nightmares: Kidnapping-related nightmares are common in individuals with PTSD. These nightmares can be vivid and recurring, exacerbating disturbance and sleeplessness.

Anxiety: Anxiety is a central symptom of PTSD. Hostages may experience constant worry, restlessness, fear, and a general sense of insecurity.

Depression: Depression is another common emotional response in people with PTSD. Hostages may feel sad, apathetic, lose interest in activities they once enjoyed, and experience a general sense of hopelessness.

Avoidance of trauma-related stimuli: Individuals with PTSD often avoid situations, places, or people that remind them of the trauma, such as avoiding discussing the kidnapping or places related to the traumatic event.

Hypervigilance: PTSD can make individuals constantly alert and vigilant, seeking signs of danger or threat in their surroundings, even when there are no objective reasons to feel threatened.

Physical symptoms: PTSD can manifest in physical symptoms, such as sleep problems, headaches, gastrointestinal issues, and other physical discomforts.

It's important to note that PTSD is a natural response to traumatic situations and is a disorder that can be treated with appropriate therapy and support.

Cognitive-behavioral therapy (CBT) and exposure therapy are common approaches for treating PTSD. Early detection and intervention can help hostages recover and manage long-term symptoms.

Personality Changes: Hostages may experience changes in their personality, such as irritability, social withdrawal, and difficulties in interpersonal relationships. Personality changes are common in individuals who have been hostages in traumatic situations such as kidnappings. These changes can manifest in various ways and may persist long-term.

Irritability: Hostages may become more irritable and prone to frustration after a kidnapping. The traumatic experience can leave them with a lower emotional tolerance threshold. Social withdrawal: Many hostages may become more withdrawn and cautious in social interactions. They may avoid situations or places that remind them of the kidnapping and may have difficulty trusting others.

Isolation: Some hostages may isolate themselves from friends and family, feeling unable to share their experiences and emotions with others. Isolation can exacerbate symptoms of post-traumatic stress disorder and depression.

Interpersonal relationship difficulties: Traumatic experiences can negatively affect personal relationships. Hostages may have difficulty relating to others, expressing their emotions, or understanding and responding to the emotions of others.

Hypervigilance: Hypervigilance, constant concern for safety and surroundings, can lead hostages to be more critical and cautious in their interactions with others.

Changes in self-image: The traumatic experience can affect the self-image of hostages, decreasing their self-esteem and self-confidence.

Difficulty coping with stress: Hostages may have difficulty coping with stress and pressure and may experience changes in their ability to handle emotional challenges. These personality changes are a natural response to trauma. They can be a manifestation of post-traumatic stress disorder (PTSD) or other trauma-related psychological disorders. Psychological therapy and support are important in helping hostages cope with these personality changes and recover in a healthy manner. The recovery process may take time, but with the right support, many individuals can regain a sense of well-being and stability in their lives.

Hypervigilance: Hostages may develop a constant sense of alertness and vigilance, which can hinder relaxation and overall well-being. Hypervigilance is a common symptom in people who have been hostages in traumatic situations. It refers to a constant sense of alertness and vigilance, in which the person is extremely attentive to any sign of danger or threat, even when there are no real threats. This hypervigilance can be a natural response to trauma and can hinder relaxation and the overall well-being of hostages.

 Constant sense of danger: People experiencing hypervigilance often feel that they are in constant danger, even in situations that objectively pose no threat.

Difficulty relaxing: Hypervigilance makes it difficult for hostages to relax and feel safe. They may be in a constant state of alertness, which can result in chronic anxiety and tension.

Sleep problems: Hypervigilance often manifests in sleep problems, such as difficulty falling asleep, staying asleep, or frequent nightmares related to the traumatic experience.

Exhaustion: Constant vigilance can lead to physical and mental exhaustion. Hostages may feel exhausted due to chronic stress.

Relationship difficulties: Hypervigilance can affect interpersonal relationships. Hostages may have difficulty trusting others or relaxing in the company of friends and family.

Exaggerated stress responses: Hypervigilant individuals may have exaggerated responses to stress and may react intensely to situations that would not represent a significant threat to others. Hypervigilance is a response to the traumatic experience and is part of a set of symptoms related to post-traumatic stress disorder (PTSD) and other anxiety disorders. Psychological treatment, such as cognitive-behavioral therapy, can help individuals learn to manage hypervigilance and regain a sense of safety and well-being. Emotional support and understanding from family and friends are also essential in helping individuals overcome hypervigilance and its effects on daily life.

Loss of Self-esteem: The feeling of helplessness during the kidnapping and the loss of control over one's life can affect the self-esteem and self-confidence of hostages. Loss of self-esteem is a common psychological effect among hostages after a kidnapping. The feeling of helplessness during the kidnapping and the loss of control over one's life can have a significant impact on the self-esteem and self-confidence of hostages.

Feelings of helplessness: During a kidnapping, hostages often find themselves in a situation where they have minimal or no control over their fate. This feeling of helplessness can be overwhelming and can undermine self-esteem.

Loss of control: The loss of control over one's life and decisions can be profoundly disturbing. Hostages may feel that they have lost their ability to make decisions and influence their own destiny.

Guilt and shame: Hostages often may feel guilty or ashamed of their experience, even if they had no control over the situation. This can lead to a decrease in self-esteem and self-worth.

Negative self-assessment: The traumatic experience can lead hostages to evaluate themselves negatively. They may see themselves as weak, incompetent, or incapable of facing difficult situations.

Feelings of vulnerability: The vulnerability experienced during the kidnapping can lead hostages to feel that they are unable to protect themselves or their loved ones. This can undermine their self-confidence. The loss of self-esteem is a common effect of trauma, but it is possible to recover over time with the right support. Therapy and psychological support can help hostages rebuild their self-esteem and self-confidence. Additionally, understanding and support from family and friends are essential to help individuals regain a sense of worth and empowerment in their lives after a traumatic experience.

Difficulties in Reintegrating into Society: Adapting to normal life after a kidnapping can be a challenge. Hostages may feel alienated or disconnected from society. Reintegration into society after a kidnapping can be a significant challenge for hostages. The traumatic experience of the kidnapping can leave psychological and emotional scars, which can lead to difficulties in adjusting to everyday life and feeling connected to society.

Feelings of alienation: Hostages may feel alienated or disconnected from society after the kidnapping. The traumatic experience can lead them to feel that others cannot understand what they have been through. Difficulty in trusting: Hostages may have difficulty trusting others, as distrust may have developed as a survival mechanism during the kidnapping.

Post-traumatic stress: Symptoms of post-traumatic stress disorder (PTSD), such as flashbacks and hypervigilance, can make it challenging to adapt to everyday life and engage in social activities.

Personality changes: Personality changes, such as irritability and social withdrawal, can affect interpersonal relationships and hinder reintegration into society.

Stigmatization: Some hostages may feel stigmatized or judged for their experience, which can lead to further isolation.

Difficulties in work and education: Hostages may experience difficulties in maintaining jobs or continuing their education due to the effects of the kidnapping on their well-being and functioning.

Need for psychological support: Many hostages require long-term psychological support to aid in their recovery and adjustment to everyday life.

Social support networks: Support from family, friends, and therapists is essential in helping hostages reintegrate into society. These support networks can provide understanding, empathy, and guidance. Reintegration into society is a process that may take time and effort. Therapy and psychological support are crucial to help hostages cope with the psychological effects of the kidnapping and facilitate their reintegration. Additionally, the patience and understanding of friends and family are essential in providing a supportive environment during this recovery and adaptation process.

Impact on Hostages' Families:

Stress and Anxiety: Hostages' families often experience a high level of stress and anxiety during the kidnapping of their loved ones and may continue to experience it after their release. Hostages' families often experience a high level of stress and anxiety both during the kidnapping of their loved ones and after their release. Uncertainty, fear, and constant worry can have a significant impact on the mental and emotional health of the hostages' relatives.

Uncertainty: The uncertainty about the safety and well-being of their loved ones during the kidnapping can be overwhelming. Lack of accurate information can increase anxiety.

Fear for the safety of loved ones: Relatives may experience intense fear for the safety of their loved ones and may worry about their physical and emotional well-being.

Constant stress: Stress related to the kidnapping of a loved one can be constant and overwhelming. This can affect the physical and emotional health of family members.

Anxiety and panic attacks: Anxiety can manifest as panic attacks, insomnia, excessive sweating, and other physical and emotional symptoms.

Guilt and self-blame: Relatives may feel guilty or responsible for the kidnapping, even if they had no control over the situation. This guilt can increase anxiety.

Changes in family dynamics: Family dynamics can change as a result of the kidnapping. There may be increased tension and worry in the home.

Need for psychological support: Hostages' relatives often need psychological support to cope with the stress and anxiety related to the situation.

Hostages' families may also experience symptoms similar to those of post-traumatic stress disorder (PTSD) as a result of the traumatic experience they are going through. Seeking psychological support and therapy can be crucial to help relatives manage their stress and anxiety. Additionally, sharing their concerns with other family members and friends who can understand the situation can provide valuable emotional support during this stressful period.

Secondary Trauma: Families can develop symptoms similar to PTSD due to constant stress and worry. The uncertainty about the fate of their loved ones can be overwhelming. Secondary trauma, sometimes called vicarious trauma, is a phenomenon in which people who have not directly experienced a traumatic event, such as the kidnapping of a loved one, develop symptoms similar to post-traumatic stress disorder (PTSD) due to constant stress and worry. Hostages' families are vulnerable to secondary trauma because of the ongoing distress and uncertainty about the fate of their loved ones.

Symptoms similar to PTSD: People experiencing secondary trauma may develop symptoms similar to those of PTSD, such as flashbacks, nightmares, anxiety, depression, and intense emotional responses.

Feelings of helplessness: The feeling of helplessness in the face of a loved one's kidnapping can contribute to the development of secondary trauma symptoms. People may feel unable to help or influence the situation.

Constant worry: Constant worry and distress about the well-being of their loved ones can generate a high level of emotional stress. Changes in family dynamics: Family dynamics can change due to the tension and stress related to the kidnapping. This can have an impact on the mental health of family members and increase the risk of secondary trauma.

Emotional support: Emotional support from therapists, counselors, or support groups can be crucial in helping people cope with secondary trauma and learn to manage their stress and anxiety.

Secondary trauma is not limited to hostages' families and can affect anyone providing support to someone who has experienced a traumatic event. Seeking help and psychological support is essential to address secondary trauma and learn to manage the emotions related to the traumatic experience. Therapy and support from mental health professionals can be valuable resources for those facing secondary trauma.

Changes in Family Dynamics: The experience of kidnapping can change family dynamics. Families may become more protective or, conversely, may find it difficult to communicate and support each other.

Changes in family dynamics after a kidnapping are common and can vary significantly depending on the circumstances and how the family copes with the traumatic experience. These changes can affect both family relationships and how the family supports each other.

Increased protection: After a kidnapping, it is natural for family members to become more protective of their loved one who has been a victim of a kidnapping. They may express their concern more visibly and take steps to enhance the overall family's security.

Impaired communication: In some families, communication can be affected after a kidnapping. Family members may have difficulty discussing the traumatic experience or may avoid the topic for fear of triggering intense emotions.

Emotional difficulties: Changes in family dynamics may be accompanied by emotional difficulties. Family members may be dealing with stress, anxiety, fear, and other emotions related to the traumatic experience.

Adapting to new rules and routines: Families may need to adapt to new rules and routines to ensure the safety of their loved one. This may include additional safety precautions or changes in daily life.

Mutual support: Despite the challenges, many families find ways to support each other after a kidnapping. Emotional support and solidarity can strengthen family bonds.

Need for professional help: In some cases, families may require the assistance of mental health professionals, such as therapists or family counselors, to address changes in family dynamics and emotional difficulties.

How a family reacts and adapts to a kidnapping can vary depending on the circumstances and the personalities of the family members. Emotional support and mutual understanding are essential to help families face these challenges. Seeking professional help when necessary can be beneficial in addressing the effects of the kidnapping on family dynamics and the mental health of its members.

Feelings of guilt and responsibility: Families often blame themselves for the kidnapping of their loved one, even if they have no control over the situation. Feelings of guilt and responsibility in the families of hostages are a common emotional response in kidnapping situations. Relatives often blame themselves for the kidnapping of their loved one, despite having no control over the situation and not being responsible for what has happened. These feelings can be overwhelming and can further complicate the family's emotional situation.

Irrational guilt: Relatives may feel guilty for not having done enough to prevent the kidnapping or for not having protected their loved one in some way, even when they had no control over the situation.

Self-imposition: Relatives often put significant pressure on themselves, thinking that they should have acted differently to prevent the kidnapping.

Feelings of helplessness: The sense of helplessness and lack of control over the situation can contribute to feelings of guilt and responsibility.

Emotional difficulties: Feelings of guilt can exacerbate anxiety and depression in relatives, making it more challenging to provide support to their loved one and themselves.

Impaired communication: Relatives may avoid discussing their feelings of guilt for fear of increasing distress within the family, which can affect communication and emotional support.

It is important for the families of hostages to understand that kidnappings are traumatic and violent situations that are beyond their control. They are not responsible for the actions of the kidnappers. Recognizing and addressing these feelings of guilt is an important step in emotional recovery. Seeking emotional support and, if necessary, therapy or counseling can help family members cope with feelings of guilt and face the situation in a healthier way. It is also essential for family members to provide mutual support and understanding during this difficult period.

Need for Support and Treatment: Both hostages and their families can benefit from psychological support and treatment to address the long-term psychological effects of the kidnapping.

Both hostages and their families can benefit from psychological support and treatment to address the long-term psychological effects of the kidnapping. Kidnapping is a traumatic experience that can have a lasting impact on the mental and emotional health of the individuals involved.

For Hostages: Hostages may experience a variety of psychological effects, such as post-traumatic stress disorder (PTSD), anxiety, depression, personality changes, and adjustment issues. Psychological therapy, such as cognitive-behavioral therapy (CBT) or exposure therapy, can be effective in addressing these issues and aiding in recovery. Therapy provides a safe space for hostages to talk about their experiences and emotions, learn to manage stress, and develop coping strategies.

For Families: Hostages' families may also need psychological support to cope with stress, anxiety, guilt, and other emotional effects of the kidnapping. Family therapy or individual counseling can be valuable resources to help family members understand and address their emotions, communicate effectively, and maintain healthy relationships.

Support Groups: Both hostages and their families can benefit from participating in support groups. These groups provide a space where individuals can share their experiences, feel understood, and receive support from those who have gone through similar situations.

Long-Term Support: It is important to recognize that recovery from trauma is often a long-term process. Support and treatment may be necessary for months or even years to help individuals fully recover.

Holistic Approach: A holistic approach to mental health and well-being, including physical, emotional, and social care, is essential for long-term recovery.

Psychological support and treatment are valuable resources to help individuals recover from the effects of kidnapping and return to a healthy and fulfilling life. Seeking early professional help and having the support of friends and family are important steps in the recovery process.

The long-term psychological impact on hostages and their families can vary significantly from person to person. Some individuals may recover over time with the appropriate support, while others may experience more lasting effects. Psychological support, such as therapy and counseling, can be crucial in helping individuals cope with these challenges and recover in a healthy manner.

347